Cases in Consumer Behavior

Houghton Mifflin Company

HOUGHTON MIFFLIN COMPANY

Boston   New York

Vice President and Publisher: Charles Hartford
Vice President, Editor-in-Chief: George T. Hoffman
Associate Sponsoring Editor: Joanne Dauksewicz
Editorial Assistant: Rachel Zanders
Production/Design Coordinator: Bethany Schlegel
Manufacturing Manager: Florence Cadran
Senior Marketing Manager: Steven W. Mikels
Marketing Associate: Lisa E. Boden

Printed in the U.S.A.

ISBN: 0-618-44155-7

1 2 3 4 5 6 7 8 9   CRS 07 06 05 04 03

CONTENTS

Introduction to the Case Method

We learn best by doing.

Anonymous

In view of the diverse objectives of courses on strategic marketing management, the specific contents of such courses may vary substantially. This book approaches these subjects through business cases. A case is a description of an organizational situation and frequently contains detailed information about complex issues.

The case method is a Socratic teaching method designed to help you apply theories and concepts that you have learned to actual situations. Most cases focus on some core problem or problems, but the cases can be lengthy and comprehensive. As a student, you are asked to identify those problems and to solve them.* The solution may require you to take advantage of strategic opportunities, and sometimes you may need to propose tactical actions. At other times you will simply be asked to analyze what a firm did correctly, not what its problems were.

Cases are usually written by professors or students or by people involved in the organizational situation. Cases almost always involve real situations. Occasionally, the identity of the organization involved is disguised, but often you will know the identity of the company. Thus you will be able to obtain additional information about the organization if you wish or if your instructor asks you to. However, it is often not wise to research past the date in which the business situation occurred (unless specifically requested by the instructor). For example, if the case describes a situation that occurred in June of 1998, then gathering information that is more current may be dysfunctional. Knowing what the company actually did in the situation is extremely difficult to ignore, and students almost always assume what the company did was the correct thing to do. This knowledge of action taken may render the learning experience offered in the business situation less effective because students think they know the correct answer and fail to consider alternative actions and learn from the discussion of all the alternatives.

Cases may be accompanied by (or contain) industry notes. Your instructor may choose to utilize these industry notes or to ignore them. When used, they are supportive materials for a specific case situation, not a replacement for case materials. As you approach any case, you should obtain as much information on the company's industry as you need to understand the situation described in the case.

*This section is adapted from two sources: James M. Higgins and Julian W. Vincze, *Strategic Management: Text and Cases,* 5th ed. (Orlando, FL: Dryden Press, 1993), pp. 467–472, and Charles W. L. Hill and Gareth R. Jones, *Cases in Strategic Management* (Boston: Houghton Mifflin, 1998), pp. C2–C9. Copyright © 1998 by Houghton Mifflin Company. Used with permission.

OBJECTIVES

The case method's objectives are

1. To add realism to the classroom and to enable students to apply what they have learned
2. To help students to integrate knowledge of the functional areas and to employ concepts of strategic marketing management
3. To improve students' decision-making ability, primarily through practice in making decisions
4. To help students see how actions are related and what they mean in a practical as well as a theoretical sense
5. To encourage students to be effective oral communicators through participation in class, through defense of their ideas, and through the need to "seize the floor" in order to participate
6. To improve students' overall communication skills

APPROACHES

Case analyses may be oral, written, or both. They may be structured or unstructured. Students may be asked to take the role of the CEO, a consultant, or some other person involved in the situation. Normally, the outside consultant's role is preferred because it forces the student to be responsible for communicating his or her basis of analysis, their reasoning that resulted in suggestions, and in addition their complete thinking relative to proposals for action and the implementation of chosen alternatives.

TYPES OF ORGANIZATIONS ENCOUNTERED

Cases cover both goods and services marketing in consumer and business-to-business marketing situations in organizations of various sizes, missions (profit and nonprofit), and geographic market penetration (local, national, multinational, and global). The problems encountered by all these organizations are similar yet distinct.

CASE PROBLEMS ENCOUNTERED

Most of the problems encountered in the cases in this book involve the formulation and control of marketing strategy or tactics. Some require lengthy analysis—which will be explained in detail by your instructor. A few cases involve social responsibility and ethical issues. All require the student analyst to work diligently to acquire an in-depth understanding of the business situation described in the case and, by doing so, to maximize his or her learning opportunity.

Group versus Individual Analysis

Students can engage in preclass and class analysis of a case in either of two ways—in a group or individually. The group method is used when the course is designed to teach people to work in teams and when it is feasible for people to meet in groups. Always be certain of the instructor's expectations relative to individual versus group case analysis. When group analysis is used, the workload should be distributed fairly, but in all groups some people do their fair share and some do not. Appropriate peer-group evaluation should be carried out. Students should resist pressures to conform and be self-reliant in group meetings. Before the group meets, each student should go individually through the steps of analysis outlined in the following section. When the individual method is used, the student prepares all work by himself or herself.

PREPARING A CASE: A SUGGESTED COURSE OF ACTION

1. Read the case; become familiar with the situation. If possible, put the case aside for awhile.
2. Reread the case.
   a. Summarize pertinent information. Use what you have learned in other courses.
   b. Identify vision, mission, goals, objectives, past marketing strategies, current strategies, key success factors, constraints, and SWOT (strengths, weaknesses, opportunities, threats).
   c. Pay special attention to information in exhibits, take notes, and perform analyses:

ratios, financial statements, forecasts, pro forma financial statements.

    d. Answer any questions your instructor has provided.

3. Establish a decision framework.

    a. What are the major problems?

    b. How do you know?

    c. What are the decision constraints?

    d. What are your strategic assumptions?

4. Try to get a comprehensive view of the problem. Do you have the strategic picture in mind? Do you see the interrelationships of the key variables? If not, mull over what you do know until you obtain an overall perspective.

5. Search for and delineate alternatives. Match strengths and weaknesses against opportunities and threats. Be sure to use applicable concepts such as the various product and business matrices, the product lifecycle model, and basic strategic options, and ensure that alternatives address the problems you identify.

6. Choose the appropriate alternatives. Match your choices against vision, mission, goals, objectives, and SWOT. The evaluation process is largely rational but partly intuitive. Once you have finished your analyses, your intuition must function to help you put the complex pieces together.

7. Set priorities for your solution.

8. Be prepared to implement your recommended decisions with a plan of action. You should know how to obtain support for your choices, and you should, if your professor desires, budget for your intended actions.

CLASS PARTICIPATION

The effectiveness of the case method depends in large part on students' contributions in class. Unlike a lecture class, the case method requires the student to assume responsibility for learning, and for the learning of others. Interactions involved in sharing ideas, questioning for understanding, challenging comments, acknowledging issues, and defending positions are important parts of the classroom experience in the case method. In the classroom, you should

1. Participate often and intelligently. A portion of your classroom grade may be based on your participation. An A average on other work may become a B or a C (or worse) for the course if you do not participate appropriately.

2. Substantiate your reasoning and positions with analysis and interpretation of the facts in the business situation.

3. Do not participate just to participate. Contribute. You will soon learn that your professor and your classmates can tell the difference.

4. Respect your peers—you will learn from them. Recognize that others will have thought of issues, analyzed facts, and come to conclusions that you have not.

5. Be prepared to seize the floor. As part of the case method learning experience, you must share your efforts—to do this, you must be heard. If not, how will sharing occur—how will anyone know of your efforts? And your classroom participation grade will suffer significantly.

6. Recognize that your instructor is going to disagree with you, sometimes simply to see if you can defend your position. Furthermore, your classmates are often going to disagree with you to enhance their own situations. You must be prepared to defend your reasoning and analysis.

7. Be willing to take risks. If you make a mistake, you make a mistake, but if you don't try, you'll never get anywhere and you squander a learning opportunity.

8. Avoid use of weak words such as *maybe, I think, I feel, It appears, It tends to.* Be positive and persuasive. Use such words as *It is* and *The analyses reveal that.…*

9. Be prepared to change your mind during the discussion of the case. Others may have presented analyses that suggest you missed something. Revising your opinion will not help your written report, since presumably you already will have turned in your written report. But be flexible enough to change your mind in your oral communications if you see you were wrong, because it will help your class participation to do so, and more importantly, it will contribute to your learning experiences.

10. Try to maintain a general manager's orientation to what is going on in the classroom. Think of the way you should respond to the positions of others if you were the CEO of this organization, and react accordingly.

WRITING A CASE STUDY ANALYSIS

Often, as part of your course requirements, you will need to prepare a written case analysis. This may be an individual or a group report. Whatever the situation, there are certain guidelines to follow in writing a case analysis that will improve the evaluation your work will receive from your instructor. Before we discuss these guidelines and before you use them, make sure that they do not conflict with any directions your instructor has given you.

The structure of your written report is critical. Generally, if you follow the steps for analysis discussed in the preceding section, you *already will have a good structure for your written discussion.* All reports begin with an *introduction* to the case. This should explain briefly the organization of your report. Do this sequentially by writing, for example, "First, we discuss the business environment and organizational audit of company X. . . . Third, we discuss several alternatives that were considered. . . . Last, we provide recommendations and a detailed plan of action for turning around company X's business."

In the second part of the case write-up, the strategic analysis section (or business audit), do a thorough analysis of past marketing strategies that resulted in past successes both to understand how the organization adds value and to identify past and current key success factors. This should be followed by the SWOT analysis. Next, analyze the organization's structure and control systems, and then analyze and discuss the nature and problems of the company's business-level and corporate strategy. Make sure you use plenty of headings and subheadings to structure your analysis. For example, have separate sections on any important conceptual tool you use. Thus you might have a section on the product lifecycle concept as part of your analysis of the environment. You might offer a separate section on portfolio techniques when analyzing a company's corporate strategy. Tailor the sections and subsections to the specific issues of importance in the case.

In the third part of the case write-up, present your understanding of issues and decisions that managers face within the organization. Also try to state a specific "problem" statement that summarizes all the issues previously identified, and do not forget the time horizon as to when decisions must be made.

The fourth part of the case write-up contains the possible alternative solutions you considered. Some instructors will require that this section of your report contain a brief explanation of the alternative followed by an evaluation of the alternative. Evaluation may be as simple as a list of pros and cons. But it also may be a more detailed discussion of positive and negative aspects of each alternative considered. And some instructors also may expect a discussion of the justification of which alternative is the best given the specifics of the business situation.

The next part of the case write-up contains your solutions in the form of both a set of recommendations of what should be done and also a plan of action that details how to perform the recommended actions. Be comprehensive and as specific as possible, and make sure your proposed activities are in line with the previous analysis so that the recommendations fit together and move logically from one to the next. The recommendations section is very revealing because, as mentioned earlier, your instructor will have a good idea of how much work you put into the case from the quality of your recommendations.

Following this framework will provide a good structure for most written reports, although obviously it must be shaped to fit the individual case being considered. Some cases are about excellent companies experiencing no problems. In such instances, it is hard to write recommendations. Instead, you can focus on analyzing why the company is doing so well, using that analysis to structure the discussion. Following are some minor suggestions that can help make a good analysis even better.

1. Do not repeat in summary form large pieces of factual information from the case. The instructor has read the case and knows what is going on. Rather, use the information in the case to illustrate your statements, to defend your arguments, or to make salient points. Beyond the brief introduction to the company, you must

avoid being *descriptive;* instead, you must be *analytical.*

2. Make sure the sections and subsections of your discussion flow logically and smoothly from one to the next. That is, try to build on what has gone before so that the analysis of the case study moves toward a climax. This is particularly important for group analysis, because there is a tendency for people in a group to split up the work and say, "I'll do the beginning. You take the middle. And I'll do the end." The result is a choppy, stilted analysis because the parts do not flow from one to the next, and it is obvious to the instructor that no real group work has been done.

3. Avoid grammatical and spelling errors. They make the paper sloppy.

4. Some cases dealing with well-known companies end in 1993 or 1994 because the decision was an important one and represents an unusual learning opportunity (also often no later information was available when the case was written). If expected or requested by your instructor, do a library and/or World Wide Web search for more information on what has happened to the company in subsequent years. Following are sources of information for performing this search:

The Internet with its World Wide Web is the place to start your research. Very often you can download copies of a company's annual report from its Web site, and many companies also keep lists of press releases and articles that have been written about them. Thoroughly search the company's Web site for information such as the company's history and performance, and download all relevant information at the beginning of your project. Yahoo is a particularly good search engine to use to discover the address of your company's Web site, although others work as well.

Compact disk sources such as Lotus One Source and InfoTrac provide an amazing amount of good information, including summaries of recent articles written on specific companies that you can then access in the library. *FINS Predicasts* provide a listing on a yearly basis of all the articles written about a particular company. Simply reading the titles gives an indication of what has been happening in the company.

Annual reports on a Form 10-K often provide an organization chart.

Companies themselves provide information if you write and ask for it.

Fortune, BusinessWeek, and *Forbes* have many articles on companies featured in the cases in this book.

Standard & Poor's industry reports provide detailed information about the competitive conditions facing the company's industry. Be sure to look at this journal.

5. Sometimes instructors hand out questions for each case to help you in your analysis. Use these as a guide for writing the case analysis. They often illuminate the important issues that have to be covered in the discussion.

If you follow the guidelines in this section, you should be able to write a thorough and effective evaluation.

ADDITIONAL PERSPECTIVES

As you engage in case analysis, the following additional issues may arise.

Degree of Difficulty

Sometimes the point of the case will be obvious. At other times it will be necessary to read, reread, and reanalyze the case in order to identify the major problem or opportunity. Many cases contain problems of technique that are not the major problems, only symptoms of a major problem.

Viewpoint

One factor to be considered is the viewpoint of the student. Should he or she envision himself or herself as a consultant or as a member of the organization? The ease with which solutions may be implemented is related to the choice of viewpoint. Be certain you understand the viewpoint your instructor expects you to use as a case analyst!

Results

Most of the time your predicted results will be attainable, but in some situations, no matter what the decision, the results may be ineffective. Many factors, especially external environmental factors, are completely beyond the control of an organization. In such situations, the best decisions may be those which allow an organization to minimize its losses.

Strength of Analyses

Most students will not uncover all the factors that eventually will be revealed in the classroom discussions. This constitutes one of the most important learning factors gained from use of the case method—the realization that there is always something the individual will overlook. This is very much like real life.

Perspective

For both the student and the instructor, the case method is a difficult process. In traditional classroom learning situations, students have been assigned the roles of listeners and nonparticipants. To be effective, the case method requires that students think, act, and participate. In order for students to receive good grades, they must achieve these more active levels of learning as opposed to being merely receptive and passive members of a lecturer's audience. The role of a strategic marketing manager, too, demands this kind of behavior.

Case Bias

One must be aware of the inherent bias in a case. The case is related as it is perceived by someone else—the case writer. The reader of a case does not have the benefit of knowing how the information was obtained or what factors the individual considered in writing the case. What is presented as fact may not be as clear-cut as it seems. How facts are presented, which facts are included, and which facts are left out are critical factors. Occasionally, facts may be distorted, especially facts related to statements about the personalities of individuals. Often, individuals' personalities are the key problems in a case, yet the reader can never be sure that the statements about these personalities are exactly accurate.

Answers

There are no right answers in a case situation. Some answers, however, are better than others. The only true test of the decision is in its implementation, and unfortunately, the case method does not allow for implementation of decisions. The right answer, then, is unknown. Only the better answer can be determined. Students whose decisions are based on insufficient analysis usually come up with worse answers and correspondingly worse grades. It is the analysis and interpretation of facts on which decisions are based that are important; several acceptable solutions may be derived from them.

Will Old Navy Recreate Past Successes for Gap Inc.? (1995)

This case was prepared by Julian W. Vincze, Professor of Marketing, Crummer Graduate School of Business, Rollins College.

In the multi-billion-dollar apparel market, Gap Inc. recorded more than $3 billion in sales in 1994 through its various stores: the Gap, Banana Republic, GapKids, BabyGap, Gap Warehouse, and Gap Shoes. Increasingly, however, it had seen competitors take what was basically known as the Gap "look" and sell it for less to a mass middle market that did not want to pay for, or could not afford, the prices for Gap clothes.[1] In the United States there are 754 Gap, 178 Banana Republic, 283 GapKids, and 45 Gap Warehouse stores. Internationally, there are 103 Gap and GapKids stores.[2]

GAP'S HISTORY

Gap Inc. has headquarters located on the waterfront at the eastern edge of San Francisco Bay, where the fog rarely reaches. From the modest white Gap building there is a clear view across the blue-gray waters of the bay. Inside the building you find few people in the art gallery ambience of the Gap cafeteria. Instead, you find most of the people who are working their 60-hour weeks in their blond-wood offices drinking coffee out of shining blue Gap mugs, wearing informal Gap cotton at their white desks. Gap Inc. is sufficiently big (second only to Levi's in sales) and unusual (making big profits over the last few years) to have become a major international competitor. Established in 1969 by Donald Fisher, when he couldn't exchange a pair of Levi's at a San Francisco department store, Gap's name is purported to be based on a remark that his wife made about "the generation gap." Mr. Fisher opened his first store, selling flared Levi's, records, and tapes. However, with the hippie wave receding, he quickly dropped the music and began advertising "Four Tons of Levi's."[3] In the next 15 years, Gap stores spread across the United States, but by the seventies and early eighties, the Gap was filled with terry-cloth polo shirts, chocolate-colored fatigues, and T-shirts with zip-off sleeves, squeezed onto pipe rails. "Fall into the Gap" jingled television and radio advertisements, and people did—but lured by almost continuous discounting.[4]

The Gap's explosive growth can be traced to the 1983 hiring of Millard "Mickey" Drexler, who was given the task of taking the Gap upmarket when 1984's profits fell 43 percent. Mickey asked the company's designers why they never wore Gap clothes themselves. "We don't like them. They're junk," said Patricia DeRosa, now executive vice-president.[5] Mr. Drexler liquidated the "junk" and put new clothes on tables in the stores so that customers could easily touch them. The new stock was clever—both old-fashioned ("classic" American styling) and daring (rejecting conspicuous consumption for what the *Los Angeles Times* called "stealth wealth").[6] And the marketing was even more clever: using glitzy stars like Kim Basinger to sell ascetic white T-shirts. After this, Mickey just repeated the winning formula. As in a lot of family businesses (the Fisher family owned more than a third of the shares), decisions were highly centralized (and still are), with standard store layouts dictated to managers from headquarters every few months. Mickey Drexler was constantly visiting stores to ensure compliance to policies. For example, all customers were supposed to be subjected to the GAP-ACT. The GAP-ACT was a process that involved the following six steps: Step 1: Greet customers within 30 seconds; Step 2: Approach and ask, "Can I help you?"; Step 3: Provide product information; Step 4: Add-ons: Suggest more buys; Step 5. Close sale honestly; if it looks bad, say so; Step 6. Thank customer.

By the early nineties, the Gap was the success story of the decade. It had become almost totally self-sufficient, controlling design, manufacturing, marketing, and sales. The Gap did not franchise. All stores were company owned and operated. Stock prices peaked in early 1992, and Mr. Fisher, in an uncharacteristically immodest moment, predicted breakneck growth for another 5 years. But profits fell in 1992, to $211 million from the prior year's $230 million, and more important, sales per square foot—retail's benchmark—stalled, after rising at least 10 percent each year since the mid-eighties.[7] In reaction to this setback, the Gap re-launched Banana Republic—acquired in 1983 as a more cutting-edge complement to existing Gap stores. This re-launch of Banana Republic was viewed by many as simply a re-emphasis of Banana Republic's operations, which had been somewhat ignored by senior executives at Gap during the late 1980s and early 1990s—but sales expectations weren't reached. "It has a really unsavory name," said Alan Millstein, a New York fashion retail analyst, "and it's just a higher-priced Gap."[8] By 1993, as Gap stores continued to falter, with profits down an additional 8% in the first quarter and 24% in the second, Mr. Fisher said: "We are not pleased with these results." And neither was Wall Street, where Gap's share price had dropped 50 percent from its 1992 high. Mr. Millstein said: "Their salad days are over."[9]

Gap Uncool

For Christmas of 1994, 17-year-old Lucas Swanson told his family, "Please, no more gift certificates from the Gap."[10] Was he tired of Jeans? Sick of T-shirts? Not really! The high-school senior, wearing exactly that clothing, said he purchased his clothing from a secondhand store. "I just don't dig the Gap anymore," he said.[11] The Gap, which once offered the epitome of cool, with basic T-shirts and jeans that looked like designer clothing without the arrogance—no fancy labels, logos, or inflated price tags—may be suffering a "Gap-lash" of sorts. Once of enormous appeal for the middle-class and middle-aged, Gap attire and advertising have become the butt of jokes and the target of resentment by teens and Generation Xers. Hugh Gallagher, a writer of satire for Los Angeles's *Grand Royal* magazine, said: "Their clothes promote a straight, white, lame lifestyle, which is just how THEY [big government] want us to be."[12] Comic Ellen DeGeneres, of the popular ABC TV program "Ellen," in the ultimate put-down, calls her navy-and-khaki-clad neighbors "Gaps."[13]

Gap Inc. until recently could ignore comedic put-downs and snide essays in trendy publications because many on Wall Street had bet it would have strong, double-digit profit growth into the next century. But could Gap be losing its edge with its more important clientele: shoppers under age 30? In Leo Burnett Co.'s biannual "What's hot among kids" survey for 1992, about 90 percent of teens said Gap clothes were "cool," but by the summer of 1993, that figure was 83 percent, falling to 75 percent by winter of 1993 and to 66 percent in the two 1994 surveys. Moreover, sales at Gap stores open for at least a year increased by only 1 percent in 1994.[14] To Stanford University senior Jerry Chang, Gap's appeal is its simple, casual clothing. But he said: "I think the Gap has dropped out of mainstream college kids' lives. The Gap relies too much on its name and hasn't given us new and fresh styles."[15] Meanwhile, 24-year-old Brannigan Waycott, who remembers Gap stores in the 1980s as carrying a wider variety of clothes, said now "They're trying to appeal to a larger mass of people, like homogenized cheese or something."[16]

In fact, some industry observers believe the Gap has been struggling for the past 3 years to offer a more effective advertising and merchandise mix. They note that Gap cited "mixed reviews" when pulling the plug early on 1992's TV ad campaign featuring New York poet Max Blagg rambling about "jeans/that fit like a glove/like a lover coming back for more." Gap's 1993 print ad copy, "Commingle. It's how you marshal every fact and contraction, how you make the universe of choice suit you. Classic Gap, for individuals," was judged to be incomprehensible by many customers. Mickey Drexler has responded by stocking more trendy, fashionable items like leather vests and long crepe skirts. "We can't afford not to change," he said at the time.[17] To some industry observers, however, it is too late. The Gap has become part of the establishment and fair game for mockery. The Gap, once considered brilliant for convincing customers that unobtrusive clothing actually illuminated a person's unique look, in 1994 moved a group of seven New York artists to create an anti-Gap art exhibit. One of them, 23-year-old Daniel McDonald, declared, the Gap is "promoting individuality as a tool to sell totally banal clothing."[18]

Still Cool in the United Kingdom

After 6 years in the United Kingdom, little has disturbed the Gap's smooth expansion; there are 40 stores, and each sells more (of exactly the same) clothes than those back in America. But it's a very defensive empire, one that has a minimal press office in its most successful outpost—Britain—and which avoids dealing with the fashion press. Despite its apparently relentless growth and its famed in-house advertising, Gap Inc. remains secretive. "We rarely do any interviews at all," said Richard Crisman, the company's only spokesman located in Britain.[19] "The Gap is still very cool," said *GQ* fashion editor Jo Levin. "People enjoy carrying Gap carrier bags. Almost everyone I know shops at the Gap for something."[20]

ESTABLISHING MASS-MERCHANDISING DIVISION

The Gap first entered the mass-merchandising market in 1989 when it opened Gap Outlets. Merchandise in the Gap Outlets was made up of irregulars and Gap leftovers. With this move, the Gap initiated an attempt at a three-tiered retailing strategy, with its Banana Republic chain at the high end of the market, Gap in the middle, and Gap Outlets at the low end. However, growth of Gap Outlets was not as quick as expected, given that Gap Inc. saw the low end as the fastest-growing segment of the industry. Therefore, in 1993, 13 of the Gap Outlets and about 40 poorly performing Gap stores were converted into the Gap Warehouse division, which stocked merchandise specifically manufactured for the division.

Old Navy Clothing Co.

Then in early 1994 the Gap, headquartered in San Francisco, began the latest metamorphosis of the mass-merchandising division when it opened its first three Old Navy Clothing Co. units in the Bay Area and one near Los Angeles. With expectations for a rollout of up to 45 strip-mall stores in 1994 and early 1995, Gap would not comment on volume projections, but industry sources estimated that the division could reach annualized sales of $240 million, based on a potential core of about 80 stores.[21] The annual clothing mass market generally was estimated to total over $200 billion. Perhaps Old Navy was the inspiration of Gap executives who came face to face with an economic reality in the early 1990s: that scores of consumers were jobless or working two jobs to make ends meet and couldn't afford the pricey goods in regional malls where most Gap stores operated. Wall Street analysts said Old Navy stores, by offering a timely mix of lower prices and decent-quality clothes, albeit a few notches below the Gap merchandise, would make Old Navy successful.[22] Old Navy merchandise generally was priced about 30 percent lower than Gap clothing and also had specially designed products. "We're really going to school on this business," said Millard Drexler, Gap president. "It's too early to make predictions, but we will be aggressive about expanding the business."[23] Products made for Old Navy are no different from what was made for Gap Warehouses, but by using lighter-weight and less expensive fabrics than those used for regular Gap merchandise, Old Navy was able to meet its low price structure. For example, Old Navy Jeans were priced at $22 as compared with Gap's $34.

Initial Locations

The Old Navy locations in the Bay Area included one converted Gap Warehouse and two new properties, while the City of Commerce (near Los Angeles) location also was a converted Gap Warehouse. Old Navy stores were expected to average about 15,000 square feet and have nondescript exteriors and a friendly industrialized interior environment that featured appetizing fashion basics. The layout placed men's wear on the left, women's on the right, and children's in the rear. Baby clothes and large sizes also were carried later. Salespersons in black logo T-shirts paired with jeans or khaki pants greet shoppers by offering oversized black mesh Old Navy shopping bags (initially priced at $3) in shopping carts, many with baby seats. Store aisles were wide and boldly labeled, and the checkout counters were surrounded by impulse items such as socks and baseball caps. Another example of cost cutting was Old Navy's serviceable concrete floors, compared with Gap's hardwood floors and lush extras, such as inviting seating areas and abundant displays of fresh flowers, which were reserved for Banana Republic's locations. One industry observer commented that the Old Navy interior reminded one of a visit to the supermarket.

Creating an Image

Startup advertising for Old Navy was limited to full-page or double-page ads in regional newspapers and local billboards. The word *Gap* was used only on exterior store signs shown in the ads and was expected to be a short-term strategy to use the corporate name. Mr. Drexler said: "We wanted to help launch the business by trading on the equity of the Gap."[24] The ads listed a toll-free telephone number for potential customers to call to get further information, and when called, a recording gave product news, detailed the 30-day return policy, and provided directions to the nearest Old Navy. The recording also asked callers to leave a message on how they heard about the store. The name *Old Navy* was purported to be more about mental imaging than fashion reality—a denim work shirt is the closest thing to a nautical theme. Old Navy does not sell Navy-style or nautical-themed clothing. It was reported that Gap executives saw the name originally on an old building in Europe and liked it. When asked what is the store for, Richard Christman, vice-president of communications for Gap Inc., first pointed out that Old Navy was not an outlet shopping center store used to sell over-stocked Gap leftovers. "It's for the consumer without as much disposable income," said Christman. "You'll find great clothes at great prices. There's a great need for casual clothing at these price points," he said. "We've been getting a tremendous response."[25]

Competitors had taken what was known as the Gap "look" and underpriced it to reach the mass market. By opening Old Navy, Gap Inc. began to sell its own version of less expensive look-alikes. But Old Navy looked different than its Gap siblings. In between a cement floor and exposed-pipe ceilings, clothing was hung on and stacked in metal shelves. And customers purchased their bargains through check-out counters. But the clothing styles were pure Gap. Old Navy was awash in denim blue, khaki tan, navy, black, and white, and roughly 20 percent of its merchandise cost less than $22. But looking at the way the clothing was displayed and at the fixtures in Old Navy was to be reminded of the elan and quality of a retailer with pricier goods, whether it be Gap Inc.'s own Gap and Banana Republic stores or others like A/X Armani Exchange or a Ralph Lauren/Polo or a Tommy Hilfiger section in a department store. Unlike much of the apparel in this price range, Old Navy's clothes were distinctive, made from higher-quality fabrics like linen-and-cotton blends and with an attention to detail like embroidery. The store's layout included high-school lockers, stripped to bare metal and bereft of some doors, that serve as chic display cases. The overhead storage space so characteristic of budget retailers was concealed with canvas flaps that lend a vaguely nautical quality. Checkout counters were crafted from polished pressed board and galvanized metal—no Formica. The light to indicate that a cashier is free was a clever adaptation of the signal light one might find on a factory floor—not the generic bulb behind a plain plastic box.[26] One observer noted that Old Navy was the type of store you wished you could have shopped in when you were in college.[27] But in reality Old Navy was a one-stop location for families, since it had both men's and women's sections and also had baby and kids' clothing in the $10 to $20 range, thereby allowing an individual to spend a virtual lifetime attired in T-shirts, khaki, and denim.

GROWTH POTENTIAL AT GAP INC.

During an October 1994 consumer conference held by Roberson Stephens & Co. in New York, Warren Hashagen, senior vice-president for the Gap Inc., noted that Old Navy (then operating 28 units) could become Gap's largest division by the end of the decade by adding between 50 and 100 stores. Mr. Hashagen said: "It's a major growth vehicle for us, and we're very excited about the potential." To avoid cannibalization of the flagship Gap stores, Hashagen said that Old Navy stores would be located in different markets. "We've gone after a different customer and real estate base," he said. While the Gap division opts for regional malls and urban areas, Old Navy units generally were located in strip centers or power centers and targeted a more moderate customer than the Gap, noted Hashagen. He observed that there had been no "significant" negative effects on the Gap stores if the two concepts were located nearby but that the company tried not to "go head to head" with the two divisions.[28]

Growth of Old Navy coincides with a time of struggling with sluggish sales at the 866-unit Gap division. Mr. Hashagen noted that the Gap division is far from dead but has the challenge to "adapt and redefine the business" and is working hard to offer "a balance between fashion and basics" while seeking merchandise to tempt customers into making "incremental" purchases, including offering new product categories such as shoes and personal products such as fragrances, shampoos, conditioners, soap, bath gels and salts, and some gift items. Mr. Hashagan said that product-line extensions also would be offered in GapKids stores, including such merchandise as toys and shoes. Although Mr. Hashagan stressed that the Gap stores will not cut prices and that its initial markups will remain the same, they will begin emphasizing "value" and will tout price in both print ads and in-store signage.[29]

Mr. Hashagen made additional comments to the effect that Banana Republic had been "turning out positive comp-store sales" and "margin improvements" and that the division was expected to "hit double-digit operating profit this year." He further noted that another growth vehicle for the Gap Inc. was its international division. He noted the Gap had stores in Canada, the United Kingdom, and France, with plans calling for opening Gap stores in Japan and Germany and Banana Republic stores in Canada in 1995. Mr. Hashagen said that the "only constraint" to international growth was high occupancy costs in Europe, particularly in the United Kingdom. Therefore, the Gap had taken to opening stores in basements or second floors rather than limiting locations to only ground level. "That has made a difference," he said. "But we won't take bad sites just to grow the business."[30]

Some Additional Outsider Viewpoints

While younger shoppers may avoid the Gap when they want the latest styles, many are still shopping there even if it's only for khakis or jeans. "It used to be cool, and it still is," said 28-year-old Richard Nardi of Pacific Heights, California. "It's prolific. You can't help [but] go in there."[31] A more positive viewpoint was taken by Alan Millstein, chairman of Fashion Network, in early 1995 when he made the observation that visibility will keep the Gap a force in the youth market. "They have the best locations of all the mall-based retailers and all the big stores [in cities]," he said. "The youth market for 14- to 22-year-olds who shop in suburbia is addicted to the Gap."[32] Barry Bryant, of Ladenbur, Thalmann & Co. Inc. (industry analysts), noted a switch to a higher percentage of fashion-forward styles from basics and said: "I suspect that women's fashion is driving the Gap store business."[33] Mr. Bryant noted that he was impressed with Gap's earnings, given that the company cut its promotions significantly in 1994, and he added that he believed that the Gap had succeeded in differentiating itself from the higher-priced Banana Republic division.

Positive observations also were made by Mr. Millstein when he said this about Old Navy: "It offers great prices and interesting ambience, and the first pilot stores that have opened have been outstanding successes. It is probably the most successful innovative specialty idea of the 1990s."[34] Kelli Arena, CNN correspondent on "Business News," who had a rather more skeptical viewpoint, said: "But the new chain won't help the Gap meet all its new challenges. Analysts say there are already too many Gap stores, with prices that are too high and a selection that's too limited. Plus, the Gap is cutting back expansion plans for Old Navy. Perhaps the hardest crowd to please are investors, who saw Gap stock fall 23 percent last year [1994], despite solid earnings growth. Word is they're waiting on the sidelines to see if the specialty retailer is really special after all."[35]

Outside Consultant

Mr. Drexler in mid-1995 decided that it would be wise to involve an outside consultant in analyzing Gap Inc.'s current situation with regard to both Old Navy and Gap stores. He was concerned about the viewpoint expressed by Kelli Arena and others (noted earlier) that there were too many Gap stores, that Gap prices were too high, and that Gap's merchandise selection was too limited. At the same time he was in a quandary about what rate of expansion to use in developing Old Navy stores. Expansion had not occurred as quickly as originally expected for Old Navy, and although no formal announcement of a slowdown had been made by Gap Inc., he was aware that many industry observers had the opinion that expansion of Old Navy had been purposely slowed by Gap executives. Mr. Drexler wondered about the effect Old Navy would have on sales from existing Gap stores. Would future growth be in the low end of the apparel market served by Old Navy? Or would future growth be best achieved by concentrating on revitalizing the Gap stores?

Questions

In order to answer these questions, the case analyst is expected to adopt the viewpoint of an outside consultant, as noted earlier.

1. Are there too many Gap stores?
2. Are Gap prices too high and merchandise selection too limited?
3. How effective have the Gap's recent advertising efforts been?
4. Which of the following alternatives offers the most likely opportunity for future growth? Why?
   a. The Gap stores in the United States after revitalization
   b. The Gap stores through expansion of international locations
   c. The Old Navy division stores
5. Given your answer to Question 4, what would be your recommendation for how quickly Gap Inc. should expand the Old Navy division? What would be the optimal size (in number of stores) for this division?

Endnotes

1. Tom Vasich, "Mass-Market Clothing: With Old Navy Clothing Co., the Gap Imitates Itself with Lower Prices for a Vast Retail Audience Searching for Low Prices," *Orange County Metropolitan,* Business Dateline, August 1, 1994, Sec. 1, p. 46.
2. Pamela Street, "Three Tiers for the Gap: Company Profile," *Women's Wear Daily,* March 23, 1994, p. 5.
3. Andy Beckett, "FASHION/How We Fell into the Gap; Does the Gap Look Ordinary Now? Was It Just the Stars Who Made It Look Great? In America the Boom Is Over, But Is It Here?" *The Independent,* November 28, 1993.
4. *Ibid.*
5. *Ibid.*
6. *Ibid.*
7. *Ibid.*
8. *Ibid.*
9. *Ibid.*
10. Christina Duff, " 'Bobby Short Wore Khakis'—Who's He, and Who Cares?" *Wall Street Journal,* February 26, 1995.
11. *Ibid.*
12. *Ibid.*
13. *Ibid.*
14. *Ibid.*
15. Max Hicks and Wendy Tanaka, "The Gap Losing Its Cool Edge with Younger Set? Hip Gives Way to Mainstream Fashion," *San Francisco Examiner,* Business Section, February 17, 1995, p. 1.
16. *Ibid.*
17. Duff, *op cit.*
18. *Ibid.*
19. Beckett, *op cit.*
20. *Ibid.*
21. Street, *op cit.*
22. Cathleen Ferraro, "Gap's Low-Priced Store View for Last Cherry Creek Spot," *Rocky Mountain News,* July 12, 1994, p. 31A.
23. Steet, *op cit.*
24. *Ibid.*
25. Vasich, *op cit.*
26. Stephanie Strom, "How Gap Inc. Spells Revenge," *New York Times,* April 24, 1994, Late Edition, Final, Sec. 3, p. 1.
27. Vasich, *op cit.*
28. Jean E. Palmieri, "Gap Sees Old Navy Evolving into Its Biggest Division; Company Exec Details Growth Plans for Unit at Monday Conference; Gap Inc. Senior VP-Finance Warren Hashagen," *Daily News Record,* October 4, 1994, p. 3.
29. *Ibid.*
30. *Ibid.*
31. Matt Hicks and Wendy Tanaka, "The Gap Losing Its Cool Edge with Younger Set? Hip Gives Way to Mainstream Fashion," *San Francisco Examiner,* February 17, 1995, p. B-1.
32. *Ibid.*
33. Jennifer L. Brady, "Gap's Net Jumps 55% in Quarter," *Women's Wear Daily,* August 12, 1995, p. 2.
34. Kelli Arena, CNN "Business News," February 9, 1995.
35. *Ibid.*

Priceline.com: Act III–From Dot.com to "Real Business"

This case was prepared by Carol H. Anderson, Crummer Graduate School of Business, Rollins College, and Alexander T. Wood, University of Central Florida.

Jeffrey Boyd and Richard Braddock were discussing Priceline.com's financial results for the second quarter of 2001. Boyd, Priceline.com's President and Chief Operating Officer, said, "We are pleased that our airline ticket sales have substantially recovered, despite the difficult airline travel market and competition from heavy discounting by the major carriers. It is also encouraging to see the continued rapid growth of our hotel and rental car products, which we believe have a substantial inventory advantage over the competition, and broad consumer appeal."

Braddock, the company's Chairman and Chief Executive Officer, stated, "We expect Priceline.com to continue the steady growth of customers beyond our current 11 million customers." He added that this could be accomplished through more efficient database marketing tools, and by building on the company's repeat business ratio.[1]

With reference to the future, Mr. Braddock said, "On-line travel appears to be one of the few sweet spots in e-commerce....With our renewed brand strengths, our product offerings robust and expanding, our customer base growing on both new and repeat bases, and our margins well above industry averages and sustainable, we believe Priceline.com is now positioned to be one of the Internet's pre-eminent, profitable, e-commerce brands.[2]

This case was written based on published documents. It is intended to be used as a basis for class discussion rather than to illustrate either effective or ineffective handling of the situation. Reprinted by permission of the authors.

Neither Boyd nor Braddock had any way of knowing that their company and the travel industry would face new challenges in the wake of the September 11, 2001 attacks on the World Trade Center in New York City.

PRICELINE.COM: COMPANY HIGHLIGHTS

Priceline.com, the "Name Your Own Price" Internet pricing system, was introduced in 1998 to sell airline tickets, hotel rooms, and other goods and services to consumers at bargain prices. From its inception, Priceline attracted attention as a leader among the growing number of dot.com competitors who offered bargains on line. Investors were attracted by the promise of founder Jay Walker's patented business model that was designed for a variety of audiences. For consumers, it is a travel agent or collector of bargain offers. For vendors, it is an alternative way to distribute products, or to get rid of distressed inventory without a negative association with cheap prices. Vendors also can use Priceline as a direct marketing channel, and a source of information to assess customers' levels of price elasticity. Investors were attracted to the idea of an easily expandable business platform where there were no physical products, and inventory risks were minimal. (A more detailed description of the Priceline business model follows in a later section.)

JAY WALKER, PRICELINE.COM FOUNDER

According to one observer, Jay Walker is a "self-styled serial inventor, who uses the Internet to devise ways of revolutionizing business much as other inventors use their toolsheds to refine mousetraps or build rockets."[3] Priceline.com, a website for bargain-hunting customers, is the most prominent of the over 300 novel business models registered by Jay Walker's think tank, Walker Digital Corporation. This innovation briefly made an $8 billion fortune on paper, and the company was called the most successful Internet business model of the year in spring 2000.

A year earlier (1999), Mr. Walker said that there was no category in which Priceline's business model could not be successful. However, in late October 2000, the company was forced to close two affiliates, WebHouse Club and Perfect Yardsale, where consumers bid for cut-price groceries, gasoline, and other small-ticket goods. Priceline invested $363 million in about a year in these unsuccessful attempts to extend the name-your-own-price model into new product categories. Investors' confidence in "name-your-own-price" online retailing was badly undermined by the WebHouse Club and Perfect Yardsale closures, and share prices fell to $1.31 by the end of 2000. (WebHouse is discussed further in a later section.)

In December 2000, Jay Walker stepped down from the board of Priceline in order to focus on rebuilding Walker Digital Corporation, his closely-held new business incubator. At that time, Walker was the largest shareholder of Priceline, but did not hold an executive position.[4] He sold a significant number of Priceline.com shares at very low prices, instituted cost-cutting measures at Walker Digital, and stopped construction on his $7.5 million, 24,000 square foot mansion in Connecticut.

THE NAME-YOUR-OWN PRICE BUSINESS MODEL

Jay Walker said that he is " ... a theorist who wants to understand the abstract levels at which things operate, then turn those abstractions into commer-

cial value."[5] Walker developed many successful ventures with this philosophy, particularly through his Walker Digital Corporation laboratory. Priceline.com was developed from a system that allows a company to dispose of excess inventory at optimal prices. A double-blind method is used so the provider can maintain brand image and charge full price for non-surplus goods. Investors were so attracted to this model they gave the company $13 million during its IPO in March 1999. Walker Digital's patented business processes were widely believed to be a key to success.

The Priceline model was built on the premise that there were only four ways to create value in the New Economy: information, entertainment, convenience, and savings, and that businesses in an electronic network blend these in some proportion. Walker believed that information and entertainment were not a good basis for business models, but the real battle was over the balance between convenience and savings—and the greatest of these was savings. Further, the Priceline model separated the information component from the physical component in the Information Economy. Information was treated as a separate element, and had its own source of value. For example, FedEx delivers packages physically (as an industrial company), but it's an information company when you can track your package, know your discount and billing, and so forth. Customers can decide which is more important to them— the information component or the industrial component.

Priceline generates revenue in two ways in the airline travel business. (1) It keeps the difference between the consumer's bid and the lowest fare given to Priceline by the airline partner. Both the consumer's bid and the airline's lowest fare are unpublished, although the airline price is visible to Priceline. (2) "Adaptive marketing" and "cross-subsidy" promotional programs give consumers the chance to increase the value of their bids. If an airline ticket customer signs up for a new credit card, for example, Priceline might add $20 to the consumer's bid (no charge to consumer) to improve the odds that the bid will be matched. However, Priceline keeps the difference between the $20 added to the bid and the $50–$75 it gets for each new credit card customer, and so on. (A number of other fees may be obtained from business partners and customers.)[6]

When Priceline introduced Priceline.com in April 1998, Walker's concept was unique, and at first shoppers and investors loved it. Priceline.com expanded its product lines from airlines to other goods and services, including a new car buying service launched in July 1998, hotel rooms launched in October 1998, and rental cars launched in February 2000. Other online services followed. Some were successful and some were not. As of November 2001, Priceline's services spanned four broad product categories: travel service (leisure airline tickets, hotel rooms, rental cars); personal finance service (home mortgages, refinancing and home equity loans through an independent licensee); automotive service that offers new cars; and telecommunications service (long distance telephone services).[7] The primary focus was on travel services.

WEBHOUSE CLUB: AN ATTEMPT TO EXTEND THE PRICELINE.COM BUSINESS MODEL

WebHouse Club was conceived as an extension of the Walker Digital name-your-price model used by Priceline.com, with the idea that large numbers of grocery and gasoline customers would bring in more frequent customers than Priceline. Jay Walker said, "Once you achieve critical mass, you can build a very large and profitable company."[8]

Some analysts predicted that the Priceline model would revolutionize the world of retailing, and there was great excitement late in 1999 when the company opened WebHouse Club, operating as an independent licensee. WebHouse made it possible for customers to bid on gasoline and groceries. The company selected William Shatner (Star Trek's Captain Kirk) as its pitchman for WebHouse Club in a series of "campy" ads on television and radio. Shatner predicted "This is going to be big—really big."[9] (Unfortunately, the appeal seemed to wear off in a matter of months.)

The media enthusiastically hailed WebHouse Club's entry into the name-your-price Internet grocery business during the last months of 1999.[10] The first launch was in the New York metro market, serving millions of residents of the New York–New Jersey–Connecticut region. Members did not pay a fee to belong to WebHouse Club, and could expect to reduce their grocery bills significantly, comparable to shopping at Sam's Club or Costco—but without the need to buy in such large quantities. Customers could register online, and have their card mailed to their home or they could pick it up at participating grocery stores. New York test area stores included A&P, ShopRite, King Kullen, Waldbaum's, D'Augustino's, and Gristede's.

WebHouse's approach was that they deliver prices, not boxes of products. They did not need a distribution facility, just the ability to get prices their customers wanted. How did this work? When a customer wanted to place an order, he or she logged on to Priceline.com and linked to the WebHouse Club site. Next, he named his desired price for national brands of grocery products in any of the 140 categories listed (excluding deli and dairy products). Customers had to pick two acceptable brand names. A minute later, WebHouse was to respond with a match. (Customer's credit card was charged at this point.) Then the customer printed out the statement and took it to his/her participating store where the WebHouse membership card and grocery list were presented at checkout. The manufacturer covered the discounted cost of the groceries directly to the retailer. Many customers were initially sold on this new method of shopping for groceries at a lower price, in spite of the need to shop online, then go to the grocery store to fill an order.

Eventually, questions were raised about the name-your-own-price grocery service. In a December 1999 *Chain Store Age* article,[11] the author described his WebHouse experience one week after the site opened for business as follows: "Consumers … go onto www.priceline.webhouse.com and select from 140 grocery categories. They either choose one of three pre-set bids for items or create a bid of their own. They are then given a list of which bids were accepted [credit cards are charged], and they print out a list of items." "At the store, shoppers take the lists they printed out from the Web site and meander around collecting the groceries. They then hit the checkout line, swipe their WebHouse card and leave." The author had no problems, but identified some critical issues based on his experience:

- Inventory—consumers had to return to the store for out-of-stock items.
- Logistics—consumers who forgot to take their printed out list, or lost the list, had to log back on to the Web and print out another copy.

• Convenience—The WebHouse frequent shopper card made it possible to deduct prepurchased items at checkout, but the customer had to separate these items from regular grocery items.

At the end of 1999, WebHouse managers faced a number of important issues: (1) they had not closed a deal with any major brand manufacturers; (2) member savings were subsidized by WebHouse's company funds, and the early consumer response resulted in significant losses and use of cash; (3) questions were raised about where and how quickly to expand; and (4) Walker was recognized as a brilliant innovator and marketer, but was considered to be an entrepreneur whose strength was in ideas, not in managing a company with complex processes.[12]

By October 2000, headlines were very unfavorable. As one headline announced, "Priceline's WebHouse Club Abandoned as Investors Balk."[13] However, analysts felt that there would be little direct financial impact on Priceline from WebHouse Club's shutdown since it was set up as a separate venture. Another headline proclaimed, "There's just one thing wrong with name-your-own-price businesses: You're not naming your own price."[14] The author maintained that this was a "propose-your-own-price" business, which was a different model. He suggested that people of Western capitalism had agreed over the past few centuries that it is more efficient not to haggle over everyday goods, and that there is a difference between saving several hundred dollars on an airline flight versus pennies on a jar of peanut butter. He questioned the price elasticity in something with a long shelf life (e.g., cereal), and said that for many consumers, the advantage of shopping on the Web is to reduce haggling and bargaining for purchases.

WebHouse discontinued operations in October 2000, after only 10 months of being in business. Investors refused to infuse more money into the company, which was losing money on the deep discounts it was forced to absorb in order to keep its two million price shoppers coming back. Jay Walker and other WebHouse executives attributed the venture's failure to the current investment climate, rather than their business model. They identified their typical WebHouse customer as a female, shopping for her family, who was flexible about brands she would buy, and who wanted to save money.[15]

PRICELINE.COM'S PROFITABILITY PITFALLS

A series of news events illustrate the company's dilemma during the last two quarters of 2000:[16]

• July 2000: Six of Priceline's supplier airlines (America West, American, Continental, Northwest, United, and US Airways) decided to operate their own website, Hotwire.com, to sell vacant airline seats directly to customers at discounted prices. (Hotwire started service in October 2000, and customers found it easier and faster than Priceline's process.)[17]

• September 29, 2000: Priceline warned investors that revenues would not meet expectations due to weak airline ticket sales. Since this represented Priceline's core business, it seemed doubtful the company could become profitable anytime soon.

• October 2000: Walker announced that he was shutting down WebHouse Club, Priceline's innovative online grocery and gasoline business.

• October 2000: The Connecticut Attorney General's Office announced that it was probing complaints of incomplete and inaccurate disclosure of the company's sales policies—particularly in the case of airline tickets.

• Early November 2000: The company reported that fourth-quarter revenue would slow down, and that it was cutting back its work force by laying off 16 percent of its employees (87 of 535 employees were fired).

• November 3, 2000: Priceline chief financial officer, Heidi Miller, resigned—considered a significant loss of a star executive.[18]

• November 3, 2000: Notice was given that a class action lawsuit against Priceline.com, Inc. and its senior executives was being pursued in the U.S. District Court for the District of Connecticut, "seeking to recover damages on behalf of allegedly defrauded investors who purchased Priceline securities between January 31 and October 4, 2000.[19]

• November 18, 2000: Another high-profile executive, Maryann Keller (former auto analyst), resigned as head of Priceline's auto-services business.[20]

• Negative publicity: CBS Television program, "48 Hours," aired consumer complaints about

Priceline.com, and announced that the Connecticut Better Business Bureau had revoked Priceline's membership because the company did not resolve the complaints.

- Fall 2000: Numerous class action suits were filed against Priceline because of declining stock value. This activity was costly and time consuming, and took the company's attention away from running the business.
- Warrants: The company's cash position was threatened by a financial burden in the form of warrants held by Delta Air Lines and other suppliers.
- Challenges to patents: Priceline charged Microsoft's Expedia with patent infringement.[21] Other patent challenges also were in process.
- Brand association: Priceline WebHouse Club's grocery business was on the Priceline.com website, leading WebHouse customers to believe they were dealing directly with Priceline.[22]

Jay Walker and other Priceline executives remained positive in the face of the many challenges that confronted them going into the fourth quarter of 2000. The company had the advantage of being the best-known name in Internet travel sales, with an ample supply of inventory that was available for them to sell. Priceline's customer base was constantly growing, with an estimated 8 million shoppers at that time. It offered an extensive product line, and had experienced significant increases in its core business of airline tickets. In the third quarter 2000, Priceline sold 1.29 million airline seats. This was twice as many as were sold in the same quarter the previous year. However, analysts were not optimistic about Priceline's survival going into the fourth quarter of 2000. At the same time, airlines were discounting their own fares, and headlines contained negative publicity about Priceline.[23]

PRICELINE PERFORMANCE

Wall Street was delighted when Priceline went public in April 1999, and very soon the company's stock traded as high as $162 per share. Then it fell to around $50 during fall 1999, and surged to nearly $100 during spring 2000. By late summer it was down to about $25. By fall 2000, a series of events took the stock down to single digits. Priceline's much-needed investors were losing confidence in the company.[24] In March 2000, the company's market capitalization reached more than $17 billion, and Wall Street was positive about Priceline's future profitability. Priceline's name-your-own-price model seemed like a sure winner. Three months later, the company's stock fell to an all-time low of $4.28, a 97 percent drop from its April 1999 high of $165.[25]

In the first quarter 2000, Priceline.com's net loss narrowed, as revenue grew to $313 million due to significant increases in demand for airline and hotel booking services. As a result, Wall Street analysts said, "Priceline's performance demonstrated the strength of the company's business." Analysts appeared to favor the idea of patenting a method that allowed customers to name their own prices—which Priceline could accept or not—for purchasing services. The company's executives said that the first quarter 2000 results showed the benefits of its diversified product expansion strategy over the past year, and the ability of every shopping service introduced by Pipeline to take advantage of the company's existing customer-support lines, technology, and other infrastructure. This was believed to give Priceline a better chance to be profitable than more narrowly focused Internet retailers.[26]

At the end of the third quarter 2000, Priceline showed improved performance in revenues and gross profit over the same period for 1999. The company had positive operating cash flow for the second quarter in a row, with $131 million of cash and short-term investments. Comparisons of pro forma results for the first and third quarters of 1999 and third quarter of 2000 indicate improved performance in revenues, gross profit, operating loss, net loss, and loss per share, as the company appeared to be heading toward anticipated profitability. (See Exhibit 1).

Given high expectations and the promise of satisfaction for customers, suppliers, and investors, it is not surprising that the company's results have been both a source of satisfaction and disappointment for each of these groups over the past several years. Although Priceline.com was not profitable until the second quarter of 2001, the company maintained a relatively strong cash position during several years of typical dot.com performance ups and downs. Priceline.com Inc. reported record revenues for second quarter 2001, and its *first-ever profit*. Revenues reached $364.8 million, compared to $352.1 million in second quarter 2000. Pro forma net income reached $11.7 million or $0.06 per basic share. Gross profit for second quarter

2001 was a record $60.1 million. (See comparative data in Exhibits 1 and 2.)

During the first two months of the third quarter 2001, Priceline.com generated about $245 million in revenue and was well on its way to continued growth in revenue and profits. In spite of the infamous 9/11 attack, Priceline was able to generate $302 million in revenues and $50.4 million in gross profits for the third quarter. Pro forma net income

was $6.3 million (GAAP net income before preferred stock dividend was $5.0 million), and gross margin reached 16.7% for the period. Priceline's consumer franchise grew to nearly 12 million customers, and repeat business reached a record 63%. (See Exhibits 1 and 2 for additional financial data.) [27]

According to Priceline.com, demand for travel products recovered substantially after the 9/11 attacks. However, unit sales and revenue from travel

EXHIBIT I

Priceline.com Pro Forma Results—1999–2000 (in $thousands)

	1 Q 99	1 Q 00	2 Q 99	2 Q 00	3 Q 99	3 Q 00	4 Q 99	4 Q 00	4 Q 00 vs. 4 Q 99	
									$ Change	% Change
	49,411	313,798	111,564	352,095	152,222	341,334	169,213	228,169	58,956	34.84%
Gross profit	5,752	49,027	10,900	55,176	18,594	54,435	24,109	35,055	10,946	45.40%
Operating profit/loss	(17,237)	(9,994)	(15,895)	(4,358)	(14,255)	(4,488)	(12,745)	(26,986)	(14,241)	111.74%
Net profit/loss	(16,779)	(7,279)	(13,876)	(1,633)	(11,899)	(2,224)	(9,988)	(25,003)	(15,015)	150.33%
Net profit/loss per share	(0.18)	(0.04)	(-0.10)	(0.01)	(0.08)	(0.01)	(0.06)	(0.15)	(0.09)	150.00%

EXHIBIT 2

Priceline.com Pro Forma Results—2000–2001 (in $thousands)

	1 Q 00	1 Q 01	2 Q 00	2 Q 01	3 Q 00	3 Q 01	4 Q 00	4 Q 01*	3 Q 00 vs. 3 Q 99*	
									$ Change	% Change
Revenues	313,798	269,704	352,095	364,765	341,334	301,989	228,169		(39,345)	−11.53%
Gross profit	49,027	43,115	55,176	60,106	54,435	50,432	35,055		(4,003)	−7.35%
Operating profit/loss	(9,994)	(8,024)	(4,358)	9,919	(4,488)	4,193	(26,986)		8,681	−193.43%
Net profit/loss	(7,279)	(6,248)	(1,633)	11,735	(2,224)	6,289	(25,003)		8,513	−382.78%
Net profit/loss per share	(0.04)	(0.03)	(0.01)	0.06	(0.01)	0.03	(0.15)		$0.04	−400.00%

*4 Q 01 not available 11/01.

product sales were not able to keep up with that demand due to refunds following the attacks, and pressure from deep discounting by airlines, hotel, and rental car companies to stimulate demand. Recovery also was slowed down by schedule changes and disruptions in available air, hotel, and rental car inventories.

In spite of any setbacks caused by the terrorist attacks, Priceline.com's top executives were confident about the future. They expected continued growth and financial success for the fourth quarter 2001, and beyond. President and COO, Jeffrey Boyd, attributed the rapid recovery of consumer demand for the company's travel products to brand equity, customer loyalty, and the value offered to consumers. Hotel and rental car unit sales exceeded airline ticket sales for the first two quarters of 2001, and continued strong during the third period, accounting for 42% of all booked offers (including air), compared to 28% for the same period in 2000. The company's "look-to-book" ratio[28] of 12.8% exceeded that of leading competitors Travelocity (8.0%) and Expedia.com (5.5%). Richard Braddock, Chairman and CEO, stated that the steadily growing customer base, record level of repeat business, and a strong look-to-book ratio have provided a strong customer franchise, and positioned Priceline.com favorably for the future. He said, "Our Name Your Own Price proposition is now a preferred way of purchasing for millions of loyal customers, who come back to Priceline.com again and again for their travel and other purchases." (See Exhibit 3 for comparative data on offers and customer activity for Priceline.com's airline, hotel, and rental car businesses.)

PROBLEMS FACED BY INTERNET MARKETERS[29]

Priceline was not the only rising star dot.com that faced problems in the new economy. Other Internet companies experienced similar difficulties, raising questions about the underlying business models that previously seemed to promise great returns. Fall 2000 saw many examples of this. Healtheon/WebMD Corp. announced that it would cut 1,100 jobs at its Atlanta medical—services site. Amazon.com Inc.'s stock took a downturn on an

analyst's questioning whether it could succeed with its huge product assortment, and Yahoo!'s stock plunged on slowing growth and smaller margins related to an expected downturn in advertising expenditures. Webvan Group Inc. decided to delay its launch of delivery services in several key regions (and filed for Chapter 11 bankruptcy protection in July 2001).

Jim Horty, president of a forensic accounting firm that gauges valuations on startups, said: "A lot of these Internet companies view the technology as their business, rather than having a business." Many have realized that making money on the Internet has been more difficult than many expected. This is a problem, because dot.coms traditionally have relied on venture capital and hyped valuations to fund expansion plans, but now many investors have lost enthusiasm and have become wary of promised future earnings.

A number of key problems that have confronted Internet marketers include:

- Lack of control over cash flow issues
- Underestimating capital costs
- Lack of control over suppliers
- Lack of control over the products the company sells (e.g., Priceline finding discount gasoline in the middle of an oil crisis)
- Lack of control over demand—after the novelty of shopping on the Internet had worn off for some customers
- Scrambling—while Internet companies struggled to redefine themselves, traditional established businesses with "deep pockets and staying power" were rallying (e.g., Toys 'R' Us.com). John Barbour, CEO of Toys 'R' Us said (referring to WebHouse Club), "But they didn't have a business model, they don't have a path to profitability and they don't have a compelling consumer benefit." Target's president of financial services and new business, Gerry Storch, added, "The stupid era of the Internet is over. It's time to start doing things that make business sense." While "old economy" methods and business models were considered passé by the dot.com innovators, it appears that some of the experience and wisdom of the past may help dot.coms become profitable.

EXHIBIT 3

Offer and Customer Activity (in thousands)—By Segment (Jan. 1999–Sept. 2001)

	1Q99	2Q99	3Q99	4Q99	1Q00	2Q00	3Q00	4Q00	1Q01	2Q01	3Q01
Priceline.com: Airline Tickets											
Tickets Sold	186,521	440,339	623,848	707,343	1,250,416	1,288,592	1,290,096	809,327	1,075,555	1,435,936	1,183,981
Net Unique Offers	570,947	822,887	1,077,111	1,129,711	1,820,918	1,753,273	1,290,096	1,242,967	1,392,747	1,683,661	1,445,575
Offers Booked	108,917	280,471	397,355	442,089	801,204	869,408	1,756,236	590,088	709,576	963,167	779,319
Bind Rate (%)	19.1	34.1	36.9	39.1	44.0	49.6	50.5	47.5	50.9	57.2	53.9
Air product was launched 4/6/98											
Priceline.com: Hotel Rooms											
Room Nights Sold	45,580	92,134	179,508	192,795	409,514	432,463	526,450	367,372	432,884	680,604	879,922
Net Unique Offers	68,740	168,543	220,613	208,991	383,708	431,249	511,396	319,501	351,952	516,816	647,446
Offers Booked	15,717	36,854	78,047	83,824	180,343	195,517	244,655	176,712	432,884	680,604	879,922
Bind Rate (%)	22.9	21.9	35.4	40.1	47.0	45.3	47.8	55.3	53.5	60.2	61.0
Hotel product was launched 10/28/98											
Priceline.com: Rental Cars											
Days Sold					229,998	429,622	579,866	522,242	607,336	922,545	895,601
Net Unique Offers					90,639	175,878	217,760	207,436	229,581	325,235	313,389
Offers Booked					37,706	70,351	107,058	93,757	105,970	162,053	160,603
Bind Rate (%)					41.6	40.0	49.2	45.2	46.2	49.8	51.2
Rental car product was launched 2/3/00											

Explanation of terms:

Net Unique Offers = New customer offers + repeat customer offers.

Bind Rate = offers booked/net unique offers.

Priceline once seemed to symbolize the Internet's limitless potential as a place to invent new ways of doing business—not just a new place to do business. It has become evident, however, that just inventing a new business model is insufficient. "Innovative pricing mechanisms are useless without the ability to figure out when 'new' also means 'better.'" Another new startup, iDerive, offered another model: name your own price. If you don't save, the company pays you a predetermined amount. Most customers of price-oriented companies like Priceline and iDerive are savvy about gathering information online that will help them with their asking prices.

PRICELINE.COM'S INITIATIVES FOR IMPROVED PERFORMANCE

The Star Trek image of going boldly where no man had gone before was severely challenged for Priceline.com. Jay Walker has been referred to as an "indefatigable entrepreneur."[30] Many successful entrepreneurial ventures preceded Walker Digital Corporation, which is Walker's laboratory developed for the sole purpose of developing strategic theories and concepts that eventually could be converted into businesses, and patented. The focus was on Internet applications.[31] By the fourth quarter of 2000, Priceline.com had suffered serious setbacks that threatened to cause its demise. However, it was hoped that Walker's past successes and fervent belief in his name-your-own-price model would attract the necessary capital to keep the business afloat until it could achieve profitability.

At the end of the third quarter 2000, Daniel H. Schulman, president and chief executive officer of Priceline.com, reviewed positive aspects of the business, and presented a number of initiatives that were expected to improve Priceline.com's performance.[32] He cited the positive cash flow experienced by the company for the second consecutive quarter. While disappointed in airline ticket sales for the third quarter, he reported that the customer base grew to 8 million, and that more than half of the purchase offers were made by an increasing number of repeat customers. He further stated that 19 percent of revenues for the period came from Priceline.com's non-air business, versus 12 percent

the previous year. An increase in cross selling resulted in Priceline.com's airline ticket customers making up about half of hotel and rental car sales, as well as a large number of long distance sales from existing Priceline.com customers.

According to Mr. Schulman, a number of initiatives to improve cost structures and achieve long-term profitability by the end of 2000 were being implemented by Priceline. Customer satisfaction and service were being given top priority. This initiative included an educational program to demonstrate the Priceline value proposition more clearly to customers. This was to be accomplished through an improved website, product delivery, and consumer and third-party feedback.

The company realigned its operating management, and implemented a new compensation program designed to motivate and retain key employees (consisting primarily of equity-based compensation). Other initiatives included significant reduction in staffing, and amended terms of warrants held by Delta Air Lines. (These measures had a negative impact on fourth quarter 2000 results.) Mr. Schulman concluded at this time that although recent results were hurt by a weakness in airline ticket sales, the company was confident that customer metrics and performance on other fronts indicated a positive outlook for the business. He said, "We believe we are taking the right steps to position Priceline.com for future profitable growth in our core businesses." By spring 2001, analysts were favorable toward Priceline's chances for profitability. As an analyst for Goldman Sachs wrote on May 2, 2001, "Priceline has successfully 'right sized' its cost structure and now better controls its destiny."[33] On May 8, the company announced that Richard Braddock would reassume the position of chief executive, replacing Mr. Schulman, since Mr. Braddock was a "more seasoned executive who could turn the company around." At this time, Jeffery Boyd, chief operating officer, was promoted to the position of president.[34]

The clearest signal of a turnaround for Priceline was its first-ever profit report for the third quarter of 2001. This was attributed to "cutting costs, tempering advertising spending, and reviving sales in an economic environment that appears to favor its discount-driven model" ... after being "counted among the nearly dead dot-coms six months ago." The third quarter profitability figures reflect items such as a $5.4 million charge for severance pay and forgiven loans for Mr. Schulman. The downturn in the travel industry had a positive effect on profits. Revenue was increased by more airlines and hotels who offered discounted seats and rooms through Priceline.com during the quarter—but the

economic downturn also exerts pressure on prices throughout the industry and increases competition for customers.[35]

Richard Braddock outlined the company's plan for an improved earnings outlook in the fourth quarter of 2001 and on into 2002.[36] He credited this outlook to key operating efficiencies that were instituted over the past year as part of Priceline's turnaround plan. He outlined the reasons why he believes that priceline.com will continue to be a winning e-commerce company, despite the current challenges in the travel business:

- demand driven recovery in Priceline.com's U.S. travel business.
- strong, loyal consumer franchise.
- broadened product scope to reduce reliance on air product (e.g., increased strength of hotel and rental car business, and progress to date in building its mortgage business).

Braddock also cited significant developments for Priceline.com during the 3rd quarter 2001:

- customer care following the 9/11 crisis; exceptional customer service at emergency response levels.
- deepening strategic relationship with Cheung Kong (Holdings) Limited and Hutchison Whampoa Limited. These companies purchased over 7 million additional shares of Priceline.com stock in September 2001, and raised their equity to 30%; provides opportunity to introduce similar service in the Asian markets.[37]
- expansion of Priceline.com's travel products (e.g., hotel service in Mexico, Bahamas, Caribbean; beta test in 50 cities and towns in Europe; online test for cruise product; software developed for vacation package product).
- acquisition of 49 percent equity stake in PricelineMortgage.
- broadening of key supplier relationships (e.g., VISA USA).

THE MARKETING CONSULTANT'S CHALLENGE

Priceline.com has hired you as a marketing consultant. You have been asked to determine the following:

1. the optimal service mix for the company.
2. the most important actions that the company should take to achieve profitability in each of its industries.
3. a short-term marketing plan for the 4th quarter 2001 and 1st quarter 2002.

You have an appointment to meet with Richard Braddock and Jeffery Boyd tomorrow morning to present your recommendations for continued growth and prosperity.

Endnotes

1. Repeat business ratio is defined as the number of unique purchase offers coming from repeat customers divided by the number of total unique purchases.
2. *Business Wire,* "Priceline.com Reports Profitability and Record Revenue for 2nd Quarter 2001 (July 31, 2001).
3. Edgecliffe-Johnson, Andrew, "Under the Hammer: Priceline Preached A Revolution. Consumers Were Not Ready, Says Andrew Edgecliffe-Johnson," *Financial Times (London),* Comment and Analysis Section (October 9, 2000), p. 27.
4. Angwin, Julia, "Priceline.com Founder Leaves Board To Focus on Incubator Walker Digital," *Wall Street Journal* (December 29, 2000), p. A13.
5. Rothenberg, Randall, "Jay Walker: The Thought Leader Interview," *Strategy + Business* (Second Quarter 2000), pp. 87–94.
6. Eisenmann, Thomas and Jon K. Rust, "Case Study: Priceline WebHouse Club," *Journal of Interactive Marketing* (Volume 14, Number 4, Autumn 2000), pp. 47–72.
7. *Business Wire,* "Priceline.com Reports 3rd Quarter 2000 Financial Results; Announces Measures to Strengthen Core Business," (November 2, 2000); *Business Wire,* "Priceline.com Reports Pro Forma Earnings Per Share of $0.03 for 3rd Quarter 2001 (November 1, 2001).
8. Angwin, Julia and Nick Wingfield, "Discounted Out: How Jay Walker Built WebHouse on a Theory That He Couldn't Prove—Priceline Offshoot Ended Up Eating Millions in Costs to Subsidize Customers—Savvy Schemes at the Pumps," *Wall Street Journal* (October 16, 2000), p. A.1+.
9. Lavoie, *op. cit.*
10. Corral, Cecile B., "WebHouse Club Puts Priceline In Grocery Biz," *Discount Store News* (October 4, 199), pp. 3, 48; Anonymous, "Priceline Strategy Extends to Online Grocery Shopping," *Supermarket Business* (October 15, 1999), p. 11+.
11. Hanover, Dan, "WebHouse Is Good, but Could Be Better," *Chain Store Age* (December 1999), p. 224.
12. Eisenmann, Thomas and Jon K. Rust, *op. cit.*, p. 49.

13. Hansell, Saul, "Priceline's WebHouse Club Abandoned as Investors Balk," *New York Times* (October 6, 2000), p. C.1.

14. Race, Tim, "New Economy: There's Just One Thing Wrong With Name-Your-Own-Price Businesses:You're Not Naming Your Own Price," *Wall Street Journal* (October 23, 2000), p. 4.

15. Race, *op. cit.*

16. Ali, "Priceline Shares Hit All-Time Low as E-Commerce Firm Struggles to Survive," *The Star Ledger*, http://www.nj.com/news (November 8, 2000).

17. Loomis, Carol J., "Inside Jay Walker's House of Cards," *Fortune* (November 13, 2000), pp. 127–138.

18. Also see Angwin, Julia and Joann Lublin, "Priceline Loses Finance Chief, Issues Warning," *Wall Street Journal* (November 3, 2000), pp. A3, A12.

19. *Business Wire*, "Dyer & Shuman, LLP Announces Shareholder Class Action Against Priceline.com, Inc. (November 3, 2000); Priceline.com is charged with violations of the antifraud provisions of the Securities Exchange Act of 1934, and alleges that Priceline issued a series of materially false and misleading statements that resulted in artificially inflated Priceline securities prices during the class period. Note that other lawsuits against the company also are pending.

20. Angwin, Julia and Karen Lundegaard, "Priceline Auto-Services Executive Quits," *Wall Street Journal* (November 18, 2000), p. B6.

21. Loomis, *op. cit.*, p. 138.

22. Loomis, *op. cit.*, p. 134.

23. Ali, *op. cit.*

24. Lavoie, Denise, "Priceline.com—The Rise and Fall of the Perfect Internet Company," *Associated Press State and Local Wire, Business News Section* (November 8, 2000).

25. Ali, Sam, *op. cit.*

26. Wingfield, Nick, "Priceline Loss Narrows as Revenue Soars Amid Demand for Bookings," *Wall Street Journal* (April 25, 2000), p. B6.

27. *Business Wire*, "Priceline.com Reports Pro Forma Earnings Per Share of $0.03 for 3rd Quarter 2001."

28. The "look-to-book" ratio is a metric used in the travel industry to measure the percentage of people who actually buy a product after visiting or contacting the travel company.

29. Most of this section is based on Kerstetter, Jim, Linda Himelstein, Rob Hof, Louise Lee, and Pamela Moore, "Analysis and Commentary: The Internet," *Business Week* (October 23, 2000), pp. 44–45.

30. Loomis, *op. cit.*, p. 138.

31. Rothenberg, *op. cit.*

32. Business Wire, "Priceline.com Reports 3rd Quarter 2000 Financial Results….," *op. cit.*

33. Angwin, Julia, "Priceline Surges on Turnaround Progress," *Wall Street Journal.* (May 2, 2001), p. A3.

34. Sandberg, Jared, "Priceline Replaces CEO With Chairman," *Wall Street Journal* (May 8, 2001), p. B7.

35. Angwin, Julia, "Priceline.com Posts a Profit, Crediting Stringent Cost Cuts, Escalating Demand," *Wall Street Journal* (August 1, 2001), p. A3.

36. *Business Wire*, "Priceline.com Reports Pro Forma Earnings Per Share of $0.03 For 3rd Quarter," (November 1, 2001).

37. See *Business Wire*, "Priceline.com Agrees to Connect Its Name Your Own Price Travel Services to the Amadeus Global Travel Distribution System," (November 6, 2000) for other opportunities to expand globally through Priceline.com's November 2000 agreement with Amadeus Global Travel Distribution, whereby its international Global Distribution System (GDS) could be used to process ticket purchase requests from Priceline.com's customers and international licensees.

Embassy by Waterford Wedgwood PLC (1995)

This case was prepared by Julian W. Vincze, Professor of Marketing, Crummer Graduate School of Business, Rollins College.

The headline, "A New Brand Restores Sparkle to Waterford," I caught Jane Mills' attention. As a bride-to-be, Jane had just registered her choices for Waterford crystal stemware and Wedgwood china at the bridal registries2 of two local upscale department stores. Since the wedding was still several months away, Jane wondered if she had registered her choices too quickly. The article noted that in 1990, Waterford Wedgwood's future had looked grim. U.S. sales (Waterford's main market) were falling as the economy depressed and customers had turned away from prestige purchases. Jane recalled that in 1994 many large U.S. retailers had been in bankruptcy proceedings, and competition from low-cost producers in the former eastern European block was hot. But Jane now read that 1994 sales of Waterford crystal and Wedgwood china were both up and that the company's share of market had increased seven percentage points from 1990 to a current 34 percent. After several years of losses, the company was profitable again. (See Exhibit A for details.) The article seemed to attribute this turnaround to the 1990 decision by Waterford to introduce Marquis, a midpriced brand and the first new brand for Waterford in 200 years. And now Waterford seemed to be hoping for the same impact on Wedgwood, with 1995 plans to introduce Embassy, a midpriced brand of porcelain dinnerware. Jane, an MBA stu-

dent, decided to find out more about what had happened at Waterford Wedgwood, thinking it would be an interesting topic for discussion in her marketing strategy class.

WATERFORD WEDGWOOD HISTORY

Waterford Wedgwood PLC (WW), the Irish holding company, had two divisions—Waterford Crystal and Wedgwood Group. Waterford, with about 60 percent of WW's revenue and world renowned for quality crystal, dated back to 1783 and the southeast Ireland port city of Waterford, where its main factory and headquarters still remain. Wedgwood, with about 40 percent of WW's revenue and based in Barlaston, England, and also world renowned, was acquired in 1986 and dated from 1759. The Wedgwood Group consisted of Josiah Wedgwood and Sons, Ltd. (its main operation, suppliers of high-quality tableware and ornamentalware in fine bone china, fine earthenware, oven-to-tableware, Jasperware, and Black Basalt); Johnson Brothers, Ltd. (makers of fine earthenware and tableware); Coalport China, Ltd. (fine bone china tableware and ornamentalware); Masons Ironstone, Ltd., and William Adams and Son (Potter), Ltd.; Wedgwood Hotelware, Ltd. (suppliers of bone china to the hotel and catering industries); and Precision Studios, Ltd.

This case was written based on published documents. It is intended to be used as a basis for class discussion rather than to illustrate either effective or ineffective handling of the situation. Reprinted by permission of the authors.

EXHIBIT A

Waterford Wedgwood PLC Key Financial Items (in 000s U.S. dollars)

	12/31/93	12/31/92	12/31/91	12/31/90
Sales	449,577	444,163	511,594	
Gross revenue	319,200	273,604	292,121	
Total operating expense	304,400	269,939	284,164	
Operating income	14,800	3,965	7,957	
Pretax income	10,100	−17,030	−2,630	
Total return on equity	9.56	−14.45	−3.75	−39.88
Operating margin %	4.64	1.45	2.72	3.23
Return on assets %	5.68	−4.70	0.17	−4.92
Quick ratio	1.36	1.13	1.24	0.85
Current ratio	2.93	2.76	2.95	1.83
Inventory-days held	185.18	222.52	222.69	233.79
Inventory turn ratio	1.94	1.62	1.62	1.54

Source: W/D Partners Worldscope.

(manufacturers of high-quality transfers for ceramic, glass, and enamel cookware). WW was a major international supplier of crystal and china, with about 32 percent of its 1993 sales from the United States, 54 percent from Europe (including the United Kingdom), 9 percent from the Far East, and the remaining 6 percent from other countries.

CONSORTIUM TAKEOVER

In 1990, a consortium led by Morgan Stanley & Co. and H. J. Heinz Company's chairman, Anthony O'Reilly, bought a 30 percent stake in WW (Dr. O'Reilly became chairman in 1993). Since that time, WW had undertaken severe cost-cutting measures that resulted in savings of 35 million Irish pounds through wage reductions, automation, cutting staff from 10,392 to 7000, and reducing overhead. For example, the crystal division's three Irish plants in Waterford, Kilbarry, Dungarvan, and Butlerstown, undertook a 3-year cost-cutting program that involved 800 redundancies[3] and was expected to result in a further reduction of 300 workers.[4] Dr. Paddy Galvin, Waterford Crystal chairman and chief executive, said: "Gradual restructuring [at Waterford] will continue,"[5] although industry observers

believed radical restructuring had been completed. At WW's annual meeting held in Dublin on June 15, 1994, when asked about the lack of dividend payments since 1988, Dr. O'Reilly responded by noting that key financial goals directed WW's actions. The goals were to recommence dividend payments as soon as prudent, to deliver above-average capital growth and sustain an above-average price-earnings ratio, to strengthen the balance sheet, and continually to enhance the quality of earnings. O'Reilly said: "Further advance is imperative for the Group [WW]. Its orientation is clear: strategic repositioning of our brands, their increased development and enhanced recognition, sustained development of multisourcing opportunities for all Group [WW] brands, and sustained development of cost-efficient manufacturing units in the Group." When asked where the Waterford Crystal business would go in the future, O'Reilly said: "The strategy is to build on the firm foundations laid, through the further enhancement of the prestige image of Waterford Crystal as a world brand in world markets through increasing and sustained investment; the continued development of multisourcing opportunities for our crystal brands; the capture of a greater market share for Marquis in the midprice segments of world crystal markets; the unremitting development of the Waterford manufacturing plants as cost-efficient producers of premium quality, world-beating crystal; and the penetration of new and underdeveloped markets by Waterford brands."[6]

LAUNCH OF MARQUIS

The decision in 1990 to launch Marquis was a calculated risk because it was the first time outsourcing of production would be used by Waterford. The plants that produced Marquis were located in Germany (former East German location), Slovenia, Slovakia, and the Czech Republic. Also, Marquis was introduced to sell at about 20 percent less than traditional Waterford. Redmond O'Donoghue, Waterford's head of marketing, noted that Marquis sales were not intended to cannibalize existing, more expensive Waterford brands but were aimed at garnering added new sales and extra market share at the expense of competing brands (especially in the United States). The Marquis price range was not cheap; for example, in the American market, a stemware glass from Marquis would be priced at $30 retail, while regular Waterford prices would be $40 to $50. Christopher McGillivary, chief executive officer of Waterford's U.S. operations, suggested that the challenge would be to lure customers from the competition, which were such heavyweights as Brown-Foreman Corp. (U.S. maker of Lenox crystal and china) and Hoya Corp. (Japan) and Baccarat (France).

MARKETING STRATEGY

As a result of marketing research that involved focus groups in three countries and reviewing 30 hours of taped interviews with consumers, Waterford concluded that customers, although price conscious, were still willing to pay for sensible consumption. "Status isn't gone; it has just been redefined," said Mr. O'Donoghue.[7] Waterford decided on a three-tier market strategy with the old-line Waterford at the top, Marquis a rung lower, and a third lower tier "which we didn't want to be in," noted O'Donoghue.[8] The results were better than expected, and within 2 years, Marquis had sold more

than US$13 million, had become the number six brand in the U.S. market, and had increased the number of bridal registrations from 613 to 10,376. In the same period, Waterford bridal registrations remained virtually constant at 12,475. "Bridal registrations are hugely important to us—they are inevitably the beginning of a crystal collection," says Mr. O'Donoghue.[9]

"I admit I was skeptical at first, but Marquis has been more successful than I would have ever guessed," said Susan Azar, crystal buyer for Dayton Hudson Corp.'s Marshall Field department stores. Ms. Azar expects that Marshall Field's combined sales of Waterford and Marquis will be up 30 percent in 1994. Marquis was given a distinctly different design—one that was simpler and lighter looking than traditional Waterford—while the company freshened up the original Waterford products by introducing colored crystal, new limited-edition sculpted pieces, and new designs such as the Doors of Dublin bowl, which reflected Irish tradition. Mr. O'Donoghue attributed the success of Marquis to keeping it sufficiently different from traditional Waterford while still allowing the new brand to benefit by association with the Waterford name.[10]

RESTRUCTURING

The downsizing and cost-cutting efforts (restructuring) had begun shortly after the consortium's buy-into WW and at about the same time as the decision to launch Waterford's new brand, Marquis. By September of 1993, the crystal division had installed more efficient production processes aimed at further lowering Waterford's cost base and boosting margins to the 50 percent required to sustain manufacturing. Dr. Galvin said: "We are well on the way to making crystal manufacturing more competitive, but we still have to complete the turnaround. Now that we are back in profit, it means we can approach the future with more enthusiasm and the workers have had the burden of uncertainty lifted." But Dr. Galvin was very cautious about the future and said: "Can anybody seriously suggest that we are already out of the woods?" since over the previous 5 years accumulated losses totaled 137 million Irish pounds.[11]

WEDGWOOD STRUGGLES

During this same 1990–1993 period, the Wedgwood fine china division also had struggled to cut costs by closing three plants and restructuring.[12] Profits remained level at approximately 8.6 million Irish pounds,[13] and Wedgwood was the U.K. market leader with about 20 percent market share, followed closely by Royal Doulton, then several larger firms, and finally, three or four dozen small firms. In the U.S. market, which accounted for 13.4 percent of Wedgwood's gross revenue, versus the United Kingdom's 61.3 percent, Wedgwood also was the market leader, although Japanese brands such as Noritake were fighting for leadership. In the Japanese market, Wedgwood was the leading import brand, although sales recently had turned downward. The distribution channels for tableware and giftware were dominated by department stores but included variety stores; specialist china or china and glass stores; hardware, cookware, and kitchenware shops; superstores; specialty gift shops; tourist shops; craft fairs; and even home shopping sources and supermarkets. Media advertising of china and earthenware products traditionally had been relatively limited, with the bulk of expenditures occurring by department stores via newspaper ads and/or color supplements. In the United States, restrictive consumer legislation had tightened controls on the amount of lead permitted to be released by tableware. In California, legislation known as Proposition 65 was even more restrictive than federal and other state laws. There, labeling regulations required products to carry the appropriate lead leaching warnings. In a recent lawsuit, California's state attorney alleged that Wedgwood, Royal Doulton, Noritake, and others had not complied with Proposition 65. The manufacturers, without admitting guilt or liability, paid US$1.2 million for expenses and penalties and agreed to establish a lead-reduction program.[14]

EMBASSY BY WEDGWOOD

Introducing the new porcelain brand Embassy might prove more difficult for Wedgwood than Marquis had been for Waterford. True, both Embassy and Marquis were aimed at being priced about 20 percent below the traditional premium pricing of their parent brand—hence the midprice description. For example, Embassy was expected to be priced at about US$80 for a five-piece place setting, compared with US$100 to US$400 for a Wedgwood china setting. However, Wedgwood had produced only premium china for almost 250 years, and a porcelain brand was clearly a step down in quality and prestige. Adrian O'Carroll, an analyst at Dillon Read, Ltd., in London, said: "Marquis was still a crystal. But with Embassy, Wedgwood is talking about introducing something completely different from fine china."[15] Mr. O'Carroll said that the porcelain line Embassy may have its greatest chance of success in continental Europe, where the Wedgwood name is not as closely associated with fine china as it is in Britain and where porcelain tableware is popular. One key aspect of the Embassy launch will not be known for some time: Waterford is counting on customers who buy Marquis and Embassy to eventually trade up to the more expensive Waterford crystal and Wedgwood china lines as their buying power increases.

Dr. O'Reilly said: "We believe that it will move Wedgwood into a new era. The objective is to capture further market share in the international ceramics market. The strategy is to penetrate the midprice sector of the tableware market through a distinctive range of new designs—less formal, more affordable, and more accessible. The tactics will involve a judicious outsourcing campaign, vigorously overseen to ensure that the quality and technical standards, traditional in the Wedgwood brand product, are fully upheld." O'Reilly confirmed that further investment would be made to enhance internal systems at Wedgwood to improve management information and logistical support to both manufacturing and marketing. He said: "This new brand will be endorsed by the Wedgwood heritage, values, and quality and will develop a character of its own, distinct from Wedgwood's formal fine bone china pedigree, yet reflecting its core brand values. It will reflect the growing trend toward a less formal lifestyle, embodying a new style of design: more loose, fresher, lower-priced certainly, and widening the perception of Wedgwood to embrace both the 'traditional classic' and the 'contemporary classic,' whilst improving the operating margin from sales. It will be supported by an array of giftware products calculated to achieve deeper market penetration and profitability."[16]

JANE'S PUZZLEMENT

After gathering all the information she could readily find on WW, Jane was faced with a dilemma. She knew that if she were to begin an in-class discussion of the WW situation and describe the launch of Marquis in 1990 with its subsequent success and then note WW's plans for launching Embassy by Wedgwood, someone was bound to ask her what she thought of WW's plans. The professor might even ask her if she approved of WW's plans for Embassy. Jane knew that she had to form a firm opinion either for or against launching Embassy.

Questions

1. What are the key differences between the Waterford situation in 1990 when the decision was made to launch Marquis and the 1995 situation Wedgwood faced in deciding whether to launch Embassy?

2. What other issues were important to Waterford Wedgwood corporate officers in early 1995?

3. If you agree that Embassy should be launched during 1995, then detail your reasons for this viewpoint.

4. If you believe that launching Embassy in 1995 is inappropriate, then detail your reasons for this viewpoint.

5. What, if any, other action options are available to Waterford Wedgwood?

Endnotes

1. Judith Valente, "A New Brand Restores Sparkle to Waterford," *Wall Street Journal,* November 10, 1994.
2. Bridal registration is a U.S. system where a couple getting married register their favored crystal and dinnerware design with a department store to ensure that they receive that particular design and no other as wedding presents. The system is usually computerized and means that the retailer will know what items have already been purchased for the couple and thus eliminates the possibility of the couple receiving the same present twice.
3. Redundancies are employee positions that are determined to be no longer necessary—thus the employee is laid off or dismissed. Downsizing and re-engineering are terms sometimes used in the United States for a similar exercise of redesigning the workforce and working processes.
4. Mary Canniffe, "O'Reilly Says Results Justify Strategy," *The Irish Times,* September 2, 1994.
5. Mary Canniffe, "Waterford Wedgwood in Good Shape," *The Irish Times,* September 2, 1994.
6. "Waterford Wedgwood PLC: Chairman's AGM Statement," *PR Newswire,* June 15, 1994.
7. Judith Valente, "A New Brand Restores Sparkle to Waterford," *Wall Street Journal,* November 10, 1994.
8. Brendan McGrath, "Waterford Steps Up Marketing Drive: Plans Involve New Technology, Fewer Jobs, and an Aggressive Marketing Campaign," *The Irish Times,* September 24, 1993.
9. *Ibid.*
10. Judith Valente, "A New Brand Restores Sparkle to Waterford," *Wall Street Journal,* November 10, 1994.
11. Brendon McGrath, "Waterford Steps Up Marketing Drive," *The Irish Times,* September 24, 1993.
12. "Key Note Report: China and Earthenware—An Industry Sector Analysis," 1994 Key Note, Ltd., February 1, 1994.
13. Victor Kuss, "Waterford Breaches Pain Barrier," *The Irish Times,* April 1, 1994.
14. "Key Note Report: China and Earthenware—An Industry Sector Analysis," 1994 Key Note, Ltd., February 1, 1994.
15. Judith Valente, "A New Brand Restores Sparkle to Waterford," *Wall Street Journal,* November 10, 1994.
16. "Waterford Wedgwood PLC: Chairman's AGM Statement," *PR Newswire,* June 15, 1994.

Calgene Inc.: Marketing High-Tech Tomatoes

This case was prepared by Julian W. Vincze, Crummer Graduate School of Business, Rollins College.

BRUISED PRODUCT PROBLEM

By the late 1990s, few customers had had the opportunity to taste the bioengineered and trademarked MacGregor's tomatoes grown from FlavrSavr tomato seeds. MacGregor's tomatoes, which were introduced with a flurry of publicity by Calgene Inc., had not achieved wide distribution. Why had this occurred? The answer was that Calgene's research and development (R&D) department, after overcoming complex technological, regulatory, and environmental obstacles through years of effort and considerable expense, seemed to encounter totally unexpected tomato distribution problems. MacGregor's tomatoes were designed to have several outstanding product features such as longer shelf life, better taste, and juicier flavor. These features were expected to differentiate MacGregor's tomatoes from ordinary fresh tomatoes. Unfortunately, during the growing season, Calgene had realized that its product was not able to withstand the normal rigors of the standard picking, packing, and shipping methods used in the fresh tomato packing industry. Early shipments became

bruised on their way to market, so Calgene had to undertake a costly overhaul of its packing methods (detailed later).

This damage to product, which was both unexpected and very late in the R&D cycle, had a major impact on Calgene's timetable for widespread distribution and market introduction of the MacGregor tomato. Industry analysts believed this difficulty contributed to a cash drain that had forced Calgene to sell assets and cut its workforce by 10 percent. "This tomato has brought them to their knees," said Stan Shimoda, an analyst with BioScience Securities Inc. of Orinda, California. "The question is, can they get up again?"[1]

CALGENE'S HISTORY

Calgene Inc., an agricultural biotechnology company involved in developing, through genetic manipulation, a portfolio of genetically engineered plants and plant products for the food, seed, and oleochemical industries, focused operations in three core crop businesses (as detailed below). Headquartered in Davis, California, Calgene was formed in 1982 and became involved in the development of improved plant varieties and plant products and was the first company to introduce genetically engineered products in the fresh tomato, cottonseed, and industrial and edible plant oils (canola) markets, where it believed biotechnology could provide substantial added commercial value in consumer, industrial, and seed markets.

Fresh Market Tomato Core Crop No. I

Fresh tomatoes currently were the most visible and probably also the most important of Calgene's core crops. After 12 years of R&D efforts, Calgene's first apparent success was when the U.S. Food and Drug Administration (FDA) announced its determination that the MacGregor tomato had not been significantly altered with respect to safety or nutritive value when compared with conventional tomatoes. This FDA approval allowed Calgene to begin to market MacGregor's tomatoes. However, this success was tempered by the apparent ongoing difficulties encountered in achieving widespread distribution and therefore market availability of MacGregor's tomatoes (as noted above). These difficulties caused Calgene's non-genetically engineered tomato production to be scaled back and eventually resulted in curtailment of much of Calgene's Mexican operations. Calgene had made agreements with both Campbell Soup Company and Zeneca A.V.P. (the original financial backers of the R&D that produced MacGregor's tomatoes) whereby Calgene received worldwide, exclusive royalty-free rights to produce and sell fresh market tomatoes containing the FlavrSavr gene. Prior to these agreements, Calgene's commercialization rights were limited to North America and had required royalty payments to Campbell Soup Company.

Tomato Packing Methods

The traditional tomato packing method was called the *gassed-green method,* which began with either mechanical or hand field picking. The field picking occurred while the tomatoes were green and rock hard. This green picking was necessary for traditional tomatoes so that they could withstand the rigors of the remaining steps in the packing process. These additional steps included being moved by conveyor belts, being dumped into large bins, being subjected to high-pressure gas spraying, and then being boxed. If field picking was mistimed until after the tomatoes began to ripen, they would start to soften too quickly as

a result of an enzyme called *polygalacturonase* (PG). If this softening occurred, the tomatoes were prone to being damaged during packing and shipping to retailers and/or by the handling that occurred within retail stores. In addition, late picking lessened the shelf life of the tomatoes at the retail store.

Customers' Reactions of Gassed-Green Tomatoes

However, the problem with the green picking and packing process was that the ultimate consumers did not want to buy green and unripened tomatoes. Therefore, the packing process included the high-pressure gas spraying step. The gas used in the spraying step was ethylene, a hormone that triggered the beginning of the reddening and ripening process. Thus almost all fresh field-grown tomatoes ripened during the packing and shipping process because the ethylene spray eventually caused the green tomatoes to turn red. However, these artificially induced ripe tomatoes did not achieve a deep red color. Instead, they turned a pale red and were somewhat mushy and to many customers were tasteless. These traditional tomato packing methods were considered by the industry to be very efficient because they minimized costs and resulted in relatively low retail prices for consumers. Unfortunately, these traditional packing methods had such a deleterious effect on the taste of tomatoes picked while still green and rock hard that many customers equated this taste with cardboard. The tomatoes certainly did not compare favorably with vine-ripened, freshly picked field tomatoes. In fact, one industry observer noted that a U.S. Department of Agriculture report gave an 84 percent dissatisfaction rate among customers of gassed-green tomatoes.[2]

Development of MacGregor's Tomato

Cognizant of this criticism of tasteless tomatoes, and anxious to capitalize on what they perceived to be a market opportunity, Calgene's geneticists bioengineered the ordinary tomato to delay softening and rotting (the maturation process) in order to enhance taste and lengthen retail shelf life. They used what was then cutting-edge technology of gene splicing. Calgene's scientists developed a procedure that prevented tomatoes from producing PG by creating an antisense, or mirror, image of the gene that carried instructions for producing the enzyme. By then inserting the antisense gene into the tomato's DNA, production of the enzyme was blocked. This began the ripening process, which in turn was responsible for breaking down the wall of tomato cells. This antisense gene also was expected to allow growers to wait until the MacGregor's tomato was turning red before harvesting.[3]

The concept seemed straightforward and rather simple: that is, the stronger the cell walls, the easier it would be to transport tomatoes without damage; the more advanced the maturation process was before picking and packing, the better the flavor and the longer the retail shelf life. However, delayed maturation, which allowed for longer time ripening on the vine, also resulted in a softer tomato when picked. With hindsight, it now seemed that Calgene had rushed to commercialize its MacGregor's Flavr-Savr tomato without considering that its tomato would not tolerate traditional packing house processes without bruising.

Cotton—Calgene's Core Crop No. 2

Calgene's second core crop and genetic engineering program focused on reducing farmers' growing costs through the development of cotton varieties that required fewer pesticides (and also the creation of cotton varieties that produced natural colors). It was estimated that U.S. cotton farmers spent over $200 million annually on herbicides and from $225 to $400 million on insecticides. Therefore, when Calgene could create herbicide resistant and insect resistant cotton varieties, the result would be not only reduced production costs for farmers but also improved crop yields and environmental benefits. Calgene believed that these product features would translate into premium pricing opportunities.

Calgene's BXN trademarked cottonseed received U.S. Department of Agriculture (USDA) deregulation in 1994. Calgene marketed conventional cottonseed varieties and their BXN cotton through its Stoneville subsidiary, which had experienced a revenue growth of 19 percent during the 1994 fiscal year. In April of 1995, Calgene introduced two new genetically engineered varieties of BXN cotton that were

resistant to the herbicide bromoxynil (commonly used cotton crop herbicide) at a 45 percent price premium over Calgene's non-genetically engineered cottonseed. These two new BXN cotton varieties, like all of Calgene's BXN cotton, also were genetically engineered to contain a Bt gene for resistance to *Heliothis*, the principal cotton insect pest.

Plant Oils—Calgene's Core Crop No. 3

Calgene's third core crop was industrial and edible plant oils. This program focused on genetically engineering rapeseed oils with a broad range of food and industrial applications. Calgene's scientists had successfully genetically altered canola rapeseed varieties that produced substantial quantities of laurate, an important ingredient in detergents that was not naturally present in canola or other nontropical oil plants. In March of 1994, Calgene received a U.S. patent on the bay thioesterase gene. This gene in rapeseed plants resulted in the production of laurate, while in June of 1994, Calgene successfully purified the LPAAT enzyme. Introduction of the gene that produced this LPAAT enzyme increased laurate levels significantly beyond the 40 percent level that had been achieved previously. Thus, by July of 1995, Calgene's Laurical trademarked canola sales were reported to be 1 million pounds.

The Plant Oils Division also was conducting its eighth season of field trials with canola plants that had been genetically engineered to produce oil with increased stearate levels. Stearate had the potential to substitute for hydrogenated oils in margarine, shortening, and confectionary products. Therefore, Calgene had begun to establish strategic relationships with Procter & Gamble, Unilever, and Pfizer Food Science to explore the potential commercial opportunities for its plant oil products.

KEY STRENGTHS AND BUSINESS STRATEGY

In a recent president's letter to shareholders included in Calgene's Annual Report, Roderick Stacey said:

> As we look to the future, I believe the key strengths of Calgene are as follows:

1. We are the scientific and regulatory leaders in agricultural biotechnology, particularly in the science of plant oils modification. All technical hurdles are behind us in our first tomato, cotton, and oil products. We have the only FDA and USDA approvals for genetically engineered plant products.

2. Our proprietary position is strong. We resolved all of the issues regarding tomato technology with Zeneca and Campbell and have worldwide royalty-free rights to the FlavrSavr gene in fresh tomatoes. We have successfully negotiated favorable cross-licenses with Monsanto, Mogen International nv, PGS, and Agracetus to obtain freedom to operate in the most important core plant genetic engineering technologies. Seven oils gene modification patents have been issued in Europe, and U.S. counterparts (patents), starting with the Laurate gene patent, are beginning to issue. We remain confident that we will prevail in our litigation with Enzo Biochem, Inc.

3. We are in excellent position to commercialize on our scientific successes. We have a conventional operating business base which generated $35 million in product revenues. We have a seasoned senior management group and an experienced and capable field production team in each of our core crops. The supply of our MacGregor's tomatoes grown from FlavrSavr seeds will be increased in October. Field results of BXN cotton have exceeded expectations, and market launch is set.

We are positioned to realize the promise of our 12 years' investment in plant science, regulatory innovation, and business planning.[4]

However, despite this optimism voiced by Mr. Stacey, several industry observers were skeptical of the basis for his optimism and openly wondered if Calgene could successfully market its high-tech tomatoes. However, in 10-K financial filings, Calgene noted that its business strategy was to build operating businesses in their core crop areas to facilitate the market introduction of genetically engineered proprietary products and to maximize the long-term financial return from such products. Calgene believed that implementing this strategy would provide direct access to markets where Calgene could sell fresh and processed plant products having improved quality traits or cost-of-production advantages or both. For details about Calgene's financial situation, refer to Exhibits A and B.

CALGENE REACTS TO BRUISING PROBLEM

Once aware of the bruising problem, Calgene's first response was to approach experienced packing companies to ask them to devise gentler handling procedures; however, none could meet Calgene's requirements. Calgene then decided to build its own processing plant near Chicago for the purpose of developing gentler handling procedures. However, by the time tomatoes grown in fields in the southern states arrived at the plant, many were bruised or split or both. Finally, Calgene announced that it would spend up to $10 million building three facilities nearer its growing areas. These facilities would be equipped with high-tech "soft touch" machines that included optical sensors to distinguish tomato size, shape, and color and which were designed originally to sort peaches.

The first location, a 90,000 square foot facility in Immokalee, Florida, was proclaimed to be on-line and operational by late March. A second location in Lake Park, Georgia, was a 65,000 square foot packing and distribution facility that was scheduled to begin operations in May. The third location, in Irvine, California, was a modification of an existing structure that was also expected to be on-line for packing and distributing by May. "We now have the facilities in place to supply demand for FlavrSavr tomatoes across the U.S.," said Danilo Lopes, CEO of Calgene Fresh, the wholly owned subsidiary of Calgene Inc. that grows, packs, distributes, and sells fresh produce.[5] In addition, Calgene noted that it would rely more heavily on manual labor in picking and packing its tomatoes grown on approximately 2000 acres in California, Florida, and Georgia. "The combination of increased acreage, new packing and distribution facilities, and an experienced management team should enable us to achieve our target

EXHIBIT A

Calgene Inc. Balance Sheet (000's)[16]

	Year 5	Year 4	Year 3	Year 2	Year 1
Assets					
Cash	11,753	5,286	15,009	9,511	5,548
Marketable securities	10,283	15,457	24,773	31,748	30,632
Receivables	6,697	4,792	2,666	2,864	3,163
Inventories	8,148	5,068	4,774	4,461	5,529
Other current assets	1,699	2,278	6,023	7,814	7,363
Total current assets	38,580	32,881	53,245	56,636	52,235
Property, plant, and equipment	38,044	32,363	26,561	21,982	20,872
Accumulated depreciation	15,524	12,872	11,023	9,909	8,432
Net property and equipment	22,520	19,491	15,538	12,073	12,440
Investment and advances to subs	0	1,415	1,551	3,432	3,710
Intangibles	26,224	23,677	17,308	12,205	14,180
Deposits and other assets	1,907	848	759	877	571
Total assets	89,231	78,312	88,401	85,223	83,136
Liabilities					
Notes payable	7,761	8,650	7,597	9,083	7,039
Accounts payable	6,487	7,916	5,327	1,977	2,457
Current long-term debt	1,494	1,728	1,241	1,037	527
Accrued expenses	2,049	1,803	1,562	3,735	4,278
Other current liabilities	9,968	8,088	3,211	2,502	5,057
Total current liabilities	27,759	28,185	18,938	18,334	19,358
Long-term debt	14,671	4,204	3,694	4,378	5,065
Other long-term liabilities	750	1,500	N/A	N/A	N/A
Total liabilities	43,180	33,889	22,632	22,712	24,423
Minority interests	N/A	N/A	N/A	N/A	948
Preferred stock	N/A	N/A	N/A	29,506	29,627
Common stock (net)	30	27	24	18	15
Capital surplus	223,161	190,934	169,482	111,101	86,488
Retained earnings	−177,140	−146,538	−103,737	−78,114	−58,198
Other equities	N/A	N/A	N/A	N/A	−167
Total shareholder equity	46,051	44,423	65,769	62,511	57,765
Total liabilities and net worth	89,231	78,312	88,401	85,223	83,136

expanded distribution," said Mr. Lopez.[6] Roger Salquist, Calgene's CEO, said the company was on target to have its tomatoes in 2500 stores by June and added that sales of the company's tomatoes in the Midwest were "doing great."[7]

Mr. Shimoda's response to these statements was: "The technology didn't do what they thought it would do, and so they had to reinvent the wheel to deal with a soft tomato."[8] Another industry observer, Andre Garnet, analyst at A. G. Edwards, asserted that "Calgene's distribution system is all screwed up, and it costs more to produce than to sell."[9] Mr. Garnet believed that Calgene would be forced to raise additional cash.

EXHIBIT B

Calgene Inc. Income Statement (000's)[17]

	Year 5	Year 4	Year 3	Year 2	Year 1
Net sales	55,431	38,433	27,237	21,877	26,104
Cost of goods sold	57,114	46,703	26,633	20,316	19,727
Gross profit	−1,683	−8,270	604	1,561	6,377
R&D expenditures	11,937	12,847	10,260	11,256	11,151
Selling, gen. and admin. exp.	16,081	21,279	16,494	11,318	10,161
Income before depreciation	−29,701	−42,396	−26,150	−21,013	−14,935
Nonoperating income	38	389	1,644	3,274	1,515
Interest expense	924	729	673	813	898
Income before taxes	−30,587	−42,736	−25,179	−18,555	−14,318
Provisions for income tax	15	65	44	61	61
Net income before extraord.	−30,602	−42,801	−25,223	−18,616	−14,379
Extraordinary items	N/A	N/A	−400	−1,300	−12,600
Net income	−30,602	−42,801	−25,623	−19,916	−26,979

Key Annual Financial Ratios	1994	1993	1991
Quick ratio	0.91	2.24	2.41
Current ratio	1.17	2.81	3.09
Sales/cash	1.85	0.68	0.53
Receivables turnover	8.02	10.22	7.64
Receivables days sales	44.89	35.24	47.13
Inventories turnover	7.58	5.71	4.90
Net sales/working capital	8.18	0.79	0.57
Net sales/total assets	0.49	0.31	0.26
Net sales/employees	113.707	73.021	77.578
Total liabilities/total assets	0.43	0.26	0.27
Times interest earned	−57.62	−36.41	−21.74
Total debt/equity	0.13	0.08	0.09
Net income/net sales	−1.11	−0.94	−0.91
Net income/total assets	−0.55	−0.29	−0.23

COMPETITOR TOMATO: ENDLESS SUMMER

Although there is currently only one other firm attempting to market genetically engineered fresh market tomatoes, competition is expected to intensify rapidly as existing gassed-green tomato producers react to competitive pressures by growing and marketing traditionally developed vine-ripened tomatoes. The existing direct competitor was DNA Plant Technology Corporation (DNAP) of Oakland, California, which developed a competitor to Mac-

Gregor's tomato which they called the Fresh World Farms Endless Summer. FDA clearance to market Endless Summer was granted in early 1995.[10] DNAP claimed that Endless Summer tomatoes required no special handling, even though they too stay ripening longer on the vine than the so-called gassed-green tomatoes. The secret was a more-recent technology that regulated a tomato's ethylene production and slowed down the overall ripening process, including softening. This allowed Endless Summer to be picked earlier than FlavrSavr tomatoes while they were still relatively hard and therefore able to withstand traditional packing house processes. Yet because of the slowed ripening, Endless Summer tomatoes outlasted FlavrSavr on shelf life because they stayed fresh for 30 days after harvest. The relative taste factors of these two competitor high-tech tomatoes had not yet been determined by the market place. However, Carolyn Hayworth, a Calgene spokesperson, said: "It's a huge market—a $3 1/2 billion market for fresh tomatoes in the U.S.; let's just let the consumer decide."[11]

Endless Summer, grown in Florida and California, was in test market in Rochester, New York, and national rollout was predicted for the fall of 1995. DNAP intended to apply its technology to other foods as well. Potential candidate foods for its process were noted to include bananas, pineapples, peas, peppers, and strawberries.[12] Mr. Shimoda thought Endless Summer stood a better chance of success than MacGregor's tomato, and George Dahlman, an analyst with Piper Jaffray Inc. and once a Calgene advocate, seemed to agree. Mr. Dahlman said: "The future of this company [Calgene] is more controversial than ever." However, Carolyn Hayworth, a Calgene spokeswoman, noted: "We're building a business, and we believe we know what we are doing."[13] Roger Salquist, Calgene's CEO, insisted that Calgene would not have to raise more money and that the fiscal year ending in 1996 would be profitable.

CONSUMER REACTIONS UNCERTAIN

Both MacGregor's tomato and Endless Summer were the result of gene-transfer technology used to develop tomatoes that could ripen longer on the vine yet not spoil on the trip to market. The goal appeared to be a year-round tomato with flavor and juiciness. However, consumer reaction to genetically altered foods remained uncertain. When MacGregor's tomatoes were offered in Seattle's Fred Meyer stores (an upscale supermarket chain) in November and December, "We had a very positive response. The stores have been asking for more as a result of requests by shoppers," said assistant vice president Rob Boley.[14] The tomatoes carried a label noting that they were grown from genetically modified seeds and a sign that gave additional details.

However, some industry observers were critical of both Calgene and DNAP for not publicizing any marketing research studies that they may have carried out prior to or during the development of MacGregor's tomato and Endless Summer. This failure to publicize any research relative to the acceptability to customers of bioengineered fresh tomatoes was interpreted by some to indicate that little, if any, actual customer opinion surveys had been carried out by either company and that in their rush to apply the technology, the whole aspect of consumer acceptance was overlooked. If R&D scientists had pressed for quick development and upper management had not expended scarce resources on customer surveys, then, without any indication of customer acceptance of bioengineered fresh tomatoes, the probability of immediate acceptance by consumers was viewed as questionable at best and perhaps improbable in a worst-case scenario. This lack of market research therefore could represent an unexplored opportunity or potentially a tremendous oversight fraught with perils. Still other industry observers were more trusting that good management existed at both Calgene and DNAP and that such a major oversight could not have occurred. They argued that surely these two management teams had not only looked at the supply side of the market but had thoroughly analyzed the demand aspects as well. Since neither company had publicized such demand analyses, actual retail trials would have to be relied on to judge potential customer acceptance rates. And results from trial markets were not being made public by either firm.

Controversy about Genetically Engineered Food

Controversy had surrounded the idea of genetically engineered food. For example, with MacGregor's tomatoes, the use of marker genes added to the tomatoes in order to determine whether the gene for slow ripening was transferred successfully had become a public controversy. The controversial aspect of the process related to the fact that the marker genes were resistant to certain antibiotics, and critics said that such resistance might create antibiotic resistance in people who ate these altered tomatoes. Even though Food and Drug Administration (FDA) scientists had concluded that such development of resistance to antibiotics by people consuming genetically altered foods was not a possibility, the rumor still existed.

In addition, a national coalition of prominent chefs as early as mid-1992 had begun to call for a boycott of genetically engineered foods.[15] This coalition claimed support from some 1000 of their colleagues, including such nationally known figures as Wolfgang Puck of Spago in West Hollywood, Jimmy Schmidt of the Rattlesnake Club in Detroit, Jean Louis Palladin of Jean Louis in Washington, D.C., and Mark Miller of Red Sage in Washington, D.C., and was led by chef Rick Moonen of the Water Club in New York. Despite this protest, the FDA declared that genetically engineered foods were safe and special labeling was unnecessary regardless of customers who had professed to having religious or health concerns.

THE FUTURE

What does the future hold for Calgene and its Mac-Gregor's tomato? Many investors and industry analysts are pondering this question. Stan Shimoda indicated that MacGregor's tomato had brought Calgene to its knees—his question was, Could they get up again? Others held similar views, only differing in degree of pessimism. Countering these views, however, were the optimistic statements of the management of Calgene, which implied that Calgene was on the verge of a huge success in the marketplace. Which view is the correct one? Would the MacGregor's tomato be a marketing success story? What would you predict? If you were to unexpectedly inherit $25,000 would you invest it in Calgene stock?

Questions

1. Do a traditional SWOT (strengths, weaknesses, opportunities, and threats) analysis of Calgene's situation in the spring of 1995.

2. What is your assessment of the product development procedures used by Calgene to develop the MacGregor's FlavrSavr tomato? Were they effective, or could they be improved?

3. What is your assessment of Calgene's knowledge about customer acceptance of bioengineered foods and specifically the FlavrSavr tomato? Do you think there has been an oversight, or do you agree that Calgene management has effectively considered market demand for the product?

4. Diagram the consumer purchasing process you believe is used by the average household when purchasing fresh tomatoes. List what

you believe are the evaluative criteria applied when deciding which alternative fresh tomatoes to purchase?

5. Calgene seems to be planning to introduce MacGregor's FlavrSavr tomatoes to the market by traditional channels of distribution. Is this the best channel to use? What other channels might be used?

6. How much of a technological lead does Calgene enjoy over DNAP? Does the FlavrSavr tomato have a market leadership position over Endless Summer tomatoes?

7. What are the barriers to entry in the fresh tomato producing and marketing industry?

8. Assume that you have unexpectedly inherited $25,000 today. Would you invest it in Calgene?

Endnotes

1. Ralph T. King, Jr., "Low-Tech Woe Slows Calgene's Super Tomato," *Wall Street Journal*, April 11, 1995, pp. B-1, B-6.
2. Barbara DeLollis, "High-Tech Tomato Had Growing Pains; Developing the Technology Was Only Half of the Challenge," *The Fresno Bee*, April 10, 1995.
3. Del I. Hawkins, Roger J. Best, and Kenneth A. Coney, "Calgene, Inc. versus the Pure Food Campaign," *Consumer Behavior: Implications for Marketing Strategy*, 6th ed. (Homewood, IL: Irwin, 1995), p. 384.
4. *1994 Annual Report to Shareholders*, Calgene Inc., Davis, California.
5. "Calgene Tomato Packing and Distribution System Nears Completion; Senior Produce Executives Join Calgene Fresh Team," PR Newswire, March 28, 1995.
6. *Ibid.*
7. Herb Greenberg, "I Say Tomato, Some Say Tomorrow, What's Really Going On?" *San Francisco Chronicle*, January 16, 1995.
8. "Calgene Tomato Packing and Distribution System Nears Completion; Senior Produce Executives Join Calgene Fresh Team," PR Newswire, March 28, 1995.
9. Lauren Dermer, "Calgene Short Seller Stomps on Biotech-Enhanced Tomato," *Portfolio Letter*, February 6, 1995.
10. "Calgene and DNAP Vie in Tomato War," *Industries in Transition*, February 1995.
11. Judith Blake, "High-Tech Tomato May Roll onto Market Soon," *Seattle Times*, February 1, 1995.
12. "Calgene and DNAP Vie in Tomato War," *Industries in Transition*, February 1995.
13. Ralph T. King, Jr., "Low-Tech Woe Slows Calgene's Super Tomato," *Wall Street Journal*, April 11, 1995, pp. B-1, B-6.
14. Judith Blake, "High-Tech Tomato May Roll onto Market Soon," *Seattle Times*, February 1, 1995.
15. "Chefs Vow Boycott of Genetically Engineered Foods," *Nation's Restaurant News*, August 10, 1992.
16. *Annual Reports to Stockholders*, Calgene Inc., Davis, California.
17. *Ibid.*

North Country Bank & Trust

This case was prepared by Brian G. Gnauck, Dean and Professor of Marketing, and Samuel P. Graci, Professor of Accounting, Northern Michigan University.

On the evening before the deer season opened, Mr. John Crocker was indeed excited. John was at his camp in Michigan's Upper Peninsula with six lifelong, deer-hunting buddies. After dinner, John brought out his old rifle case and displayed his brand new 340 Weatherby magnum. "Wow!" said Pete, his hunting buddy of 15 years. Tim Compton chimed in, "That set you back a buck or two." Ed, John's best friend, said, "That is quite a weapon; let me see it." John, responding to Tim's comment, said, "It didn't cost me a dime." Tim immediately responded, "How's that? Come on, you gotta be kidding?"

How John obtained the weapon and its real value were all explained in a unique marketing program of North Country Bank & Trust of Manistique, Michigan, which was just one example of their unique approach to banking.

BACKGROUND

North Country Bank & Trust, formerly First Manistique Corporation, is a branch holding company with $327.5 million in assets as of June 1996. North Country Bank operates two commercial bank subsidiaries, First Northern Bank & Trust, headquartered in Manistique, Michigan, and South Range State Bank, located in South Range, Michigan. These banks operate 23 facilities (branches) in 20 communities in Michigan's Upper Peninsula. North Country Bank also owns and operates three other businesses: First Manistique Agency, which sells annuities as well as life, accident, and health insurance, First Rural Relending Company, a nonprofit relending company, and First Northern Services Company, a real estate appraisal company.

The company has experienced significant growth in assets as a result of acquisitions, having acquired two banks, one branch, and substantially all the banking assets and liabilities of a third bank since 1994. Effective January 31, 1996, the company acquired all the outstanding stock of the South Range State Bank, with assets of approximately $40 million. This acquisition may have an adverse effect on earnings because past results cannot be ensured in the future. The company is continuing to seek acquisitions in its existing or adjoining market areas

EXHIBIT A

North Country Bank & Trust,
Manistique, Michigan, Selected Consolidated Financial Data

	1995 ProForma*	1994†	1993	1992	1991
Interest income	$ 24,990	$ 13,798	$ 7,942	$ 8,035	$ 8,085
Interest expense	11,001	6,053	3,543	3,788	4,551
Net interest income	13,989	7,745	4,399	4,247	3,534
Security gains (losses)	(19)	75	175	191	323
Provision for loan losses	811	330	125	239	232
Other income	1,587	1,037	795	577	407
Other expenses	11,076	6,101	3,715	3,277	2,714
Income before taxes	3,670	2,426	1,529	1,499	1,318
Cumulative effect of change in accounting for income taxes	0	0	13	0	0
Income taxes	1,047	458	260	331	321
Net income	$ 2,623	$ 1,968	$ 1,282	$ 1,168	$ 997
Per share					
Earnings	$ 1.25	$ 1.14	$ 1.05	$ 0.95	$ 0.82
Dividends	0.41	0.20	0.49	0.31	0.29
Book value	11.87	10.72	8.12	7.57	6.92
Ratios based on net income					
Return on average equity	11.44%	14.25%	13.33%	13.25%	12.24%
Return on average assets	.87%	1.01%	1.13%	1.15%	1.11%
Dividend payout ratio	32.80%	17.54%	46.67%	32.63%	35.37%
Shareholders' equity as a percent of average assets	7.58%	7.11%	8.45%	8.67%	9.46%
Financial condition					
Assets	$320,646	$253,098	$117,279	$106,798	$ 94,237
Loans	248,527	183,168	87,145	73,108	61,958
Securities	30,882	35,795	17,183	21,107	25,005
Deposits	277,014	223,436	103,717	94,257	82,786
Long-term borrowing	15,351	3,553	2,250	2,000	1,000
Shareholders' equity	25,006	22,483	9,943	9,260	8,467

*Gives effect to the company's recent acquisition of the South Range State Bank as if such acquisition had occurred on January 1, 1995.
†Per share data reflect 3 for 1 stock split, 23 April 1996.
Source: Prospectus.

to the extent suitable candidates and acceptable terms can be found. The company is a very aggressive bidder in the event a bank within its geographic region is for sale or agreeable to a merger. The company views the acquisition opportunities as limited and takes a very aggressive acquisition stance.

North Country Bank has experienced significant growth (see Exhibit A). This growth in assets has been a combination of internal growth as well as through merger and asset-acquisition activity.

Much of the internal asset growth was attributable to North Country Bank & Trust's innovative approach to marketing. Under the leadership of Ron Ford, the bank had deviated significantly from traditional bank practices and marketing methods. Among these nontraditional methods are deposit programs featuring Weatherby rifles, Big Bertha golf clubs, diamonds, grandfather clocks, and art prints, all innovative and effective approaches to demand deposit acquisition.

The company is in the process of selling 400,000 shares of common stock, which is expected to yield $10.668 million. The proceeds will be used to retire $2.9 million in bank debt, of which $1.9 million was incurred to acquire the South Range Bank. Another $4.3 million of the proceeds will fund expected future acquisitions. The balance will be used for working capital needs and to generally strengthen the financial position of the company.

THE WEATHERBY CERTIFICATE OF DEPOSIT PROGRAM

The Weatherby certificate of deposit program was typical of all these programs. This program basically provided the customer with a Weatherby rifle or shotgun in lieu of interest on a certificate of deposit (CD) with the bank. CDs with 3-, 9-, 12- or 20-year maturities were available to secure a rifle. For example, if a customer desired an Accumark 340 Weatherby magnum, a minimum deposit of $5673 for a 3-year period was required. If the customer deposited the money for as long as 20 years, it would require only $1189 (see Exhibit B). At the end of the deposit period, principal only is returned on the CD. For example, if customers

purchased a 3-year, $5673 CD, they would receive their weapon at deposit time. At the end of the 3-year period, when the CD matures, $5673, the principal amount, is returned without any interest.

The purchase process works as follows: First, the buyer would select the firearm and fill out the appropriate information on the deposit agreement. Since a federal firearm license is required, a copy of that would be included with the purchase. In certain instances, required sales tax would be paid in addition to the deposit. North Country Bank & Trust provides free shipping as an incentive for the program, with delivery in about 4 to 6 weeks. The certificate of deposit could not be withdrawn prior to maturity. All the Weatherby products handled by the bank were new and included a Weatherby warranty as if they were purchased in a typical retail store. Since customers got the gun, they were required to pay income tax on North Country Bank & Trust's cost and were issued a 1099 for that tax year, analogous to paying tax on the CD's interest earnings.

Other certificate of deposit programs using Big Bertha golf clubs, diamonds, grandfather clocks, and prints worked in a similar fashion. Ron Ford was particularly proud of the Weatherby program. North Country Bank & Trust purchased rifles in lots of $250,000 and were consequently able to negotiate a lucrative purchase price. Typical margin on these types of weapons was 30 to 40 percent of *retail price.* The company advertised nationwide through sports magazines and operated an 800 phone number to handle inquiries and take orders. The program has been a great success and represents one of the highest-volume dealers for Weatherby rifles.

Weatherby rifles are viewed by the hunting community as a premium product. They are priced at the upper end of the mass-production weapons market. However, the typical retail consumer would seldom pay suggested retail price. Discounts of 10 to 20 percent off suggested retail occur in many markets (see Exhibit C).

Ron Ford sought out the best brands for his premium CD programs. He had tried but thus far has not been successful in securing Tiffany diamonds and Ping golf clubs. His ability to secure highly branded products like Weatherby and Big Bertha was one reason this premium program was so successful.

EXHIBIT B

North Country Bank and Trust:
Weatherby Certificate of Deposit Program

Code	Package Description	Minimum Deposit Amount and Term Required to Earn Bonus				
		3-year	6-year	9-year	12-year	20-year
	ACCUMARK *"New for 1996"*					
1	.257, .270, 7 mm, .300, .340 Weatherby Magnum, 7 mm Remington Magnum, .300 Winchester Magnum, 26" bbl.	$5673	$2838	$2037	$1636	$1189
	MARK V DELUXE					
2	.270, 7 mm, Weatherby Magnum .30-06 Springfield, 24" bbl.	$6318	$3160	$2268	$1832	$1324
3	.240, .257, .270, 7 mm .300, .340 Weatherby Magnum, 26" bbl.	$6619	$3311	$2376	$1919	$1386
	LAZERMARK					
4	.257, .270, 7 mm, .300, .340 Weatherby Magnum, 26" bbl.	$7090	$3546	$2544	$2055	$1485
5	.460 Weatherby Magnum, 26" with Accubrake	$9638	$4818	$3456	$2791	$2015
	MARK V SPORTER					
6	7 mm Remington Magnum, .300 Winchester Magnum, 24" bbl.	$4064	$2034	$1461	$1181	$ 854
7	.257, .270, 7 mm, .300, .340 Weatherby Magnum, 26" bbl.	$4247	$2126	$1526	$1234	$ 892
8	.30-06 Springfield, 22" bbl.	$4064	$2034	$1461	$1181	$ 854
	MARK V SYNTHETIC					
9	7 mm Remington Magnum, .300, .338 Winchester, 24" bbl. .257, .270, 7 mm, .300, .340 Weatherby Magnum, 26" bbl.	$3542	$1774	$1274	$1030	$ 745
	MARK V STAINLESS					
10	.257, .270, 7 mm, .300, .340 Weatherby Magnum, 26" bbl. 7 mm Remington Magnum, .300, .338 Winchester, 24" bbl.	$4688	$2346	$1684	$1361	$ 984

Source: North Country Bank & Trust's marketing literature.

EXHIBIT C

**List Price and Probable Retail Selling Price
of Weatherby Rifles**

	List Price	Probable Retail Selling Price
Accumark	$ 1,199	$ 959.85
Mark V Deluxe	1,399	1,149.95
Lazermark	1,499	1,197.00
Mark V Sporter	899	714.95
Mark V Synthetic	749	599.95
Mark V Stainless	999	789.95

Source: Lindquist Sporting Goods.

LAISSEZ-FAIRE BANKING

North Country Bank & Trust differentiated itself from other Upper Peninsula banks and banks in general by promoting an "easy going" informal style. Casual clothes are worn instead of the traditional blue or black suits. This is true of tellers as well as the CEO.

In addition, the bank presents itself in a friendly, almost homelike atmosphere. Popcorn is always available in the lobby, as well as coffee and pop. The bank provides pharmacy delivery and free legal advice. All these were significant deviations from traditional bank practices. They were, however, consistent with Mr. Ford's philosophy of meeting customer needs and style. He observed often that customers did not dress formally in the market served by North Country Bank & Trust. The bank, therefore, complemented the lifestyle of its customers.

WELCOME TO THE TYCOON CLUB

In an effort to instill savings in children, explain how banking works, and develop lifelong banking customers, North Country Bank & Trust created the Tycoon Club and the comic character Mr. Tycoon. As of 1996, there were about 3000 members of the Tycoon Club. The club sponsored Little League teams, promoted the club with guest appearances of Mr. Tycoon at fairs, outings, and picnics, and sold an array of Tycoon clothing. Special savings programs existed for Tycoon Club members. In addition, a loan program existed for young entrepreneurs. If, for example, a teenager wanted to buy a lawn mower to start a lawn mowing business, North Country Bank & Trust would loan the youngster the money.

The character Mr. Tycoon had achieved significant popularity in the local community around Manistique, Michigan, the headquarters of North Country Bank & Trust. Children related to Mr. Tycoon in a local sense as youth relate to Mickey Mouse or Donald Duck on the national scene.

The Tycoon Club emphasized savings at an early age and encouraged parents to save for very young children (1, 2, 3, and 4 years of age). These and other promotional efforts stressed the importance of saving early and developing lifelong saving habits. All evidence indicated that this program created customer loyalty at a very early age and secured customers for the bank for many years to come.

CHARACTERISTICS OF THE MARKETS SERVED BY NORTH COUNTRY BANK & TRUST

The rural Upper Peninsula of Michigan covers 14,000 square miles with a population of 320,000 people. It is approximately 300 miles east to west and 70 to 90 miles north to south. Its major cities are as follows:

- Marquette, population 25,000

- Sault Ste. Marie, population 14,448

- Escanaba, population 14,355

- Iron Mountain, population 8,314

- Houghton, population 7,512

- Ironwood, population 7,741

Major industries of the Upper Peninsula include tourism, mining (iron ore), health care, gambling, and forest products. A long history of immigration from Finland, Italy, and Wales is partially responsible

EXHIBIT D

Rate of Return on Assets, North Country Bank & Trust, First of America, and Michigan Financial Corporation, 1993–1996

	Return on Assets, %			
Bank Holding Company	*1993*	*1994*	*1995*	*1996*
North Country Bank and Trust	1.18	1.01	0.87	0.97
First of America	1.20	0.97	0.99	1.02
Michigan Financial Corporation	0.98	1.10	1.13	1.23

Source: Sheshunoff Banking Organization Quarterly.

for a sense of rugged individualism that pervades the region.

The opening of deer season is equivalent to a "national holiday" in the Upper Peninsula. Many high schools and businesses close on November 15. Snowmobiling, cross-country and down-hill skiing, and showshoeing are major winter sports. The Upper Peninsula in its northern tier receives 150 inches of snow a year. The summertime brings lots of opportunities to sailboat or fish on Lake Michigan, Lake Huron, or the massive 31,000 square mile Lake Superior.

From a banking perspective, the Upper Peninsula of Michigan represents a $3 billion market. This market is served primarily by three bank holding companies: MFC First National, with assets of $783 million, North Country Bank & Trust, with $327 million in assets, and First of America, a $22 billion bank, headquartered in Kalamazoo, Michigan. This bank has business operations in Michigan, Ohio, Indiana, and Illinois. These three bank holding companies vary in their relative profitability. Exhibit D shows the relative rate of return on assets for these three companies for 1993 through the first 9 months of 1996.

Questions

1. Does the laissez-faire approach to banking used by North Country Bank & Trust make sense, or should it consider a more traditional approach?

2. Does the Weatherby, Big Bertha, diamond, grandfather clock, and picture premium program to secure demand deposits make economic sense from the bank's perspective as well as the customers' perspective? Are there nonfinancial implications of this program that benefit the bank? Do you believe this program should be continued?

3. Are the North Country Bank's profitability measures comparable with those of their competitors? How are these measures affected by the current rapid-expansion mode? As a potential investor, do the rapid-expansion and profitability measures add to the appeal of the forthcoming stock offering?

4. What are the marketing implications of the Mr. Tycoon program?

Service in the Skies: High-Class, Low-Class, and No-Class

A Case Study in Airline Misbehavior

This case was prepared by Carol H. Anderson, Crummer Graduate School of Business, Rollins College, and Alexander T. Wood, Educational Foundations, College of Education, University of Central Florida.

Abstract: This case provides an opportunity to analyze the challenges faced by airlines and airline passengers when individuals become unruly. Airlines, government agencies, and other organizations are concerned about the threat of air rage to air safety and customer satisfaction, and must develop measures to overcome these problems. Passengers share these concerns and want something done about it.

"Passenger's Death Prompts Calls for Improved 'Air Rage' Procedures."[1] "'Air Rage' A Threat On Flights."[2] Numerous headlines about unruly passengers underscore the airline industry's dilemma in trying to ensure safe air travel for customers and crews. Passengers are creating a growing number of critical incidents and potential disasters by "threatening crews, pilots, and the general well-being of everyone on board."[3] Passengers who do not like the cabin service often resort to verbal abuse and assault on crew members.

"Airline misbehavior" often appears to be the product of mounting tensions that are related to pre-flight, in-flight, and post-flight customer service. From the perspective of the airlines, personal safety and service quality suffer due to service disruptions caused by unruly passengers. Airline officials are concerned about increased incidents of passenger frustration and rude behavior, which leads to abuse

of flight attendants and unpleasant service experiences for other passengers. Many incidents occur when passengers have had too much to drink, and get rowdy when told they cannot have more alcohol.[4] A number of other cases involve drugs or mental illness. Drunken passengers have hit, scratched, and shoved flight attendants when they were denied another drink. One passenger was so angry that he defecated on a food-service cart and used the linen napkins as toilet paper. On another flight, 18 British travelers started a food fight aboard a Northwest Airlines flight when they were refused liquor.[5] However, airline passengers also have their side of the story. They have reported numerous indignities suffered at the hands of the airlines, and have called attention to experiences of poor service, discomfort, and lack of consideration.

AIR RAGE

Andrew R. Thomas, President of www.AirRage.org and co-author of the book, *Air Rage: Crisis in the Skies,* defines air rage as *"the aberrant, abusive, or*

Reprinted by permission of the authors.

The World Association for Case Method Research & Application has published a previous version of this paper in the publication entitled, *Creative Teaching-Act* 5, 2002, ISBN 1-877868-19-1.

abnormal behavior of passengers either on aircraft or in airports."[6] Research conducted by www.AirRage.com since the September 11, 2001 hijacking and World Trade Center bombing indicates that passenger air rage is on the rise, despite tightened security. The study included reports filed by local police, the FBI, and FAA, at 15 airports across the U.S. Hundreds of other unreported incidents have been occurring more frequently, and often at a higher level of intensity since September 11, 2001. Thomas maintains that although the more sensational incidents tend to be reported, the media, government agencies, and the airlines themselves have underreported the problem for quite some time. Prior to September 11, there were six cockpit intrusions, and the number escalated after the WTC bombing—a threat to the safety of the 1.5 billion airline passengers who fly each year. Within a little over a month after the WTC incident, several commercial airliners were forced to make an emergency landing—some with military fighter escort planes at their side, due to passengers trying to break into the cockpit. Numerous other air rage incidents have continued to be reported throughout the U.S. and other countries. The reasons behind air rage before and after September 11 are similar. However, Thomas attributes the rise in air rage incidents after the WTC bombing to higher anxiety about air travel, increased alcohol consumption to overcome anxiety, increased number of passengers smoking in the lavatory, increased mistrust of—and anger toward—"dark skinned" passengers, and mounting frustration with the inconveniences of new security measures.

Thomas, and others have called for the U.S. Congress to include the air rage problem in the new aviation security measures. He stresses the need for government, law enforcement agencies, airlines and regulatory authorities to cooperate in finding "common solutions to a common problem."[7]

INCIDENTS PRIOR TO SEPTEMBER 11, 2001

While air rage may be an extreme case of airline passenger misbehavior, it emphasizes the severity of any situation where an agitated customer is out of control in a confined space with hundreds of other people, thousands of feet above the earth. At issue is how airline personnel can deal with a situation, such as the killing of a violent 19-year-old man on Southwest Airlines Co. flight 1763, on August 11, 2000. Mr. Jonathan Burton of Las Vegas began to act wildly and tried to kick through the cockpit door about 20 minutes before landing in Salt Lake City. When he tried a second time, passengers came to the aid of the two stewardesses who were trying to restrain him at the front of the Boeing 737. Mr. Burton ended up in an exit-row seat, but flight attendants decided to move him to the back of the plane because of his comments about wanting to get off the plane. He became agitated and fought violently as six passengers pinned him to the floor in the rear of the airplane. In the end, six to eight passengers subdued and ultimately suffocated Mr. Burton. Southwest defended the action of its crew and passengers, stating that "You don't want anyone to die, but you don't want the plane to go down either."[8] A Southwest spokesman attributed the incident to an attempted hijacking, rather than a case of air rage. Authorities ruled the death a homicide, but stated that it was justified in self-defense.

Southwest Airlines is a consistently successful airline with an enviable performance record. It is the fourth largest U.S. carrier in terms of originating customers boarded, and has received numerous awards and accolades for its on-time performance, baggage handling, and low number of customer complaints compared to competitors. The company is also well known for its outstanding employee culture, "fun" service environment, and respectful attitude toward customers—leading to high levels of customer satisfaction. Southwest's low-cost, no-frills airline service strategy has resulted in 26 consecutive years of profitability, despite two major industry downturns.[9] However, like many other airlines, Southwest does not train its cabin crews in physical restraint. It is common practice for airlines to encourage attendants to summon help from other passengers. The Burton incident and others have raised questions that are being pondered by the airlines, unions representing pilots and flight attendants, the Federal Aviation Administration, and concerned citizen groups, such as the Skyrage Foundation. In general, there is a call for more training for flight crews on how to handle anything from passengers who are annoying to those who are physically abusive. However, this type of training requires a different approach, and as Colleen Barrett, Southwest's executive vice president of customers, says, "We don't want to turn any employee into a law-enforcement officer."[10] (The effect of the federal Sky Marshall program that was put in place following the September 11, 2001 WTC bombing was unknown at the time of this case.)

The August 2000 Southwest air rage incident is not an isolated case. In June 2000, the NASA Aviation Safety Reporting System stated that unruly airline passengers whose behavior disrupts pilots caused serious flying errors that threatened safety.[11] In a study of 152 passenger-aircraft rage incidents, analysts found that in 40 percent of these cases, pilots left the cockpit to handle a disturbance or had their flight routine interrupted by flight attendants who needed help. One of four of these cases involved errors such as flying too fast, flying at the wrong altitude, or taxiing across runways designated for other aircraft. In a number of recent cases deranged passengers have broken into jet cockpits before they could be subdued. Flight attendants and pilots reported the following causes of rage incidents: alcohol (43 percent), prohibited electronic devices (15 percent), smoking in lavatories (9 percent), drugs or medication (8 percent), bomb/hijack threats (5 percent), and other reasons (18 percent). According to the study, about 10 percent of pilot errors, over a 10-year period, were due to air-rage cases that disturbed the pilot's carefully choreographed routines, particularly during the critical takeoff and landing phases.

The airlines' ability to manage the service process and to deliver high quality customer service affects, and is affected by, a number of players. In order to identify issues related to airline passenger misbehavior and make recommendations for resolving this increasingly widespread problem, a number of viewpoints should be considered. In the following sections, we will consider the perspectives of airline management, front-line employees, and customers. The roles of support personnel, travel agents, and other parties that interface in any way with the airline industry and its customers also should be considered.

AIRLINE MANAGEMENT PERSPECTIVE

The deregulation of the airlines in 1978 set off the beginning of intense competition among America's airlines. Over the past two decades, airlines have added more aircraft, that travel at faster speeds, with greater fuel efficiency and safety than ever before. Operating efficiencies of larger planes that can carry larger passenger loads over greater distances make it possible to lower the cost of passenger air travel. A healthy economy and global business expansion also contribute to increased numbers of both first time and repeat leisure and business airline travelers.

In spite of this apparent success story, there are many service mishaps that must be addressed by marketing managers. Competition is fierce among the airlines as they try to give higher levels of customer service, frequently with limited resources to back it up. They struggle to be profitable, while often operating in a survival mode in an industry where operating costs are escalating and customers are more demanding. Many airlines are attempting to increase profitability by focusing on lucrative market niches, and offering these customers special amenities. Others are forming strategic alliances with other domestic and overseas carriers and adding new routes or pruning existing routes.

AIRLINE FRONT-LINE EMPLOYEE PERSPECTIVE

Observations made by flight crews and airport personnel indicate a widespread lack of consideration by passengers for other people or for established airline procedures, such as the following:[12]

- Passengers board planes in random fashion, not in the orderly fashion prescribed by the airlines.

- Passengers carry on too much luggage, cramming it into overhead bins, under seats, or anywhere they can—leaving the later arriving passengers without the storage space to which they are entitled.

- Passengers use the aisles as their personal playground or workout area, making it difficult for the flight attendants to provide service to other passengers.

- Passengers are often unreasonable—insisting on more alcohol when they have already imbibed too much; asking for special food that should have been ordered in advance;

throwing a tantrum when they do not get their way.

- Passengers have physically assaulted and verbally abused flight attendants and other airline employees—often taking out their frustrations on individual employees rather than the airline.

- Pilots express concern about safety issues that are created when they need to leave the cockpit to settle disputes in the cabin.

- Flights are long, layovers are short, and home is ... where?

In general, airline front-line employees share concerns about the inconsiderate, unruly, and often dangerous behavior of their customers. The stories of mistreatment of flight crews and other airline personnel by passengers are seemingly endless, and the problem is yet to be resolved in an industry that competes largely on the basis of price and customer service.

AIRLINE CUSTOMER PERSPECTIVE

On the 1999 New Year's weekend, thousands of Northwest Airlines passengers were left stranded on runways at the Detroit Metropolitan Airport. More than 8,000 Northwest travelers were restricted to their seats for as long as 11 hours—mostly without food, water, working toilets, or the use of their own cellular phones (they were restricted to the expensive in-flight phones)—based on airline rules for maintaining order and safety. They also were prohibited from walking around the cabin. Passengers with special needs included families with babies that did not have enough formula to feed them and individuals with medical problems.[13] This fiasco illustrates the frustrations and disappointment of many passengers with the quality of airline service.

Blizzard conditions kept more than 75 planes, most with passengers already aboard, on the field where they had already taxied onto the runways before the flights were canceled. Conditions were considered unsafe to take buses to the plane to pick up the travelers. Northwest apologized to all passengers who were inconvenienced and offered those who were delayed on the ground for more than $2\frac{1}{2}$ hours a free domestic round-trip ticket.

The Department of Transportation and the Federal Aviation Administration were given the responsibility of investigating these actions, which had been performed in the name of passenger "safety." The federal investigation concluded that Northwest Airlines violated no laws, but the Department of Transportation was "sharply critical of Northwest's lack of planning, poor communications, and other failings that resulted in thousands of passengers being trapped in its grounded planes for hours."[14] The report said, "Even if the well-being of passengers had not been an issue, the ... stranding of passengers on aircraft queued up on taxiways for up to $8\frac{1}{2}$ hours invites more serious problems and is simply unacceptable." The airline has since implemented changes in its procedures and planning, and attempted to make restitution to the inconvenienced passengers. However, a number of lawsuits have been filed against Northwest Airlines and other defendants, alleging infliction of emotional distress and false imprisonment.

PASSENGER RIGHTS: THE "CUSTOMERS FIRST" INITIATIVE

Passengers and airline employees alike have experienced an escalation in rude behavior, service quality issues, and agitation for most of the past decade, while participating in commercial airline flights. As employees feel more harassed in their work, and passengers experience poorer quality service (or perhaps expect more attention and consideration than is realistic), federal lawmakers and airline industry groups are trying to resolve the problem.

The sheer volume of air travel has increased significantly. In 1999, airlines struggled to provide service to more than 600 million passengers. Unexplained delays, canceled and overbooked flights, cramped seating, and lost luggage, resulted in consumer outcries and calls for Congressional legislation. "Passenger rights" bills were brought before Congress, and the furor against poor service by the airlines continues to attract the attention of the U.S. government.

In June 1999, the airline industry responded to pressure from the White House and Capitol Hill by instituting a "Customers First" initiative.[15] Twenty-three carriers pledged to:

- inform travelers promptly of delays and cancellations;

- assign a customer service representative to handle complaints and respond to them within 60 days;

- make food, water, and restrooms available when a plane is sitting on the tarmac for an extended period of time;

- ask the Transportation Department to consider raising the liability limit for lost luggage;

- make available information about airline policies on cancellations, restrictions, seat size, and more.[16]

"When you fly, do you feel like the focus of a cattle-herding operation? Cramped seats, endless delays and cheery flight attendants tossing bags of pretzels your way? Sorry—none of that will improve soon. But some things may get better, and an informed traveler is certainly a happier traveler."[17] From this perspective, Customers First attempts to provide the information outlined above to airline travelers. In December 1999, the Air Transport Association (which represents carriers that transport over 95 percent of all air passengers and cargo in the United States) enacted the guidelines that resulted from the Customers First initiative. These guidelines are designed to make air travel more pleasant and passengers better informed.[18] (See Exhibit 1.)

Customer complaints seem to revolve around several issues: inadequate or inaccurate information about airline policies and flight details; lack of planning for unexpected inconveniences (i.e., delayed flights, lost luggage, etc.); and lack of timely responsiveness to passenger complaints and concerns.

AIRLINE MANAGEMENT RESPONSES TO CUSTOMER AND EMPLOYEE CONCERNS

The Customers First pledge by the airline industry, described in the previous section, addresses major customer concerns related to information, unexpected inconveniences, and responsiveness. Individual airlines are pursuing a variety of strategies to improve service performance and customer satisfaction. Some examples follow.

It is interesting to note that while some airlines focus on more comfortable seats, better in-flight food from celebrity chefs, and appealing advertising, these are not at the top of travelers' minds. According to an online study of nearly 21,000 U.S. adults, what travelers want from their airlines is "dependable, no-hassle transportation at a reasonable cost, plus happy employees and strong performance."[19] The number one ranked domestic and international carriers in this study were Southwest Airlines and Singapore Airlines respectively. Southwest's on-time record, low fares, and friendly employees appear to overcome any negative aspects of no-frills service.

Although there have been great advances in package tracking technology, the use of this innovation has not been fully implemented, and airlines still have not found satisfactory answers to lost luggage. United Airlines in the Denver airport and British Airways at London's Heathrow Airport installed new higher-tech systems—but both have met with a number of problems. With heavier passenger loads, the volume of baggage that must be handled has increased greatly. However, most of the time travelers' belongings are still handled in the same way they were a generation ago. In 1997, major carriers mishandled an average of 4.96 bags out of 1,000. In 1999, this number increased to 5.08—figures that have held fairly consistent for the past decade. Today, airlines use minimal technology for luggage handling. Barcodes are put on luggage, but only used to sort at the originating airport, and not to track luggage after that point. The U.S. Department of Transportation says that 99.5 percent of all passengers' bags are handled without any problems. This sounds like a good track record until we consider that one-half of one percent of 500 million passengers traveling through the domestic system represents the mishandling of 2.5 million bags each year.[20]

Electronic ticketing has removed some of the time-consuming details of travel for passengers and is cost-effective for the airlines. United Airlines started selling e-tickets in 1994, and by 2000 about 60 percent of its sales were from e-tickets. Other airlines report similar transitions. However, occasionally travelers are frustrated by computers that crash while they are in the check-in line, computer errors, or lack of a paper ticket if a flight is delayed or canceled and the customer wants to book a flight with another airline.[21]

These are but a few examples of how the airlines are trying to improve the service process for their customers. Some other initiatives include training flight attendants to speak other languages and paying attention to the needs of special customer segments (e.g., children, disabled, college students, etc.). Many airlines are jazzing up their images by adding personal services for business-class passengers, repainting planes, and paying attention to details such as the type of tableware used to serve airplane food. While making these higher-paying passengers more comfortable with larger seats and more services, they are taking space away from the lower-fare coach section and making these seats smaller and more crowded.

The problem of unruly passengers and disruptive air rage incidents is more difficult to remedy. Airlines are generally in agreement that measures

EXHIBIT 1

Air Transport Association Guidelines

According to guidelines enacted by the Air Transport Association (ATA) in December 1999, member airlines pledge the following to their customers:

- *Fares:* Customers will be offered the lowest fare available, and will be told the lowest fare for the date, flight and class of service requested.

- *Information about delays, etc.:* Airline personnel will provide passengers with the "best available information" about delays, cancellations and diversions, in what the association calls a "timely manner." Policies on accommodating passengers who are delayed overnight will be determined by each airline individually.

- *Luggage:* Airlines will "make every reasonable effort" to get checked luggage to a passenger within 24 hours and will attempt to contact a customer whose unclaimed bag bears a name, address or telephone number.

- *Baggage liability:* The airlines petitioned the Department of Transportation to increase their baggage liability limit from $2,350 to $2,500.

- *Reservation penalties:* Airlines will not penalize customers who hold a reservation without payment for 24 hours or who cancel a reservation within 24 hours in the same span. Each airline will determine which of these policies to enact.

- *Refunds:* Refunds will be issued to eligible customers within seven days for credit card purchases or 20 days for cash purchases.

- *Special accommodations:* Each airline will disclose its individual policies for accommodating disabled and special needs passengers (e.g., unaccompanied minors).

- *Delay on runway:* Each airline will develop plans to accommodate the needs of passengers who are delayed on an airliner on a runway, and will make "every reasonable effort" to provide food, water, restrooms, and medical treatment as the situation warrants.

- *Overbooked flights:* When passengers are bumped from overbooked flights, they will be handled with "fairness and consistency," and airlines will disclose policies and procedures (e.g., check-in deadlines).

- *Disclosures:* Airlines will inform customers about changes in travel itinerary, equipment (e.g., type of plane), frequent-flier rules, cancellation policies, etc.

- *Code-sharing:* When airlines use other airlines in a "code-share" arrangement, consumers will be ensured of the partners' commitment to "comparable consumer plans and policies."

- *Customer complaints:* Airlines will respond to written customer complaints within 60 days.

Source: Carden, Lisa, "Airlines' New Guidelines: What Do They Really Mean?" *The Orlando Sentinel* (January 23, 2000), p. L-2. (Also see http://www.airtransport.org/press/1999/99-022.htm for additional information.)

must be taken, but training of customer contact employees seems to focus on customer service, with varied approaches to dealing with dangerous passenger behavior. There is not a set policy, but British Airways PLC, for example, uses role-playing and body-language awareness to teach conflict management to its crews. The airline also has stern warning letters on its planes that flight attendants can deliver to passengers who are disruptive to warn them of the consequences of their actions. Several carriers have installed redesigned cockpit doors to keep passengers from breaking in and have equipped airplanes with plastic "flex-cuffs" or wrist restraints. They are also providing more information to passengers about the consequences of unruly behavior on their aircraft.

The U.S. government and the airline industry developed a number of short-term and long-term solutions to the problems that can be attributed to air rage incidents since September 11, 2001. Short-term measures included closure of airports, heightened screening at airport check-ins, banning of carry-on luggage, and other safety precautions. Longer-term remedies included the creation of a federal Sky Marshall program whereby trained and armed individuals would fly as passengers to help to avert serious incidents, improved airport check-in procedures (both personnel and equipment), heightened airport security (including the U.S. National Guard presence in airports), and others that were still being considered at the time of this case.

SUMMARY

The need to balance airline safety, service quality, and profitability is a major challenge for U.S. passenger airlines. Assume that you are Mr. Andrew Thomas, Director of AirRage.org, and that you have been asked to present your solutions to this problem to executives from the major U.S. airlines. What would you tell them about how you would approach this problem? Airline management, front-line employees, customers (as well as the airline industry at large), and law enforcement agencies are all key players in the scenarios described in this case, and each has his or her personal view of the situation that must be considered in arriving at a solution. What can commercial airlines do to improve personal safety and the quality of service experienced by their customers? What role(s) can customers play in this process, if any?

Endnotes

1. Trottman, Melanie and Chip Cummins, "Passenger's Death Prompts Calls for Improved 'Air Rage' Procedures," *Wall Street Journal* (September 26, 2000), pp. B1, B4.
2. Levin, Alan, "'Air Rage' A Threat On Flights," *USA Today* (June 12, 2000), p. A1.
3. Dateline NBC, "Cabin Pressure; Unruly Passengers Pose Threat On Some Domestic Airline Flights" (April 9, 2000, 7 p.m. ET).
4. Nomani, Asra, "Airlines Tell Boozers to Put a Cork in It," *Wall Street Journal* (August 28, 1998), pp. W1, W7; Associated Press, "Flight Attendants Decry Abuse: It's a Jungle Up There," *Orlando Sentinel* (January 31, 1996), p. A-10; Reuters, "Rowdy Passenger Forces Down Another Flight," http://dailynews.netscape.com (June 9, 1999).
5. Associated Press, "Flight Attendants Decry Abuse: It's A Jungle Up There," *Orlando Sentinel* (January 21, 1996), p. A-10; Reuters, "Rowdy Passenger Forces Down Another Flight" (June 9, 1999), Nomani, Asra Q., "Airlines Tell Boozers to Put a Cork in it," *Wall Street Journal* (August 28, 1998), pp. W1, W7.
6. Thomas, Andrew R., "The Number of Air Rage Incidents Has Increased Since the Hijackings of September 11, 2001 Despite Security Crackdowns At Airports and On Airlines Across the US," News Release, www.AirRage.org, October 25, 2001.
7. Thomas, Andrew R., "Congress Must Include Air Rage in New Security Measures," *Aviation Daily*, October 22, 2001.
8. Trottman and Cummins, *op. cit.*, p. B1.
9. Anonymous, "Air Herb's Secret Weapon," *Chief Executive* (July/August 1999), pp. 32–42.
10. Trottman and Cummins, *op. cit.*, p. B4.
11. Levin, Alan, "'Air Rage' A Threat On Flights," *USA Today* (June 12, 2000), p. A1.
12. McCartney, Scott, "Chaos in the Aisles: Airlines Try to Speed Up Boarding," *Wall Street Journal* (March 8, 1996), pp. B1, B6.
13. Carey, Susan, "Fliers Assert Rights After Runway Ordeal," *Wall Street Journal* (January 15, 1999), pp. B1, B4.
14. Carey, Susan, "U.S. Criticizes Northwest Air's Actions in Blizzard," *Wall Street Journal* (June 3, 1999), p. A4.
15. Taylor, Lauren R., "Air Travel: Know Before You Go," *Government Executive* (August 1999), pp. 62–63.
16. For additional information about Customers First, go to http://www.airtransport.org/press/1999/99-022.htm or call the Air Transport Association at (202) 626-4000.
17. Taylor, *op. cit.*
18. Carden, Lisa, "Airlines' New Guidelines: What Do They Really Mean?" *Orlando Sentinel* (January 23, 2000).
19. McCartney, Scott, "Airlines' Reputations Hinge on the Basics, Study Shows," *Wall Street Journal* (April 27, 2000), p. B4.
20. McCartney, Scott, "Baggage Bedlam," *Wall Street Journal* (June 30, 2000), pp. W1, W4.
21. Reynolds, Christopher, "Know the Pitfalls, Pluses of Electronic Ticketing," *Orlando Sentinel* (November 5, 2000), pp. L1, L6.

Target Is Hot! What's Next for the "Upscale Discounter" (2001)

This case was prepared by Carol H. Anderson, Crummer Graduate School of Business, Rollins College, and Alexander T. Wood, University of Central Florida.

In a January 17, 2001 interview with the Star Tribune in Minneapolis, Bob Ulrich, Chairman and CEO of Target Corporation and Target Stores, expressed his confidence that Target was prepared for a soft economy. "In 25 years, Target's comp-store sales [sales from stores open at least a year] haven't fallen below a 3 percent increase in any single year, and we've had several recessions," he said. "I think we're well positioned to survive a recession, if there is one."[1] Ulrich has weathered a number of economic ups and downs during his 34-year career with Target. In recent years most of the revenue and profits for the parent company have come from the rapid growth of the Target discount store division (the focus of this case), and from the national brand recognition that is associated with the Target bullseye logo. The department store chains, Mervyn's and Marshall Field's, have not been as immune to a slowing economy, but Target Corporation has made a number of changes in these divisions that are expected to improve their performance.

Following the September 11, 2001 attacks on the World Trade Center in New York City, many retailers saw their market plunge drastically. Fewer customers were shopping in the stores and malls, and those who did shop tended to buy less and to seek greater value in their purchases. Although each of the major discount retail chains was affected by this event, Target Stores and Wal-Mart Stores, Inc. rallied as customers returned. Kmart Corp. was

the hardest hit, and did not seem to recover from this financial blow during the 2001 fall and holiday selling season. By January 2002, Kmart's stock had dropped to its lowest closing price since 1970. A contributing factor was the company's decision to cut advertising expenditures during the holidays. Target Stores and Wal-Mart were able to pull out of the downslide following the events of September 11. By January 2002, Target's share prices had gained 54 percent over the September 21 low, and Wal-Mart's shares had risen 30 percent during the same period. Kmart shares dropped 25 percent during this period, compared to a 155 percent increase in share price from the end of 2000 to their peak in August 2001.[2]

Target's performance has been outstanding in the face of past economic downturns and disasters. Bob Ulrich has many challenges ahead in 2002 and beyond. He and his company must continue to develop strategies for growth of the Target Stores division, and be able to reach the firm's desired financial goals in a slowing economy.

TARGET CORPORATION (FORMERLY DAYTON HUDSON)

Target Corporation's headquarters are in Minneapolis, Minnesota, with regional offices and distribution centers located in other cities/states. The history of the corporation dates back to the

Reprinted by permission of the author.

founding of J.L. Hudson Company in Detroit in 1881, the founding of the Dayton Company in Minneapolis in 1902, and the merger of the two chains in 1969. Target Corporation ranks as America's fourth largest retailer among general merchandisers in the 2001 *Fortune* 500,[3] and includes three divisions: Target Stores (upscale discounter), Mervyn's California (midrange department store), and Marshall Field's (upscale department store chain consisting of Marshall Field's and the former Dayton's and Hudson's stores). The company also owns Rivertown Trading (a catalog company), and Associated Merchandising (apparel supplier). Target Corporation entered the year 2002 with a total of 1,383 stores: 1,055 Target Stores (including 62 SuperTargets) in 47 states, 264 Mervyn's California stores in 14 states, and 64 Marshall Field's stores in 8 states.[4] Corporate revenue and net income for the three chains combined in 2000 were $36.9 billion (9.5% growth) and $1.26 billion (10.5% growth), respectively. Target Corporation has 255,000 employees, an 18.7% growth over the previous year.[5] Target is consistently ranked high among all U.S. firms by industry analysts, such as number 37 in the 2001 *Fortune* 500 rankings, and number 46 in Hoover's 500.

Target Stores Division

Target Stores is the largest division of Target Corporation, generating 80 percent of corporate income, while the two department store divisions contribute about 20 percent each. Target Stores is community oriented, and contributes 5 percent of its federally taxable income to its local communities through grants, special programs, team member participation, partnerships with nonprofits, and other means.

Profile of Target Stores Shoppers ("Guests")[6]

Target shoppers tend to be the youngest among major retailers, with a median age of 44. They have a median household income of $51,000, compared to the median American household income of $39,000. Eighty percent are female and approximately 43 percent have children at home. About 39 percent are college graduates.[7] According to the company,

Target guests recognize the "difference between price and the more enduring concept of value." "Target guests are smart about their purchases, savvy to trends and conscientious about their communities. They're a unique crowd for a unique store."

Some of the Major Brands Available In Target Stores—2001

- Calphalon (cookware)
- Michael Graves (décor; housewares)
- Philips (coffee maker)
- Martex (bed and bath)
- Waverly (home textiles, etc.)
- Mossimo (apparel)
- Carter's Baby Tykes (children's apparel)
- Eddie Bauer (camping products)
- And many other national and store brands with a fashion emphasis (e.g., Cherokee, Merona)

Target continues to add new brands to its merchandise mix to provide more value for its customers. For example, in January 2002, the Stride Rite Corporation announced the introduction of two new footwear brands ("Kid Smart?" and "Baby Smart?") that would be available in Target stores in Spring 2002. Stride Rite's Chairman and CEO said, "We are excited to expand our brand lineup to fill the needs of Target guests looking for stylish, value-priced children's shoes." Prices of the shoes will range from $12.99 to $16.99.[8]

Target Stores' Merchandising Approach

Store design consists of wide aisles, bright lighting, and layouts that make merchandise easy to find. Customers are able to move through checkout lanes easily. The store is operated from the perspective of a service-driven attitude, and supported with an innovative distribution network. Target's philosophy is to provide its shoppers with "Trend-driven merchandise with the everyday basics, a unique shopping experience, and a commitment to the community. It is this vision for value that has taken Target from its department store roots and made it into *the* upscale discount retailer."[9]

SELECTED HISTORY OF TARGET STORES (1962 – 2001)

1960s:

- First store opened in Roseville, Minnesota, in 1962.
- End of 1960s: Target operated 17 stores in 4 states; sales $100 million.

1970s

- 1975—Target became top revenue producer for parent Dayton Hudson Corp., and has kept that position ever since.
- End of 1970s: Target operated 80 stores in 11 states, over 18,000 team members, and $1.12 billion in sales.

1980s

- Continued expansion into many new states.
- End of 1980s: Target operated 399 stores in 33 states, and reached $7.52 in sales.

1990s

- 1990—opened first Target Greatland store in Apple Valley, Minnesota.
- 1995—opened first SuperTarget store.
  —launched the Target Guest Card, and Club Wedd bridal registry.
- 1997—began building Target House, for long-term patients and their families at St. Jude Children's hospital.
  —entered New York City metropolitan market.
- 1999—continued expansion in the Northeast in Massachusetts and Rhode Island.
- 1999—target.com established in August 1999—a Web site where both merchandise and information about the company are available. By the end of 1999, the site had almost 2,000 items and a growing number of loyal customers.
- End of 1990s: Target operated 907 stores in 44 states, and sales reached $26.02 billion.

2000

- January 2000—Corporate name was changed from Dayton Hudson Corporation to Target Corporation[10]
- February 2000—Target Corporation formed a new e-commerce unit, called "Target Direct," with responsibility for all of the company's electronic retailing and direct marketing efforts for all of the corporation's store brands and catalogs.[11]
- May 2000—Target announced that it had entered into a strategic multi-channel marketing alliance with E*TRADE. The agreement includes an in-store E*TRADE financial service center at a SuperTarget store, and the creation of a co-branded Target/E*TRADE website for Target guests (launched August 24, 2000 to offer financial services and free investment information).[12]
- August 2000—Target Stores and America Online, Inc. (AOL) announced the roll-out of joint marketing and promotional initiatives. Special edition AOL CD-ROMs are now available in over 900 Target stores.[13]
- Year 2000 sales reached $29.28 billion; pre-tax profits reached $2.223 billion.

2001

Target Stores

- January 2001—Target's corporate brand strengthened by changing names of Dayton's and Hudson's to Marshall Field's to leverage the Field's brand name nationally.
- Number of stores as of March 2001:[14] 992 Target Stores in 46 states, including 95 Target Greatland stores, 37 SuperTarget stores, 507 pharmacies, 136 optical centers, and 9 multi-level stores.
- Total number of Target Stores as of August 31, 2001 increased to 1,019.[15]
- Typical store size of 90,000—125,000 square feet; and company's total store square footage of about 125,000 square feet.
- Approximately 195,000 team members are employed by Target Stores.
- May 2001—Target Corporation announced plans to double the number of its discount

stores over the next few years, rather than expand Marshall Field's or Mervyn's.[16]

- June 2001—Target announced a partnership with VISA U.S.A. to offer a chip-embedded smart card. Cardholders can access special offers and build points toward rewards on a national basis.[17]

- July 2001—Target announced an agreement with Tupperware to sell plastic containers in SuperTarget stores. [18]

- August 2001—Target claimed victory over Kmart Corp. in a slugfest over comparative price claims by Kmart in its Dare to Compare promotion. Target claimed that 74% of the Kmart ads it surveyed not only included the wrong prices, but also referenced items that Target did not stock. Kmart denied any wrongdoing, but stopped the promotion.[19]

- September 2001—Target Stores and Nickelodeon announced an exclusive marketing partnership for the fall 2001 retail launch of SpongeBob SquarePants (a popular Nickelodeon animated character) merchandise, including school supplies, apparel for all ages, toys, and other items.[20]

- September 2001—Attack on World Trade Center took its toll on retail sales throughout the U.S. However, Target was able to recover and sustain its profitability more quickly than its competitors. Target's value proposition and sense of fashion attracted many shoppers who were concerned about the economy during the fall and holiday 2001 selling season.

- Target continued to open new stores, particularly SuperTarget Stores, as the company moved into 2002. For example, a new SuperTarget Store will open in New Tampa, Florida, in March 2002. In early January, the company attracted about 3,000 job seekers for 300 positions starting at $7 an hour as cashiers, bakers, sales, and stock personnel. (This store will offer a full line of groceries, a deli and bakery, a Starbucks coffee house, and a Krispy Kreme Doughnuts shop—in addition to clothing, electronics, music, and other products.)[21]

- January 2002—In a rare publicized complaint about Target Stores policies, a customer in Wichita, Kansas, took exception to an unpopular return policy that only allowed her to receive current clearance prices for items now on sale—although the item she returned shortly after

Christmas, was purchased at full price during the holidays. Although Target had posted signs throughout the store and at every checkout lane, customers complained that this was an unfair policy. Management listened to these complaints and revised their return policy. They still require a receipt for returns, but the company has a new receipt lookup service to help consumers who have lost their proof of purchase.[22]

Target Greatland

- Store size averages 135,000 square feet, with over 1.5 miles of shelf space
- Stores have 2,200 feet of aisles throughout the store (equivalent of 7 football fields)
- Stockroom space measures about $1/_4$ mile.

SuperTarget Stores

- A SuperTarget store is "a 175,000-square-foot box" designed with three distinct segments: clothing and furniture; grocery area; and more traditional items found in grocery stores and traditional Targets, such as health and beauty aids, and cleaning products.

- There were 62 SuperTarget stores in 14 states at the end of 2001. Longer-range plans are to open 200 SuperTargets by 2010, although some think this number could be as high as 400.

- The grocery area is stocked with name-brand groceries plus Target's house brand, "Archer Farms." At the front of the grocery area are several outlets, such as D'Amico & Sons deli, Wuollet Bakery, Starbucks Coffee, and Famous Dave's ribs. (An analyst says the way to look at this area is "that it's a lifestyle-based destination for food.") For example, the produce section has sushi, edible flowers, imported cheeses, organic foods, and other specialty foods—all part of the concept of bringing "fashion to food."[23]

Target.com Web Site

- October 2000—announced a redesigned website, www.target.com, to leverage its successful offline brand online, offering nearly 15,000 products—some are also available in Target stores; some are only available from target.com; successfully launched during the 2000 holiday season.[24]

- target.com was ranked by Net Nielsen Ratings among the top 10 online shopping sites.
- Convenient online access to Club Wedd and Lullaby Club.
- Online purchases may be returned to any Target store location.
- July 2001—Target announced that it was selling windmills and other energy-saving products online at target.com to help combat high energy prices.[25]
- August 2001—The Target Town House was opened in Manhattan—a 6,000 square foot Tribeca townhouse, styled with Target merchandise throughout. In each room, Target previewed the best of home, fashion, and beauty. (A virtual tour of the townhouse was also made available online at target.com.) The Town House opened with a gala celebration, and featured Target designers such as Sonia Kashuk, Mossimo Giannulli, and Michael Graves. At the close of the Target Town House, all of the furnishings and a charitable grant were given to the Coalition for the Homeless.[26]
- August 2001—Target Corporation launched Bullseye, a new website destination devoted exclusively to teenagers at www.target.com/bullseye. Target's senior marketing manager said that "Bullseye is at the center of today's pop culture." Bullseye has seven key site features to engage a growing teen audience: Horoscopes, Music, Quizzes (interactive), Advice, Fashion, Beauty, and Events.[27]

Target Stores Performance

See Exhibit 1 for end-of-August through December 2001 monthly sales and year-to-date sales for Target Corporation and each of its divisions. *Fortune* 500 rankings are presented in Exhibit 2 for the years 1999 and 2000. For further financial information, refer to the company's 2000 Annual Report and website (www.target.com, or www.targetcorp.com). ...

HOW TO SUSTAIN SUCCESS

Assume that you are a consultant to Bob Ulrich, Chairman and CEO of Target Corporation and Target Stores. What advice would you give Mr. Ulrich about strategies for continued growth and profitability over the next 5 to 10 years? What are some specific ways that the company can sustain its success?

EXHIBIT I

Target Corporation Sales: August—December 2001 and Year-to-Date

TARGET CORPORATION AUGUST SALES UP 9.8 PERCENT

MINNEAPOLIS, September 6, 2001—Target Corporation today reported that its net retail sales for the four weeks ended September 1, 2001 increased 9.8 percent to $3.010 billion from $2.741 billion for the four-week period ended August 26, 2000. Comparable-store sales increased 2.4 percent from August 2000.
"For the Corporation overall, August sales were essentially in line with our plan," said Bob Ulrich, chairman and chief executive officer of Target Corporation.

	Sales (millions)	Total Sales % Change	Comparable Stores % Change
August			
Target	$2,454	13.4	3.9
Mervyn's	328	(3.4)	(3.0)
Marshall Field's	190	(4.0)	(4.0)
Other	38	(7.9)	na
Total	$3,010	9.8	2.4

EXHIBIT 1 *(continued)*

Target Corporation Sales: August—December 2001 and Year-to-Date

Year-to-Date			
Target	$16,374	11.5	3.2
Mervyn's	2,056	(1.9)	(1.4)
Marshall Field's	1,381	(6.3)	(6.3)
Other	201	(8.4)	na
Total	$20,012	8.3	1.9

Source: Target Corporation news releases at www.target.com or www.prnewswire.com.

TARGET CORPORATION SEPTEMBER SALES UP 7.4 PERCENT

MINNEAPOLIS, Oct 11, 2001—Target Corporation (NYSE:TGT) today reported that its net retail sales for the five weeks ended October 6, 2001 increased 7.4 percent to $3.286 billion from $3.060 billion for the five-week period ended September 30, 2000. Comparable-store sales increased 0.2 percent from September 2000.

"Sales for the corporation were below plan in September, particularly in the second week," said Bob Ulrich, chairman and chief executive officer of Target Corporation. "Profit trends remain very good at Target Stores, and are somewhat weak at Mervyn's and Marshall Field's. As a result, we now expect third quarter earnings per share (before unusual items) to be in the range of $0.24 to $0.25, compared with $0.24 a year ago." The company previously disclosed that it will record an unusual charge of approximately $0.05 per share in this year's third quarter related to accounting for previously sold receivables.

	Sales (millions)	Total Sales % Change	Comparable Stores % Change
September			
Target	$2,672	10.6	1.3
Mervyn's	306	(9.1)	(8.7)
Marshall Field's	268	1.9	1.9
Other	40	(8.1)	na
Total	$3,286	7.4	0.2
Year-to-Date			
Target	$19,045	11.4	3.0
Mervyn's	2,362	(2.9)	(2.4)
Marshall Field's	1,649	(5.0)	(5.0)
Other	243	(8.3)	na
Total	$23,299	8.2	1.7

(continued)

Source: Target Corporation news releases at http://www.target.com or http://www.prnewswire.com

EXHIBIT I (*continued*)

Target Corporation Sales: August—December 2001 and Year-to-Date

TARGET CORPORATION OCTOBER SALES UP 8.9 PERCENT

MINNEAPOLIS, Nov 8, 2001/PRNewswire via COMTEX/—Target Corporation (NYSE:TGT) today reported that its net retail sales for the four weeks ended November 3, 2001 increased 8.9 percent to $2.873 billion from $2.638 billion for the four-week period ended October 28, 2000. Comparable-store sales increased 2.0 percent from October 2000.

"Sales for the corporation were below plan in October, reflecting particular weakness at Marshall Field's," said Bob Ulrich, chairman and chief executive officer of Target Corporation.

	Sales (millions)	Total Sales % Change	Comparable Stores % Change
October			
Target	$2,336	12.8	4.1
Mervyn's	283	(1.6)	(1.0)
Marshall Field's	226	(10.1)	(10.1)
Other	28	2.5	na
Total	$2,873	8.9	2.0
Third Quarter			
Target	$7,461	12.2	3.0
Mervyn's	917	(4.8)	(4.4)
Marshall Field's	685	(4.0)	(4.0)
Other	107	(5.3)	na
Total	$9,170	8.7	1.5
Year-to-Date			
Target	$21,381	11.5	3.1
Mervyn's	2,645	(2.7)	(2.2)
Marshall Field's	1,875	(5.7)	(5.7)
Other	270	(7.3)	na
Total	$26,172	8.3	1.7

Source: Target Corporation news releases at http://www.target.com or http://www.prnewswire.com

TARGET CORPORATION NOVEMBER SALES UP 19.4 PERCENT

MINNEAPOLIS, Dec 6, 2001/PRNewswire via COMTEX/—Target Corporation (NYSE:TGT) today reported that its net retail sales for the four weeks ended December 1, 2001 increased 19.4 percent to $3.902 billion from $3.269 billion for the four-week period ended November 25, 2000. Comparable-store sales increased 11.4 percent from fiscal November 2000.

"Sales for the corporation were slightly below plan in November," said Bob Ulrich, chairman and chief executive officer of Target Corporation.

EXHIBIT 1 *(continued)*

Target Corporation Sales: August—December 2001 and Year-to-Date

	Sales (millions)	Total Sales % Change	Comparable Stores % Change	Comparable Sales % (adjusted calendar*)
November				
Target	$3,211	23.2	13.5	1.1
Mervyn's	388	2.4	3.0	(3.0)
Marshall Field's	252	2.6	2.6	(8.8)
Other	51	34.0	na	na
Total	3,902	19.4	11.4	(0.1)
Year-to-Date				
Target	$24,592	12.9	4.3	
Mervyn's	3,034	(2.1)	(1.6)	
Marshall Field's	2,127	(4.8)	(4.8)	
Other	321	(2.6)	na	
Total	$30,074	9.6	2.9	

*Compares four weeks ended December 1, 2001 to four weeks ended December 2, 2000. Target Corporation news releases at http://www.target.com or http://www.prnewswire.com

TARGET CORPORATION DECEMBER SALES UP 7.5 PERCENT

MINNEAPOLIS, Jan. 10/PRNewswire-FirstCall/—Target Corporation (NYSE: TGT) today reported that its net retail sales for the five weeks ended January 5, 2002 increased 7.5 percent to $6.550 billion from $6.093 billion for the five-week period ended December 30, 2000. Comparable-store sales increased 0.6 percent from fiscal December 2000.

   "Sales for the corporation were well above plan in December, primarily due to exceptional strength at Target Stores," said Bob Ulrich, chairman and chief executive officer of Target Corporation. "As a result of this sales performance, we now expect our fourth quarter EPS to be moderately higher than the current First Call median estimate of $0.65."

	Sales (millions)	Total Sales % Change	Comparable Stores % Change	Comparable Sales % (adjusted calendar*)
December				
Target	$5,399	10.3	1.81	0.1
Mervyn's	639	(1.3)	(0.6)	6.1
Marshall Field's	442	(10.0)	(10.0)	(2.3)
Other	70	14.9	na	na
Total	6,550	7.5	0.6	8.6

(continued)

EXHIBIT 1 (continued)

Target Corporation Sales: August—December 2001 and Year-to-Date

Year-to-Date			
Target	$29,992	12.4	3.9
Mervyn's	3,673	(1.9)	(1.4)
Marshall Field's	2,569	(5.7)	(5.7)
Other	390	0.0	na
Total	$36,624	9.2	2.5

*Compares five weeks ended January 5, 2002 to five weeks ended January 6, 2001. Target Corporation news releases at http://www.target.com or http://www.prnewswire.com

EXHIBIT 2

Target Corporation—*Fortune* 500 Rankings (1999–2000)

Year	Rank	Revenues		Profits			Assets		Stkhldrs Equity	
		$ mil.	% change	$ mil.	Rank	% change	$ mil.	Rank	$ mil.	Rank
2000	37	36,903	9.5	1,264	90	10.5	19,490	159	6,519	114
1999	32	33,702	8.9	1,144	92	22.4	17,143	156	5,862	113

Mkt. Value 3/15/01* 3/14/00**		Profits As % Of...			Earnings Per Share			Total Return to Investors		
$ mil.	Rank	Revenues	Assets	Stkhldrs Equity	2000 $	% change	1990–2000 ann'l grwth	2000 %	Rank	1990–2000 annual rate
31,861*	80	3.4	6.5	19.4	1.38	12.7	11.8	(11.5)	307	23.1
27,166**	83	3.4	6.7	19.5	2.45	23.7	10.6	36.2	86	23.5

Endnotes

1. Moore, Janet, "Target's Ulrich Is Confident Despite Soft Economy," *Star Tribune*, Minneapolis (January 17, 2001).
2. Chicago Tribune Market Report Column, *Knight Ridder Tribune Business News* (January 3, 2002), p. 1.
3. "2001 Five Hundred," *Fortune* (April 16, 2001), pp. F-1, F-32, F-54.
4. *Target Corporation Fact Card,* Sales and Corporate Data, http://www.corporate-ir.net (January 10, 2002). Store data given were the latest available at the time of writing this case. Financial data were not available for the year 2001 as of January 2002.
5. Sources include www.target.com, www.targetcorp.com, *Target Corporation Annual Report 2000*, and http://hoovers.com.
6. Patty Morris, Target Media Relations, March 2001, and company information.
7. *Ibid. Target Corporation Fact Card.*
8. "New Children's Footwear Brands From Stride Rite Introduced at Target Stores in the U.S.; Stride Rite Continues Strategy of Bringing Expertise to Wider Audience," *Hoover's Online*, http://hoovnews.hoovers.com/ (January 7, 2002).
9. *Ibid.* Patty Morris.
10. "Dayton Hudson Corporation to Change Its Name to Target Corporation," Target Corporation News Release, www.iredge.com (January 13, 2000).
11. "Target Corp. Forms New E-Commerce Unit; Names Nitschke President of 'Target Direct,'" Target Corporation News Release, www.iredge.com (February 1, 2000).
12. "Target Announces Strategic Multi-Channel Marketing Alliance With E*TRADE," Target Corporation News Release, www.iredge.com (May 11, 2000); "Target and E*TRADE® Launch Co-branded Web Site Offering Financial Services and Free Investment Information," Target Corporation News Release, www.iredge.com (August 24, 2000).

13. "Target and America Online Launch Marketing and Promotion Initiatives," Target Corporation News Release, www.iredge.com (August 22, 2000).

14. *Ibid.*

15. Note: due to rapid growth of Target Stores, number of stores reported here may be much greater.

16. Brumback, Nancy, "Target Aims to Double Number of Stores," *Business and Industry* 75(22) (May 28, 2001), p. 3.

17. Mills, Karen, "Target Partners With Visa to Offer Smart Card," *Associated Press* (June 19, 2001).

18. Goldman, Abigail, "Tupperware Still Parties—But It's Spreading to Target," *Los Angeles Times* (July 18, 2001), Part 3, page 1.

19. D'Innocenzio, Anne, "Big Discounters Turn Warlike In Fight for Customers," *Associated Press* (August 24, 2001).

20. "Nickelodeon's SpongeBob SquarePants Makes a Splash With Major Retail Debut at Target Stores," *PR Newswire* (September 5, 2001).

21. "Thousands Apply for Chance to Work at SuperTarget Store in New Tampa, Fla.," *Tampa Tribune* (January 14, 2002).

22. "Target Stores Overturn Unpopular Return Policy," *Wichita Eagle* (January 7, 2002).

23. Moore, Janet and Ann Merrill, "Target Market; The Concept that People Will Pay More for What's Fashionable—Including Food—Is Being Tested In SuperTarget Stores," *Star Tribune* (July 27, 2001), p. 1D.

24. "target.com Redesign Leverages Successful Offline Brand Online," Target Corporation News Release, www.iredge.com (October 27, 2000); "target.com Expands Merchandise Offerings to Include Exclusive Branded Products," Target Corporation News Release, www.iredge.com (September 5, 2000).

25. "Target Selling Windmills On-line to Combat High Energy Prices: Become Your Own Utility!" *Business Wire* (July 30, 2001).

26. "Target Takes Manhattan—An Inside Look at Life and Style for Real People," *PR Newswire* (August 7, 2001).

27. "Target Aims for Teens with Bullseye Online; Bullseye Offers Cool News, Tips and Advice for Teen Guests," *PR Newswire* (August 16, 2001).

Black Diamond, Ltd.: Hanging on the Cutting Edge

This case was prepared by Steven J. Maranville, Assistant Professor of Strategic Management, University of St. Thomas, and Madeleine E. Pullman of Southern Methodist University.

Jeff Jamison looked above at the glistening ice and snow of the frozen waterfalls. He had waited 3 weeks for the ice to get to this perfect condition, thick enough to support body weight, and the correct consistency for holding the picks of the two axes in his hands and the tooth-covered crampons on his feet. On this day in early January of 1993, he was trying out a new axe, the Black Prophet, a state-of-the-art climbing tool with a light weight, composite handle, and innovative head design produced by Black Diamond Equipment, Ltd. Everyone in the mountaineering world was talking about the Black Prophet's novel design and waiting for the tool to enter the stores in the coming months. Jeff was lucky enough to have a connection with one of Black Diamond's sales representatives, giving Jeff access to the new Black Prophet before its formal release to the market.

At the top of the last pitch of the climb, he sunk the Black Prophet into the ice and suddenly felt a disconcerting snap. Jeff watched with trepidation as pieces of the broken axe plummeted thousands of feet to the canyon floor. As panic swept in, Jeff realized that he would be forced to descend with only one axe, a doable but challenging feat. During the long, arduous descent, all Jeff

could think about was how could a tool like that one have left Black Diamond's factory.

The following Monday, January 4, 1993, Mellie Abrahamsen, Black Diamond's new quality assurance manager, a recent MBA graduate from the University of Utah, entered her office and turned on her computer to scan her e-mail. The news of the axe incident was echoing from all over the plant. Research & Development, Production, Customer Service, Marketing, and the president were all demanding an explanation and a plan. With all the excitement over the new design, preseason orders for the Black Prophet had exceeded expectations. Although the tool was on back order for many customers, the first production run of the axe had already been shipped to mountaineering stores throughout the world. Highlighted at the top of Abrahamsen's e-mail listing was a priority message from Peter Metcalf, president of Black Diamond, calling an emergency meeting with all department heads to develop a plan for handling the crisis.

MONDAY MORNING MEETING

By 9:00 A.M., Black Diamond's top management team was huddled around the square butcher-block table that filled the center of Metcalf's congested corner office. As Abrahamsen approached, she could see into Metcalf's office through the two large windows that faced the shop floor. Because she was new to the company, many of the artifacts peculiar to Black Diamond still caught her attention.

Metcalf's office walls were decorated with framed photographs of mountain-climbing and skiing adventures. The management team members sitting around the table were dressed casually; many were wearing Black Diamond sportswear—tee-shirts and sweaters with the Black Diamond insignia. Abrahamsen squeezed through the office and found a seat next to Metcalf, from which she had a view out the windows.

Metcalf anxiously spoke to the group. "This incident is a devastating blow. Thank goodness the guy didn't get hurt, but now every one of our axes out there is suspect. If we have to issue a recall on the product, that will kill our axe business. If we have to discontinue our axe program, all the European competitors will step in and copy the technology that we worked so long to perfect. Yet, think of the liability implications of an accident from this tool! How could this have happened? I thought this axe had the latest and greatest technology! We've never had problems like this with our regular mountaineering axes."

Cranor, the marketing manager, added to Metcalf's fervent speech. "If customers see this axe as being of poor quality, we'll be forced to cease the axe program. But worse, if customers think Black Diamond is a company that markets unsafe products, our whole business is in jeopardy! Black Diamond must not lose its leadership image."

"My sales representatives are having a fit," Stan Smith, manager of customer service, proclaimed loudly. "They have huge back orders for the axe, and the retail shops have several customers a day asking about the tool. You folks know how this industry is—rumors about tool failures and accidents get around fast."

In a despondent tone, the designer of the Black Prophet, Chuck Brainard, said, "I can't believe this nightmare. Just as we were sitting on top of the world with the most innovative design to enter the market in years—all the competition taken by surprise, and a good ice climbing season ahead—a major stroke of bad luck hits."

"I can't help but think" said Stan Brown, the production manager, "that the cause of the axe's failure is in its design. It's great to be innovative, but I think the design is so innovative that it just doesn't work."

"Now wait a minute, Stan," Metcalf interjected, "I don't want this to deteriorate into finger pointing."

Brainard spoke, "No, no, that's all right Peter. Stan might be right. Maybe we did go too far."

Metcalf went on: "We don't know all the facts. So let's stay focused and not jump to conclusions. This is a companywide problem."

Trying to refocus the group, Cranor said, "We tried to cut the lead time on this project so that we would have at least a year of sales before the French, Swiss, and other U.S. competitors could copy our concept and steal our market share. We have the reputation as the quality and innovative design company. This incident is potentially very damaging to our reputation as the market leader for innovation."

"We've got to nip this one in the bud and find a way to reassure our customer base," contended Smith. "I need an answer as soon as possible."

John Bercaw, manager of research and development, said, "Stan, I appreciate the urgent need that you're feeling with regard to handling customer concerns, but we need more than a quick fix. We need to find out why the failure occurred and put systems in place to prevent this from happening again."

"I agree," Metcalf applauded. "As I said, this is a companywide problem."

Brainard attempted to clarify the situation: "As I see it, the possible sources of the failure are design, materials, and/or assembly."

"I can speak about the development phase of the project," stated Bercaw. "We worked hard to develop this axe and cut down on the lead time between the conceptualization and production of the final tool. Peter, you know we've been under tremendous pressure to have this new axe into the production phase and on the market in under 2 years."

Metcalf nodded. "That's been our strategy," he said, "being the firstest with the mostest."

Bercaw continued: "This project has been a real struggle; we've been working with all sorts of new technologies like composite construction and modular tool design. The vendors normally don't make tools for these types of applications. They've had a hard time meeting our specifications, and many of the vendors don't want to work on our products because of potential liability implications."

"What about the assembly?" asked Metcalf.

Brown spoke, "Well, the shop worked like crazy to get those axes out for the winter season, and I put my best people on the rush assembly. The shop has been really taxed, what with the increasing growth rate for all our climbing and mountaineering products. We're always scrambling to meet the back orders. We need more people and new machines to keep up with this demand and improve our quality."

Metcalf persisted: "Do you know of anything in particular that may have been out of the ordinary during assembly?"

Brown replied: "I'd have to talk to Brian, our lead assembler, to see if he has any clues about why that axe could have failed in the field."

Metcalf turned to his left, where Black Diamond's newest management team member was sitting. "I realize that this is all new to you and that you came in after the fact, so I doubt the Quality Assurance Department can do much about this situation now."

Caught somewhat by surprise, Abrahamsen pulled her thoughts together. "Since this job is a newly created position, I wasn't here during the design development and testing phase. I would like to see the procedures and testing information on the production lot of axes. Black Diamond wants to be ISO 9000-certified, and we would need to have all those documents for ISO 9000 certification anyway, so this is a good starting place. Meanwhile, I think we should bring all the field axes back for inspection to reinforce customer confidence and prevent what happened on Saturday from happening again."

Looking out of his office's windows, Metcalf pointed to the shop floor and remarked, "Isn't that Brian walking through the shop? Ask him to come in."

Brian Palmer, the lead assembler, entered Metcalf's office. There was no place to sit, so he remained standing. Metcalf explained to Brian the purpose for bringing him into the meeting. Brian indicated that he had heard about the climbing incident involving the Black Prophet.

Metcalf continued: "Brian, we're not on a witch hunt; we're trying to understand the full range of factors that could have contributed to the tool's failure. What can you tell us about the assembly?"

Brian spoke frankly: "I personally put together all those axes. We didn't have any procedures, because it was the first time we had made a production lot. Normally when we work on a new product, we go through a learning curve trying to

figure out the best assembly method. We make so many different types of products in the shop, it's really like a craft shop. And I'm not even sure if I have the most up-to-date prints right now. The vendor had a lot of trouble casting all those parts to the exact dimensions. But I was able to find enough parts that seemed to fit, and with a little extra elbow grease, I hammered the pieces together. I had to work overtime to meet the deadline and get all the preliminary orders out to the customers. But that's what matters—pleasing the customer."

"But is creating a defective axe really pleasing the customer?" questioned Abrahamsen. "What good is it to be first to market if the product fails in the field. Sure, we have to get to market fast, but we also have to make the axe right the first time. The way we deal in the short term with the Black Prophet situation will have some long-term implications for Black Diamond's strategy. I think we should examine the new product introduction process as well as the ongoing production processes to see how we can prevent this type of thing from happening in the future."

THE MARKET FOR MOUNTAINEERING EQUIPMENT

The established customer for mountaineering products, including mountaineering skis, had traditionally been the serious international mountaineer—professionals as well as expert amateurs. Some dedicated mountaineers worked as professional guides and explorers; nonprofessionals had other jobs, but both professionals and amateurs spent their vacations and weekends climbing in their local areas and traveling throughout the world attempting to conquer remote peaks. This traditional customer base had been primarily in North America, eastern and western Europe, Japan, and Korea, although limited numbers of participants were from other countries.

Mountaineering was as popular in Europe as basketball was in the United States, with mountaineering stars earning high incomes through competitions, product endorsements, and other media exposure. Because of the long history of climbing in Europe, the European market was the biggest segment in the world climbing market, with 10 percent of the market in France alone. Not only did the adult urban European population prefer to spend vacations in mountain villages, but increasingly, younger generations of Europeans were forsaking crowded beaches for mountain holidays revolving around mountain sports.

Starting in the 1980s, media exposure had brought mountain sports to previously ignored market segments throughout the world. Rock climbing and mountaineering images had become popular for advertising many types of products and for adding "color" to music videos and movie plots. Because of this exposure, teenage and recreational customers—predominantly in the U.S. market—were high-growth segments, with noticeable growth in the mid-1980s erupting into an explosive growth rate of 40 percent in the early 1990s. Customers in this growing market segment had no intention of traveling the world looking for untouched and ever more challenging peaks; instead, this recreational segment climbed and skied purely for fun in their local and national resort areas.

Customarily, people wishing to learn mountain sports would employ guide services and schools for acquiring the necessary skills. The newer converts, however, were bypassing this conventional route by going to indoor climbing gyms or learning skills from friends. Many industry experts speculated that this breakdown of the conventional training methods would contribute to an increased lack of knowledge regarding mountaineering safety and lead to increased accident rates. In turn, accidents would increase the chances of litigation for all firms involved in the industry. These trends were a concern to mountain-sports firms worldwide.

COMPETITION IN THE MOUNTAINEERING EQUIPMENT INDUSTRY

Located in Salt Lake City, Utah, Black Diamond Equipment, Ltd., was a major player in the burgeoning international mountaineering industry, on both domestic and global fronts. Black Diamond manufactured and distributed a full range of products for mountain sports, from rock-climbing gear to mountaineering and backcountry skis, and faced few domestic or global competitors whose business was on a similar scale. (Exhibit A is a company/product profile of the mountaineering industry.)

The industry that served the mountaineering market consisted of three groups: retailers, wholesalers, and manufacturers.

Retailers

The retail businesses serving the market's diverse variety of mountaineering customers were one of three types. The first group, the "core" mountaineering shops, were small retail operations specializing in products specific to mountaineering such as ropes, climbing protection, climbing axes, expedition clothing, packs, harnesses, and information guides for local and national areas. Because these shops were usually located in mountain areas such as the Rocky Mountains or the Alps, the shop personnel were experts in the special tools and applications for their regions. In addition, these shop personnel often had personal knowledge of other international locations.

These shops usually carried products made in their region with specialized products from other countries. The core shops competed on the basis of the expertise of their personnel and their stock of technically appropriate tools. These retailers specialized in high-quality, cutting-edge-technology products. Prices were relatively high. The majority of their customers were highly skilled mountaineers. Black Diamond operated a small retail shop in this category located next to its Salt Lake City manufacturing facility. Black Diamond's full product range sold well in this type of shop.

Because of their remote locations, many core shops made effective use of catalogues as a direct-marketing tool. Several mail-order companies, including Black Diamond's mail-order division, competed in this core area, selling products both nationally and internationally.

The second group, "mom and pop" stores, also consisted of small retail outlets, but they sold all types of equipment from camping and backpacking equipment to bikes and skis. The product mix varied depending on the geographic location. Most of these stores carried a limited assortment of climbing products—usually ropes, harnesses, and carabiners, small clips used in all climbing applications to attach the climber to rock or snow. The personnel in mom and pop stores usually had limited technical knowledge of the products being sold.

EXHIBIT A

Mountaineering Industry Competitive Product Profile

Product Category/ Manufacturers	National Market Share, %	International Market Share, %
Carabiners		
Black Diamond	50	10
Omega	10	3
SMC	10	3
Wild Country	10	20
DMM	10	20
Petzl	5	30
MSR (REI)	5	4
Climbing protections		
Black Diamond	50	20
Metolius	20	10
Lowe	10	10
Wild Country	10	25
DMM50	10	25
Harnesses		
Black Diamond	50	20
Petzl	20	50
REI	20	
Blue Water	10	10
Wild Country	5	20
Plastic boots		
Scarpa*	40	30
Merrell	25	5
Koflach	25	40
Lowe	15	5
Adjustable ski poles		
Black Diamond	60	5
Life Link	40	5
Mountaineer skis		
Rossignol	30	50
Hagen*	20	10
Climbing accessories		
Black Diamond	55	15
Omega	25	10
Petzl	20	75
Gloves		
Black Diamond	50	5
Snow climbing axes		
Charlie Moser	50	10
Black Diamond	20	5

EXHIBIT A *(continued)*

Mountaineering Industry Competitive Product Profile

Product Category/ Manufacturers	National Market Share, %	International Market Share, %
Ice climbing axes		
Black Diamond	30	10
Charlie Moser	30	15
DMM	25	30
Grivel	15	30
Rock shoes		
Scarpa*	25	20
Sportiva	25	35
Boreal	25	35
Five Ten	15	5
Ropes		
Mamutt	30	50
PMI*	20	40
New England	20	
Blue Water	20	10

*European manufacturers producing Black Diamond designs.
Source: Estimates of industry representatives.

The third group consisted of sporting goods and department store chains, ranging in size from regional chains such as Eastern Mountain Sports (7 stores) to national chains such as Recreational Equipment, Inc. (REI) (40 stores). These stores, which were located in major cities with access to mass markets, had extensive outdoor clothing departments, tents, stoves, canoes and kayaks, sleeping bags, bikes, skis, etc. Products in each category were selected for volume sales. Thus, in the climbing department, the product line covered the needs of entry-level or intermediate recreational climbers. The expertise of department store personnel was, however, generally limited.

In the United States, REI was the dominant firm in this group of retailers. REI operated department stores in Seattle, Boston, Los Angeles, and Washington, D.C., with limited national competition on this level. Because of its large size and wide scope, REI could buy in volume for all its stores and offered very competitive prices. The Canadian retailer, Mountain Equipment Coop (MEC), served a similar market in Canada, with a large store in each of Canada's major cities. In France, Au Vieux Campeur owned multiple department stores in major French cities, serving a broad customer base.

Wholesalers

Retail outlets bought their product lines from wholesalers during semiannual outdoor equipment shows held throughout the world. The wholesaler category of firms consisted of companies that either manufactured their own products or subcontracted the manufacturing of their designs and distributed their own product lines and companies licensed to distribute the products of other companies in certain geographic areas, as well as various combinations of these two. Black Diamond was in this last category. The company distributed equipment designed and manufactured in its Utah plant, equipment manufactured for Black Diamond by other firms, and merchandise designed by Black Diamond and distributed under other manufacturers' names. In all, Black Diamond offered over 250 different items, covering most mountain sports (see Exhibit B).

REI was Black Diamond's biggest wholesale customer, making up almost 10 percent of Black

EXHIBIT B

Black Diamond Product Categories

Climbing protection	Ropes and rope bags
Camming devices	Packs
Nuts	Hip packs
Stoppers	Backpacks
Pitons	Tents
Piton hammers	Snow and ice tools
Slings	Axes
Runners	Crampons
Daisy chains	Ice screws and
Etriers	hooks
Webbing	Ski tools
Belay devices	Skis
Carabiners	Bindings
Harnesses	Poles
Sport climbing	Climbing clothing
Alpine	Tee-shirts
mountaineering	Sweatshirts
Big wall	Shorts
Footwear	Pants
Mountaineering	Hats
boots	Belts
Ski boots	Chalk bags
Rock climbing shoes	

Diamond's total sales. The next biggest customer, Lost Arrow—Japan, was a Japanese distributor comprising 5 percent of Black Diamond's sales. The other major wholesale customers were North American outdoor sports department store chains, mail-order companies, and Black Diamond's own retail shop and mail-order business. Combined, the top 20 percent of Black Diamond's retail customers—roughly 60 companies—accounted for about 80 percent of total sales.

Domestically, Black Diamond's wholesaling competition came from Omega Pacific, which manufactured and distributed its own metal products, and Blue Water, which wholesaled its own lines of ropes and harnesses. Neither of these companies, however, carried a product line as extensive as Black Diamond's.

The international wholesaling segment included strong competition from two U.K. firms, Denny Morehouse Mountaineering and Wild Country, and a French company, Petzl. These firms wholesaled a full range of mountaineering products manufactured by companies with strong international reputations. Additional competition came from more regional firms. Most countries had several smaller manufacturers of specific products such as carabiners or climbing axes that were successful in wholesaling their own products.

Several issues influenced sales in the international marketplace. First, the International Organization of Standards had mandated that by 1997 "personal protective equipment" would have to meet ISO 9000 quality certification standards in order to be sold in Europe. Companies with certification stamped their products with a symbol showing that the product's manufacturer had met the relevant ISO 9000 standards. This certification was intended to give the consumer more confidence in a product's quality. Most of the European mountaineering manufacturers had initiated the certification process and were well on their way to obtaining certification. In contrast, very few American companies, including Black Diamond, had even begun the certification process. (Exhibit C provides an overview of the ISO 9000 standards.)

Second, some European countries had a long history of climbing and mountaineering, and certain manufacturers, Grivel, for example, dated back to the late 1800s. Although several European companies had well-established worldwide reputations for quality and innovative products, others relied on home country support, producing lower-quality, lower-priced products. All mountainous European countries had small factories for carabiners, skis, axes, or shoes that produced, at relatively low cost, simple products in high volume for domestic consumption.

Third, the European market was predominantly ethnocentric in purchasing behavior. French climbers preferred to buy French products, while German climbers preferred German products. Because of the risks involved in climbing and mountaineering, customers chose equipment they knew the most about and had the most confidence in. Usually, these products were from the buyers' respective countries.

Manufacturers

As a manufacturer, Black Diamond faced both domestic and international competition. Domestic manufacturing firms ran the gamut from small garage operations to large machine shops with 50 or more employees, and most produced either

EXHIBIT C

ISO 9000 Standards

The ISO 9000 standards provide the requirements for documenting processes and procedures. The intent of the standards mandates an organization "do what they say and say what they do." The standards offer three quality system models—ISO 9001, ISO 9002, and ISO 9003—with increasing levels of stringency. 9003 covers documentation and procedure requirements for final inspection and testing, 9002 adds production and installation, and 9001 includes design and development. An organization chooses the appropriate standard depending on the strategically important functional areas requiring quality procedures. In most cases, manufacturers use 9001 for covering all areas.

In order to receive ISO 9000 certification, a company will spend several years complying with the requirements in the standards. This compliance usually requires extensive documentation of the existing quality program and training for all employees involved in processes related to quality. Individual auditors, who work for the international ISO registration organization, evaluate the company for requirement compliance. The certified companies are reevaluated every two years to ensure continuing compliance.

A brief overview of the 9001 requirements are provided below:
- The entire quality system must be defined and documented to ensure each product meets specifications.
- The contractual requirements for quality between company and the customer must be defined and documented.
- Procedures are required to ensure that critical processes are under control.
- Procedures are required for inspection at all levels and for identification of nonconforming parts or products.
- Procedures are required to prevent nonconforming parts from getting damaged in storage, delivery, or packing.
- Training is required for all personnel affecting quality.
- The quality system must be audited internally to ensure effectiveness and compliance.

"software" or "hardware." The software firms worked with textile products such as ropes and harnesses. The majority of the software firms, including Blue Water, Sterling Rope, and Misty Mountain, were located in the southeastern United States. These more specialized manufacturing firms expanded their market by catering to the needs of nonmountaineering industries, such as construction safety, military applications, and spelunking. The hardware group manufactured or assembled metal products such as carabiners and other climbing tools and protection. This group of manufacturers included Friends, Rock Hardware, and Rock Exotica. These firms had reputations as producers of innovative and high-quality equipment.

REI had recently started up a small manufacturing facility for carabiners. The manager of this REI facility had many years of engineering experience with Boeing Aircraft and had designed a highly automated manufacturing system capable of both production and quality testing.

Because Black Diamond had begun as a machine shop, the company had strong capabilities in metalworking. Specifically, the Salt Lake facility manufactured cold-forged metal parts associated with carabiners, axes, and other climbing accessories and protection. Hot-forging and casting were subcontracted by Black Diamond to manufacturers specializing in this area. Black Diamond was beginning to expand into simple soft goods, such as slings and other webbing products, and intended to continue developing its in-house sewing capabilities.

Black Diamond had plans to become vertically integrated. Management believed that in-house performance of operations related to core products would enhance Black Diamond's competitiveness. Consequently, Black Diamond had started reviewing some of its subcontracting practices to determine what functions could be brought in-house. In particular, the company wanted to bring in-house all sewing of climbing gear and some metal treatments such as heat-treating.

Other products, such as skis, ski poles, foot gear, and ropes, required very specific technologies, production skills, and economies of scale for competitive pricing and quality. Black Diamond entered into subcontracting agreements with international manufacturers to design and manufacture such products. The company also subcontracted the production of its harnesses to a technically sophisticated harness manufacturer located next door to the Salt Lake City facility that made the harnesses on a semiautomated assembly line. This process required minimal human involvement, in contrast to a "garment industry" sewing process by which one person sews the complete harness from start to finish.

By the late 1980s, European competition was becoming a more significant factor in the U.S. market. In particular, Petzl, a French company with a full range of products, had taken an aggressive position in the U.S. market. Petzl, like several of the European competitors, had a well-established reputation as a producer of high-quality, innovative products. Petzl had set up a manufacturing facility in the United States within 60 miles of Black Diamond's manufacturing facility and had sponsored several professional U.S. climbers. Black Diamond, of course, was making efforts to sell its own products in Europe but faced the problem of ISO 9000 certification.

Some international manufacturing activity went on in Korea and Japan. Products produced by these manufacturers were marketed and distributed through other international companies. The majority of these products were low-cost, mass-produced items such as carabiners.

The continuing growth of copyright violations and product privacy—especially prevalent within international markets—added a further dimension to global competition. Several U.S. and European companies had used machine shops in Korea and Japan as subcontractors, supplying dies and other technological knowhow. Consequently, unlicensed clones of more expensive items were expected to appear soon in the international market.

BLACK DIAMOND'S OPERATIONS

Black Diamond Equipment, Ltd., opened for business in 1989 after a group of former managers with employee support bought the assets of Chouinard Equipment from Lost Arrow Corporation during Chapter 11 bankruptcy proceedings. The bankruptcy resulted from four lawsuits related to climbing equipment accidents during the 1980s. Chouinard

Equipment was the first U.S. company to develop and manufacture rock-climbing gear. From its inception and for the following decade, Chouinard Equipment had a reputation for innovation and quality unmatched by any national competitors.

After the purchase, the new owners chose a new name for the company that would reflect its roots yet would project a fresh beginning. The insignia of a diamond was Chouinard Equipment's previous logo. The new company decided to keep the diamond image and chose the name "black diamond" because of the different associations the name might evoke: "diamond in the rough," "rogue," "bad boy," and "unusual" (see Exhibit D for the Black Diamond Logo). Furthermore, a "black diamond" was used to identify the most difficult type of run in ski areas, and the company owners hoped the name would appeal to the "extreme" athlete, their primary targeted customer base. Black Diamond's management believed that "if you target the extremities, the recreational customer will follow."

The mission of Black Diamond was "to design, manufacture, and bring to market, in a profitable and on-time manner, innovative and technical products of high quality, high performance, and exemplary durability that are targeted toward our primary customers—climbers and backcountry skiers." The company was committed to 10 guiding principles:

1. Being the market leader, synonymous with the sports we serve and are absolutely passionate about

EXHIBIT D

Black Diamond Logo

2. Having a truly global presence

3. Supporting the specialty retailer

4. Creating long-term partnerships with companies we do business with

5. Being very easy to do business with

6. Being a fierce competitor with the highest ethical standards

7. Developing sustainable, competitive advantage

8. Sharing the company's success with its employees

9. Creating a safe, personally fulfilling work environment for all employees

10. Championing the preservation of and access to our mountain environments

In 1991, the owner-employees relocated the business from Ventura, California, to Salt Lake City, Utah, where they would be closer to the targeted customer. Black Diamond began operations with a staff of roughly 40, covering all functional areas. (See Exhibit E for Black Diamond's organizational structure.) Black Diamond was 50 percent owned by employees; the remaining 50 percent of the stock was held by outside investors, predominately distributors, customers, and friends and family of the main employee stockholders. Of the 50 percent that was employee owned, 75 percent was held by Metcalf, the CEO; Cranor, head of marketing; and Kawakami, the chief financial officer.

In 1993, Black Diamond's annual sales were expected to be approximately $12 million with a gross profit margin of about 40 percent (grossing about $4.8 million) and with a net profit margin of about 10 percent (netting around $1.2 million). From 1990 through 1993, the climbing industry had experienced tremendous sales growth of 20 to 40 percent per year. The market demanded more innovative products and faster delivery. Black Diamond struggled to keep up with the exploding customer demand by hiring more employees and upgrading shop machinery to increase productivity. Slowly, the original machinery was being replaced by automated machining centers and testing devices. By 1993, the company employed more than 100 people.

Like other metalworking shops, Black Diamond specialized in certain types of metalworking; the areas of specialization consisted of cold-forging metal parts, stamping and forming, computer numerically controlled (CNC) machining, and assembly or fabrication. Forging, stamping, and forming, along with the assembly processes, had been done for 20 years by the original Chouinard Company, and these processes were considered to be Black Diamond's technical core. These core processes used the same multiton presses that forced metal stock into a die or mold to obtain the desired shape.

Since moving to Salt Lake City, the company had expanded into CNC machines—large programmable machine tools capable of producing small to medium-sized batches of intricate parts—in an effort to reduce costs and to move more production processes in-house. These machines were expensive, although they provided the advantages of capacity and product flexibility. Many of Black Diamond's processes, however, required machinery that was too costly to justify purchase for the manufacturing of a limited number of parts. Consequently, Black Diamond subcontracted with other vendors for aluminum hot-forging, investment casting, laser-cutting steel, preshearing metals, anodizing, heat treating, welding, screw machining, wire forming such as springs, and aluminum extrusion. These processes were subcontracted to achieve economies of scale (e.g., aluminum extrusion) or because the specialized equipment and skills required were beyond Black Diamond's capabilities (e.g., hot-forging).

Black Diamond's production facility was divided into several functional areas: the machine shop, which built prototypes and constructed and maintained tool and die apparatus; the punch press room, where parts were pressed out at a rate of one per second by several multiton presses; a room with assorted machines, each operated by one person doing drilling, milling, grinding, or operating CNC machines; a tumbling and polishing room, where large batches of parts were polished; the assembly room, where parts were assembled by individuals or teams; and finally, a room for materials and shipping.

Supported by a material requirements planning (MRP) system, materials were ordered several months in advance for a full batch of products—for example, 5000 carabiners or 500 axes. When fairly common parts such as springs and aluminum rod stock were involved, the orders arrived on time and met standard quality requirements. The more complex and customized parts, such as investment-cast

EXHIBIT E

Black Diamond Organizational Structure

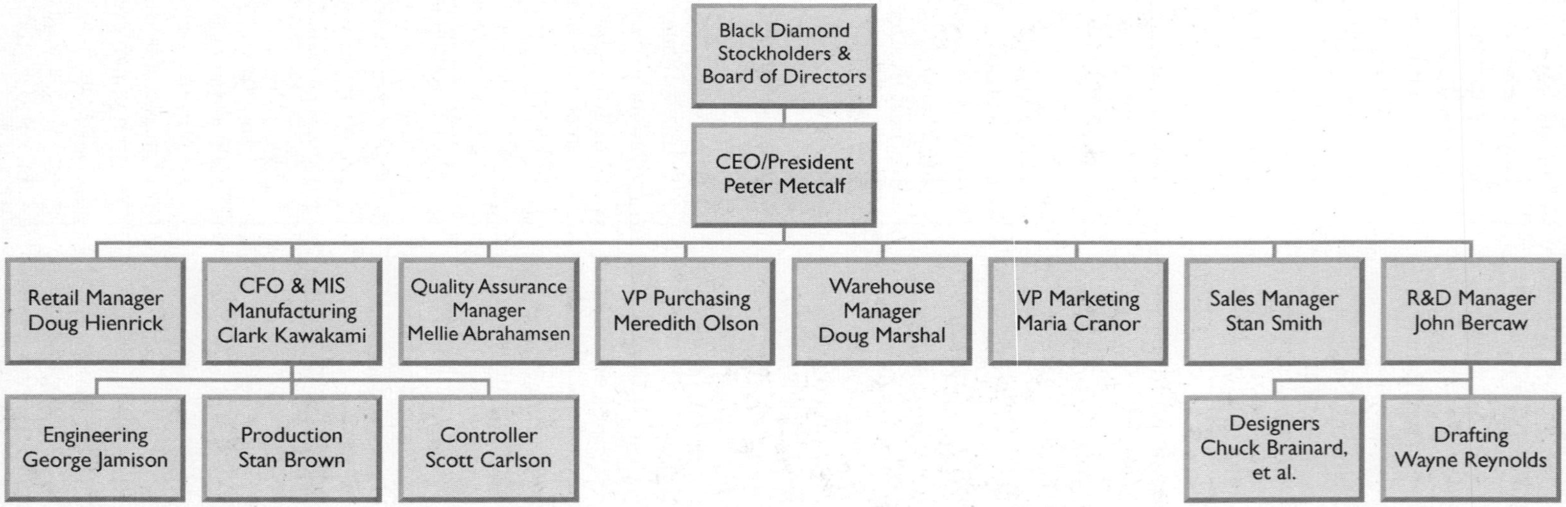

Black Diamond Stockholders & Board of Directors

CEO/President Peter Metcalf

Retail Manager Doug Hienrick

CFO & MIS Manufacturing Clark Kawakami

Quality Assurance Manager Mellie Abrahamsen

VP Purchasing Meredith Olson

Warehouse Manager Doug Marshal

VP Marketing Maria Cranor

Sales Manager Stan Smith

R&D Manager John Bercaw

Engineering George Jamison

Production Stan Brown

Controller Scott Carlson

Designers Chuck Brainard, et al.

Drafting Wayne Reynolds

axe parts, were difficult for vendors to make to specifications and thus often did not meet the assembly deadline.

When the parts arrived in the materials supply area, one person was responsible for spot-checking the order to see if the parts met specifications. For example, when 500 axe heads arrived, the inspector would randomly select 15 parts and would measure 20 different key dimensions on each part to determine if the tolerances met specifications. If one dimension was out of tolerance, the quality manager was summoned for an evaluation. Depending on the impact on other assembly processes, a larger meeting, involving all potentially affected parties, might be necessary to determine a course of action.

Most of Black Diamond's products began as a sheet of steel or aluminum rod. After receiving the metal, the incoming inspector would pull a sample of the metal to check hardness and dimensions. When production on an order was ready to begin, the metal was moved from a hallway to the press room. The press operator would receive an order for 5000 parts and would set up the press to begin cutting and smashing parts to shape. Once the dies were in place, the operator would smash a few sample parts and check with an inspector for approval.

As the dies wore down, the parts might turn out to have excess metal, or the logo engraving might be substandard. Depending on the demand for the parts, the inspector might feel pressure to pass on these cosmetically imperfect parts. Once approval was given, the operator would proceed to press out as many parts as possible in the shortest time. Often chips of metal would settle in the die and these chips would be imbedded into many parts before being discovered by the operator. When this occurred, thousands of parts needed to be scrapped.

After the smashing process, the parts usually were sent out for heat-treating to harden the metal. The heat-treatment plant was located in California, and so this procedure had a turnaround time of several weeks. When the parts returned, they went to the tumbling and drilling rooms for further processing. When color was needed, the parts would be shipped out again for anodizing, an electrolytic process by which metal is covered with a protective and/or decorative oxide film.

Finally, when the main body of a part was finished, the materials department would issue batches of all the other components needed to finish the product batch under production. All these parts would proceed to a group of assemblers, seated around tables, who were responsible for assembling the final product. The assembly room was the epitome of a craft shop environment. Large and expensive products such as axes were assembled in small batches by one individual, while products such as carabiners were assembled in larger batches by teams of people who often rotated jobs. The finished products would go through individual testing and inspection before passing to the shipping area. During inspection, one inspector might evaluate thousands of parts in a day.

Originally, the company had one employee responsible for quality assurance, and several shop employees performed quality control functions. The quality assurance person worked for the R&D department and focused on testing new products, prototypes, and work in production. As the company grew and ISO 9000 certification loomed in the future, several members of the management team decided that quality issues needed more prominent attention. Not only was testing required, but a plantwide program to ensure that defects did not occur in the first place was needed.

Black Diamond's original quality assurance officer had left the company to guide climbing expeditions, after which Black Diamond's management created a stand-alone Quality Assurance Department and hired Mellie Abrahamsen as the manager. At the time of Abrahamsen's hiring, the organization lacked a companywide quality assurance program. The members of R&D and the shop functioned along craft-shop lines. Product designers built prototypes on the shop floor, iterating between field testing and lab testing until they felt the design was ready. When the new design went into production, the shop personnel used trial and error to develop an assembly procedure. Out-of-tolerance parts often were accepted by shop personnel, who invented creative ways of adapting the parts or the procedures for assembling the products.

Implementing a quality control program would mean the introduction of formal testing and assembly procedures for both designers and shop workers. As Andrew McLean, a head designer, said:

"We are like artists here, and you just can't restrain or rush creativity and get good results." Chuck Brainard complained: "If we have to write procedures for every step of production, we'll be changing those things a million times."

Like most machine-shop workers, Black Diamond's shop employees labored under comparatively unglamorous working conditions, involving, for example, noise, grease, and monotony. Many shop workers lacked a high school education, and some could not read or write in English. Although the shop workers were the lowest-paid employees at Black Diamond, the company offered a generous profit-sharing bonus to all workers and tried to involve all of them in monthly meetings concerning the financial performance of the company. Despite these measures, the shop had a high rate of job turnover.

Because quality control programs require training in procedure writing, blueprint reading, and statistical techniques, the shop employees needed elementary math and language training before they could learn more complicated subjects. Stan Brown acknowledged that the workers needed training but said: "I can't let those people miss too much work for training; we really need everyone working nonstop to get products out the door."

Many of the professional employees at Black Diamond were avid climbers and users of the products, taking great pride in trying to make the very best products available. Marketing was concerned about keeping up the company's innovative image with new products every season. Production worried about vendor costs, delivery of parts, and the shop's ability to meet sales forecasts. R&D attempted to simultaneously develop buildable new products, reduce lead time for new product development, and improve existing products. Customer service tried to keep retailers pacified with partial deliveries and promises.

Finally, quality assurance was charged with implementing quality control procedures, conducting training, testing products, and resolving problems attributed to parts or products not meeting specifications. All functional areas faced the problems inherent in trying to achieve the simultaneous goals of meeting customer demand and ensuring the highest-quality products, and the different areas often clashed on the best means and methods of achieving these goals.

THE BLACK PROPHET

The concept for the Black Prophet axe was developed originally to round out Black Diamond's product line of axes. The product line had two other axes: the Alpamayo, a glacier-walking and snow-climbing axe, and the X-15, a versatile axe for both snow and ice climbing. The Black Prophet was designed specifically for ice climbing and incorporated an innovative ergonomic shape to reduce arm fatigue, a composite, rubber-bonded shaft construction for gripability and weight reduction, and interchangeable modular components allowing the use of different types of tools—a hammer head, picks, or an adze—for miscellaneous ice applications. (Exhibit F is a drawing of the Black Prophet and its component parts.)

Designing and producing the axe entailed several years of working with different vendors to develop the appropriate production process for each component. The axe was designed as a prototype and field tested with different constructions until R&D agreed on a specific configuration. This configuration was then reviewed by sales representatives considered to be mountaineering experts and by other company members at the quarterly meetings. If the tool did not pass the scrutiny of those examiners, R&D would begin a new phase of prototype development and field tests. This development process would continue until a company-wide consensus was reached.

The axe required five parts: shaft, head, hammer, pick, and adze. Three parts were cast metal, requiring a casting subcontractor with the ability to meet strict specifications. The composite shaft was produced by a composite and bonding manufacturer. The ice pick was manufactured in Black Diamond's plant. Black Diamond received the parts from each vendor, inspected them for conformance to specifications, and assembled the axes.

The Black Prophet, which cost approximately $80 to produce, sold as an axe with two tool accessories. The total retail price was $200; the wholesale price was $140. The initial shipment of Black Prophets for winter season 1993 was approximately 200 axes. The company expected yearly sales of the axe to reach at least 2500 units, making a significant contribution to winter sales.

Management expected the Black Prophet to be one of Black Diamond's top 10 selling winter

EXHIBIT F

The Black Prophet

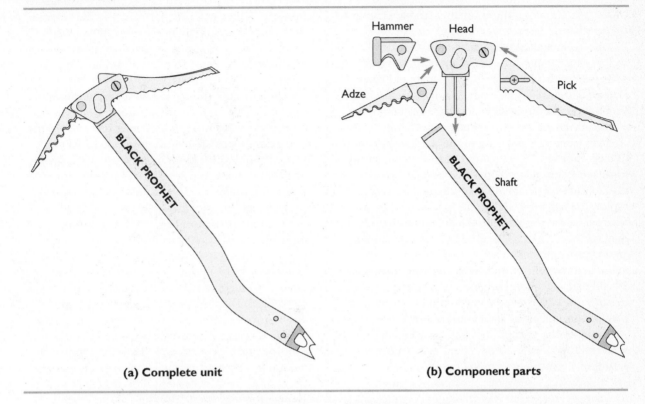

| (a) Complete unit | (b) Component parts |

products, and the entire company regarded it as a very big image item on the world mountaineering scene. Every competitor in this industry had an axe for glacier walking. Axes were especially popular in Europe, where Black Diamond foresaw superb potential for the new axe.

The axe had been well received at the previous year's outdoor product show. At that time, no other axes like it were in the wings, and the climbing industry anticipated the Black Prophet's arrival with great excitement. All major U.S. and European industry magazines had published articles about the Black Prophet, and famous mountaineers had called Black Diamond requesting Black Prophets for their upcoming expeditions.

THE DILEMMA

As the Monday morning meeting continued, Black Diamond's top management team members struggled to find answers to the questions raised by the axe crisis. They knew that the situation required both short- and long-term solutions. In the short term, management needed to address the pressure for immediate delivery confronting customer service. Should management recall all the Black Prophet axes currently on the market? A recall would come with high shipping, testing, and opportunity costs. Or should Black Diamond basically ignore the incident, assuming the accident was a one-time freak, and continue to sell the axes while refuting any rumors about the axe's questionable performance? The possibility of lawsuits had to be considered. For any accident causing injury, legal fees could be expected to run $500,000, and a catastrophic accident could bring a suit for several million dollars. While Black Diamond's insurer would pay legal expenses and any settlement involved, with a cap of $1 million, Black Diamond could expect to pay at least $25,000—the company's insurance deductible—for each legal action. In addition, there would be the costs of lost time by the employees who had to go to court (such costs might involve one or two managers' salaries for a year—at $40,000 to $60,000 per person). Several catastrophic accident cases won by the plaintiffs in a single year could put the company into bankruptcy.

Another option was to continue the sale of Black Prophets—including the axes already released as well as those in production—but require all units to be sold with a cautionary label? Or should Black Diamond just quietly and quickly sell those Black Prophets already in retail outlets and only undertake a critical view of the axes still in production?

Management's response to the short-term issue of customer service would have major implications for Black Diamond's competitive strategy. Would Black Diamond be able to meet the market's rapidly growing demand for all products while improving—or at the very least maintaining—product quality? Would Black Diamond be able to maintain an image as the recognized industry leader in the manufacture of innovative tools and equipment? Would Black Diamond be able to balance the realities of increased risk associated with innovative product design and of increased liability corresponding to the greater potential for accidents, while still establishing a dominant competitive position? Even though various members held strong—and in some cases, divergent—opinions, the management team was willing to consider enterprising alternatives.

Nevertheless, management also knew that a more long-term plan needed to be put into place. "When crises strike," Metcalf said, "there will always be some degree of needing to react to the surprise of the situation. But we need to institute a system of managing crises proactively—that means organizing the business to prevent the preventable crises."

Even though the management team thought the Quality Assurance Department should be a constructive resource in this long-term effort, the department was so new that no one had a clear idea of the Quality Assurance Department's role. Abrahamsen also questioned her role: "I was hired to implement a plantwide quality control program and to specifically work on ISO 9000 certification. Representing QA, I'm supposed to improve the efficiency of the company by reducing or eliminating defects in the whole production chain, but I'm not sure that a TQM [total quality management] approach will completely solve Black Diamond's problems. Perhaps the whole process of new product development and on-going operations would be more effective if a BPR [business process reengineering] approach were used. Either way, my challenge is to get all these other employees and departments to change the way they do things so they're both more efficient and effective."

Frigidaire Company: Launching the Front-Loading Washing Machine

This case was prepared by Kay M. Palan and Timothy T. Dannels of Iowa State University.

The Frigidaire Company, Laundry Products Division, in Webster City, Iowa, was a high-volume manufacturer of washing machines and dryers. In October of 1996, after several years of intense development, Frigidaire introduced a new front-loading (horizontal axis) washing machine in the United States. This new machine was designed and developed to offer U.S. consumers an alternative laundry product that was superior to conventional, top-loading (vertical axis) washing machines in terms of energy consumption, water conservation, and washing performance. Although an eager and receptive market for the front-loading washer did not exist, Frigidaire intended to use the new product to expand its position in the marketplace and to establish itself as the industry leader in energy-saving, environmentally sound laundry products.

Despite a $20 million investment, exhaustive development efforts, and detailed marketing plans, however, Bill Topper, vice president and general manager of the Laundry Products Division, was concerned. Initial sales were sluggish; results for the first 3 months of sales were 30 to 40 percent below projected levels. Although this early dismal per-formance was not a cause for panic, it triggered some serious concerns for the Frigidaire management staff. As Bill Topper reviewed data for the first 3 months' performance, he pondered several questions that he would need to review with the key players in his management team—Chris Kenner, market manager; John Jergens, market planner; and Dave Modtland, manager of washer engineering and project leader. Could Frigidaire create and grow a market for horizontal-axis washing machines in the United States? How could Frigidaire best encourage product adoption?

THE FRIGIDAIRE COMPANY

The Frigidaire Company, owned by AB Electrolux of Sweden, was the fourth largest producer of household appliances in the United States, behind Whirlpool, General Electric, and Maytag (see Exhibit A for a summary of the U.S. appliance market). Frigidaire had 10 operating sites within the United States, with its corporate headquarters located in Dublin, Ohio. The company manufactured all major appliances—washers and dryers, refrigerators and freezers, ranges, dishwashers, and air conditioners—under the popular brand names of Frigidaire, White-Westinghouse, Gibson, Kelvinator, and Tappan. In addition, Frigidaire manufactured appliances for the General Electric Company (under the GE label) and for Sears (under the Kenmore label).

EXHIBIT A

1996 Major Appliance Market Share in the United States*

Company	Percent Market Share
Whirlpool	35.9
General Electric	30.4
Maytag	14.8
Frigidaire (Electrolux)	11.0
Amana (Raytheon)	6.4
Others	1.5
TOTAL	100.0

*Major appliances include dishwashers, ranges, washers/dryers, and refrigerators.

Source: *Appliance Magazine,* September 1997.

Laundry Products Division

The Laundry Products Division, located in Webster City, Iowa, produced washers, dryers, laundry centers (stacked, full-size washer-dryer combinations), and now, the front-loading washing machine. Transmission assemblies for washing machines were made at a smaller plant in nearby Jefferson, Iowa. The facility in Webster City had gradually been expanded and had the capacity to produce 6500 units a day (over 1.5 million units per year).

THE FRONT-LOADING WASHING MACHINE

Background

The U.S. laundry market was dominated by the top-loading (vertical axis) washing machine—it was estimated that over 95 percent of the washing machines in the United States were of this type. Top-loading machines were developed in the late 1940s and had been the primary method of washing clothes ever since. In contrast, the horizontal-axis, front-loading washer had experienced very little success with U.S. consumers. In 1945, Westinghouse started to market a front-loading machine. These machines were often referred to as "tumble action" washers because they simply tumbled clothes clean (versus cleaning with the "agitation motion" caused by the presence of an agitator in top-loaders). However, the early front-loading machines were plagued with many problems. Aside from the many mechanical problems that were reported (front-loaders were much more technologically complex than top-loaders), consumers perceived that front-loaders did not clean very well and even tangled clothes. Furthermore, front-loaders were more costly to purchase and service. Not surprisingly, in light of all these problems, the front-load market failed to materialize, and top-loading machines evolved as the dominant laundry product in the United States.

In Europe, however, high energy costs had driven the market toward front-loading technology because front-loading washers required less water and less energy to operate. In addition, Europeans believed that front-loading machines cleaned better and were gentler on clothes, relative to top-loading washers. The European market was dominated by front-loading machines.

Aware of the success of the front-loading washing machines in Europe, Sears and Magic Chef attempted, in 1981, to market front-loading washing machines in the United States by carrying foreign-made units. However, their attempts failed to produce significant results. Westinghouse, despite the disappointment associated with the original introduction of front-loading washers in the United States, continued to carry a front-loading machine, only to cease manufacturing in 1994 due to recurring service issues and customer complaints.

Despite these setbacks and problems, Bill Topper believed that the demand for front-loading machines in the United States would increase over the next several years. Initially, the management team believed that governmental influence would lead to a new market for this style of washing machine. It had been rumored for several years that the U.S. Department of Energy (DOE) was preparing to unleash new, rigid efficiency standards that would apply to household appliances. These regulations would lead to the design and introduction of new energy-efficient machines by all appliance makers and would create consumer demand for energy-efficient appliances. Furthermore, the team believed that the growth in environmental awareness and energy/water conservation in the United States would support the presence of an energy-efficient washing machine. After all, similar machines had been used in Europe for years for reasons of energy conservation, and it was felt that this trend would eventually drift into U.S. markets. Topper hoped that the company could stimulate this market by being the first domestic appliance manufacturer to successfully produce and sell a reliable, high-quality front-loading washing machine. If the front-loading washer functioned as intended, it would cost less to operate (use less water and energy), it would be gentler on clothes, and most important, it would clean better. Likewise, it would provide Frigidaire with much needed product differentiation in an industry where differentiation and competitive advantage were very difficult to attain.

With these considerations in mind, a $20 million project to design, develop, and produce a new and better front-loading washing machine was begun by Frigidaire in 1989. The project experienced a setback in 1994, however, when the government announced that the much-anticipated DOE changes would be delayed indefinitely. Industry speculations included the possibility that the delayed DOE regulations eventually might set energy-efficiency standards that could easily be met by either revolutionary vertical-axis designs or the more conventional top-loading machines currently available. Consequently, many appliance manufacturers had chosen to discontinue development of front-loading machines. Frigidaire, however, continued with the project because the management team believed that the benefits of differentiation, combined with increasing environmental awareness, ultimately would lead to a demand for the front-loading washer.

With the delay of the DOE regulations, the market manager, Chris Kenner, could no longer be assured that a ready-made market would exist for the front-loading washer. Instead, Kenner and his team were forced to focus on the difficulties and unknowns associated with market creation.

Exactly *who* would buy a front-loader?

How much would consumers pay for a front-loader?

How could loyal consumers of top-loading washers be converted to the use of front-loaders? Could consumers be converted?

What were the direct competitors doing with respect to the development and introduction of front-loaders?

The Product

Dave Modtland, manager of washer engineering and project leader for the front-loader, was tasked with overseeing the design of this revolutionary washing machine. The front-loading washing machine represented the first major technological innovation in several years in the industry. The horizontal-axis washer used tumble action—top-loading washers used an agitator that actually forced clothes to beat against each other, while the front-loader lifted and tumbled clothes in and out of the water without rough agitation. The new washer had more capacity than previous front-loaders and used approximately 20 less gallons of water per load than conventional top-loaders, or about 8000 gallons a year. Likewise, the front-loader saved on energy costs. Using national averages, water and energy savings were calculated to be at least $86 per year. Additional savings would be gained from reduced drying time due to the higher spin speeds achieved in front loaders. The front-loader also offered many features—automatic dispensing (of detergent, bleach, and fabric softener), an extra rinse option (i.e., for infant clothing), automatic water fill (fills to needed level and eliminates waste), and dryer clothes due to its high-rpm motor. Moreover, the front-loading washer offered versatility in installation—it could be installed under a counter, stacked with a dryer, or used in a free-standing position. The washer had a unique look, and the glass door allowed the viewing of machine operation. A matching clothes dryer complemented the new washer very well.

There were, however, some disadvantages associated with the front-loading washer. The washer was very heavy and more difficult to install (due to extra internal packing needed to protect critical components during shipment). Also, the front-loading washer was more costly to service than conventional top-loaders.

COMPETITION

The laundry market represented a very competitive and demanding environment. Frigidaire currently competed with four other major appliance manufacturers in the United States—Whirlpool, General Electric, Maytag, and Amana—all of whom managed

EXHIBIT B

Major Appliance Industry Brands by Company, 1996

Frigidaire	Maytag	Whirlpool	General Electric	Amana
Frigidaire	Maytag	Whirlpool	General Electric	Amana
Frigidaire Gallery	Jenn Aire	KitchenAid	GE Profile	Speed Queen
White-Westinghouse	Admiral	Roper	Hotpoint	
Gibson	Magic Chef	Estate	RCA	
Tappan	Norge	Kenmore (Sears)		
Kelvinator				
O'Keefe & Merrett				
Kenmore (Sears)				
GE (General Electric)				

Source: Frigidaire Product Planning Department, Webster City, Iowa.

several different brand names (see Exhibit B). At the present time, Frigidaire's market share for the home laundry market was about 7.9 percent, down from 9.2 percent in 1995. However, the Frigidaire brand name itself represented only about 2 percent of the washer market (see Exhibit C). The Laundry Division's market planner, John Jergens, believed the front-loader represented a tremendous opportunity for Frigidaire to expand its position in the marketplace.

Despite delayed DOE regulations, both Maytag and Amana had announced plans to introduce their own versions of horizontal-axis machines in 1997; Frigidaire managers had noted, though, that news releases on Maytag's new washer indicated that it might not be front-loading. In addition, Whirlpool was in the process of developing a new-generation washing machine, which was rumored to be neither traditional vertical nor horizontal axis, and GE had recently released a new, redesigned vertical-axis machine. Because of the new products being developed by competitors, Jergens felt that early presence in the marketplace would be vital to the success of the front-loader.

CUSTOMER ANALYSIS

Bill Topper and his management team knew that a key to market creation was to understand the needs and wants of potential consumers with respect to washing machines. Several pieces

EXHIBIT C

1996 Washing Machine Market Share in the United States

Brand Name	Percent Market Share
Kenmore	29.0
Whirlpool	21.6
Maytag	14.7
GE	13.1
Amana	4.9
Roper	2.4
Frigidaire	2.3
Admiral	1.9
Others	10.1
TOTAL	100.0

Source: Industrial Marketing Research, Inc.

of information were available to the management team, including survey and focus group data and personal feedback from consumers who had tried early prototypes of the front-loader.

Survey Data

Results of a 1991 consumer/environmental profile suggested to Chris Kenner, marketing manager, that a potential market existed for the front-loader. Over half of surveyed households (53 percent) purchased energy-efficient appliances, while 28 percent used water-conservation devices in their homes; 46 percent of households reported considering environmental impact when purchasing products. Consumers in several geographic regions in the United States were rated above average for considering environmental issues when purchasing appliances; cities included Denver, Minneapolis–St. Paul, Houston, Washington, D.C., Salt Lake City, Seattle, San Francisco, Dallas–Fort Worth, and Hartford.

Kenner also reviewed information related to current Frigidaire users. The majority of Frigidaire brand purchasers were families (79.3 percent), followed by single females (14.5 percent), and single males (6.1 percent). Brand sales were highest in the East North Central (26.8 percent) and South Atlantic (22.0 percent) regions; New England posted the fewest brand sales (1.2 percent). Sales in the other regions of the United States varied from 4.9 to 12.2 percent. Sales of washing machines were subject to fluctuations—for example, sales tended to be lowest in January and April. However, Kenner did not find evidence of seasonal sales. Of more concern to Kenner was Frigidaire's low ranking in brand acceptability relative to major competitors (see Exhibit D).

Focus Groups

Chris Kenner also reviewed a 1993 market research focus study, which exposed consumers to the front-loading washer. Several concerns about the washer had been identified in the study:

1. Water leakage through the front door
2. Small load capacities
3. Cleaning performance without an agitator

EXHIBIT D

1996 Brand Acceptability among U.S. Households

Brand Name	Acceptability
Maytag	97%
General Electric	95%
Whirlpool	93%
Frigidaire	92%
Amana	87%

Source: Frigidaire Market Research Department, Webster City, Iowa.

4. Insufficient water savings and energy conservation to merit purchase
5. Difficult loading and unloading of the washer
6. Brand loyalty to current (i.e., familiar and proven) washing technologies

Another study, conducted by Kenner's Market Research Department, had shown that pricing of the front-loader was a potential problem. Consumer interest in the washer did not increase significantly until the price was reduced to $599 or less. Many consumers reported that a lower price and/or a manufacturer's rebate would offer the best incentive for purchase. Even with an incentive, 35 percent of those consumers surveyed indicated that they would not buy the washer.

Consumer Feedback

In 1995, Bill Topper had implemented a controlled sales program in Iowa, Wisconsin, and California. The purpose of the program was to obtain consumer feedback on the new washer prior to national introduction. Several hundred units were sold to target consumers; they were given large rebates and were asked to work with the design and marketing teams to identify the strengths and weaknesses of the product. Engineers and other manufacturing personnel stayed in close contact with these consumers—reading surveys, answering telephone calls, and visiting actual homes to discuss performance and problems. Problems were identified and corrected, and more important, Frigidaire found that many of the customers reported high levels of satisfaction with the close personal contact and attention they received from manufacturing personnel.

Market Segmentation

Using historical data obtained on previous buyers of front-loading machines (White-Westinghouse), Kenner and his marketing group identified six target segments of potential customers. Although the information was dated, the profiles were used to estimate demand potential and sales forecasts for the new washers. The six segments, representing only 16.7 percent of U.S. households, had generated nearly half the demand for the previous White-Westinghouse front-loading machines. Frigidaire's marketing department calculated that the same segments would produce a potential demand of 134,000 units per year for the new front-loading machine (the estimate included a conversion factor that assumed a 14-year life for each horizontal washer). The segmentation data is summarized in Exhibit E on pages 76 and 77.

MARKETING PLAN FOR HORIZONTAL-AXIS, FRONT-LOADING WASHER

Bill Topper and his management team concluded that in order for the front-loading machine to be successful, the company would have to implement a marketing plan that would (1) overcome consumers' negative perceptions about the Frigidaire brand name and about the front-loading technology, (2) take advantage of the environmental and energy concerns of consumers, and (3) provide close personal contact and attention to customers.

Product Introduction

The front-loader washer initially would be marketed under the Frigidaire Gallery brand name, a new professional series line recently launched by Frigidaire. This tactic allowed the new washer to take advantage of the market synergies created by the recent large-scale Gallery introduction. Introduction focused on one model, available in either white or almond. This approach streamlined production, inventory levels, and distribution.

The management team believed that it was imperative to convey the potential benefits of the front-loader to consumers, dealers, and within the company itself. Failure to do so would hamper successful introduction of the washer. Consequently, Kenner and his marketing department developed a summary of benefits to guide product introduction:

Consumer Benefits	Dealer Benefits	Frigidaire Benefits
Better washing performance	High profit potential	Increased market share
Gentler on clothes	Improved product offering	Increased profitability
Saves energy, saves water	Improved visibility/traffic	Improved product offering
Flexible installation	New laundry room options	First-mover advantages

Although the initial product introduction involved only one model, the engineering department, under the direction of Dave Modtland, continued to develop additional features and product offerings. Negotiations were underway with GE and Whirlpool to possibly manufacture front-loading washers for these major appliance companies. Commercial versions and coin-operated machines also were under development. Finally, a line of horizontal machines, with varying features and price points, was planned for future introduction. Eventual plans called for an ultra-high-end model and a low-end model that could compete with traditional top-loader price points.

Pricing

Topper wanted to competitively price the new washing machine—not so high that consumers would not even consider the washer but also not so low that profit objectives could not be attained. Consequently, a suggested retail price range for the new horizontal-axis machine was established at $749 to $849, with a target retail selling price of $799. Built into the price was a very appealing profit margin for dealers (30 percent) relative to dealer margins for top-loading washing machines (10 percent). Frigidaire's profit margin was set at about 26 percent. Frigidaire's profit margin accounted for all variable and fixed costs allocated to the front-loading washer. The price also allowed for a 12 percent return on investment (ROI) to be obtained.

Even at this price, however, the management team knew that the front-loader faced a tough challenge. There were (and would continue to be) many conventional washing machines on the market that cost much less than the front-loading washer; most top-of-the-line washers sold for less than the front-loader would sell for. In fact, only about 0.8 percent of the available washing machines on the market were priced above $700. Thus, at the targeted retail selling price of $799, consumers had the very attractive option of purchasing a conventional top-loading machine *and* a dryer or just a front-loading washer.

Merchandising

The front-loader washing machine would be marketed through existing distribution channels, catalogues, and the Internet (www.frigidaire.com). In addition, a dedicated sales manager was assigned to the new washer to help push it through the new distribution channels. High priority also would be given to the dealers. According to Chris Kenner:

> A critical step in growing this market is to educate and convince dealers of the benefits of front-load technology.

Consequently, several steps were implemented to educate dealers about the new washer and to assist dealers in sales of the washer.

First, the manufacturing facility in Webster City hosted an open house and training for dealers and district managers as a kickoff for the front-loading washing machine introduction. Dealers and district managers also received free sales and training kits to help stimulate sales. Those who could not attend the training at the Webster City facility received a free formal introduction presentation at their own facilities. Dealers and retailers also received a free floor plan to assist in the visual display of the new washer. Retailers were equipped with a variety of sales aids to enhance in-store sales efforts; for example, a sliding rule showing energy and water savings was made available to retailers.

An Inside Line Consumer Direct program was established for fully trained, certified retailers. These retailers had access to an upscale consumer database to capitalize on target markets.

Financial incentives were initiated. Dealers would earn a higher profit margin for the front-loader than for conventional washers. Discounted pricing would be implemented throughout the first year of sales, creating an even larger profit margin. District managers would receive premium commissions for their sales efforts and results. Both retail sales personnel and district managers were enrolled in the Earn a Free Washer sales contest program—free front-loading washers would be awarded based on number of units sold.

Consumer-oriented strategies aimed at assisting dealers and district managers also were implemented. Free financing for 6 months (no pay, no interest) was made available to consumers; moreover, because installing a front-loading washer was more difficult and costly than that required for conventional machines, an installation allowance would be provided to purchasers. The front-loading washer carried a full 2-year warranty, the longest available in the industry, and consumers were promised a 30-day money back guarantee if they were not fully satisfied with the cleaning performance—The Cleaner/Gentler Promise. Consumer promotions included free "low suds" detergent samples of Wisk (Frigidaire and Lever Brothers were partners in developing and marketing this low-sudsing detergent), and those customers who purchased both a new front-loading washer and a matching dryer received a free Braun steam iron.

There was a contest for consumers, too. A Watch & Win program enabled interested customers to watch an "infomercial" videotape about the front-loading washer and then answer some questions about the washer on a contest entry form. Completing the entry form provided a chance for the consumer to win free Frigidaire Gallery appliances. But the contest actually had a broader aim, which was to educate consumers about the benefits of the new washing machine.

Marketing Communications

The management team believed that the benefits of the front-loader were best conveyed to potential customers through personal communications. Although mass media reached a large number of consumers quickly, explaining the front-loading machine necessitated a complex message. Plus Frigidaire's experience with the controlled sales program had revealed that personal contact with consumers was crucial to creating satisfied customers. Consequently, mass-media advertising was limited to a brief television advertisement, to be aired in national markets in early 1997. The primary thrust of the communications plan rested on the ability of retailers and dealers to communicate and educate consumers on the benefits of the front-loader at the point of sale. Besides training all salespeople, floor displays and literature were designed to enhance and complement sales efforts.

EXHIBIT E

Potential Market Segments for Front-Loading Washing Machines

Segment	Age Group	Ethnic Background	Affluence	Psychographics	Ecological Orientation	Motivation to Buy	Expected Demand
Urban Gold Coast Elite urban singles and couples	25–34 35–54	White, Asian	High	Egocentric, amicable, conforming, self-assured Not style-conscious, impulsive, or cautious	Below Average	Space Savings	0.51%
Gray Power Affluent retirees in sunbelt cities	65+	White	Middle	Cautious, egocentric, broad-minded, reserved, brand loyal Not experimenters, ad-believers, or conformists	Low	Energy Savings	2.09%
A. Money & Brains Sophisticated townhouse couples	55–64 65+	White, Asian	High	Amicable, broad-minded, efficient, intelligent, creative Not reserved, impulsive, or economy-minded	Above Average	Space Savings Performance Environment	3.08%
B. Young Literan Upscale urban singles and couples	25–34 35–54	White, Asian	Middle				
C. Bohemian Mix Bohemian singles and couples	Under 24 25–34	Ethnic Diversity	Middle				

EXHIBIT E (*continued*)

Potential Market Segments for Front-Loading Washing Machines

Segment	Age Group	Ethnic Background	Affluence	Psychographics	Ecological Orientation	Motivation to Buy	Expected Demand
A. *Kids & Cul-de-Sacs* Upscale suburban families	35–54	White, Asian	High	Amicable, intelligent, efficient, reserved, style-conscious, cautious	Above Average	Performance Fashion	4.76%
B. *Winner's Circle* Executive suburban families	35–54 55–64	White, Asian	High	Not conformists, brand loyal, impulsive, or economy-minded			
A. *Executive Suites* Upscale white-collar couples	25–34 55–64	White, Asian	High	Amicable, efficient, brand loyal, intelligent, cautious, creative, style-conscious	Below Average	Performance Fashion	4.75%
B. *Pools & Patios* Established empty nesters	55–64 65+	White, Asian	High	Not experimenters, conformists, ad-believers, economy-minded, or impulsive			
C. *Second City Elite* Upscale executive families	35–54 55–64	White	High				
Blue Blood Estates Elite super-rich families	35–54	White, Asian	High	Amicable, cautious, intelligent, refined, efficient, self-assured, frank, brand loyal Not experimenters, impulsive, ad-believers, or economy-minded	Above Average	Performance Fashion	0.78%

Source: Claritas, PRIZM Profiles, 1994.

All communications emphasized a performance-driven product that resulted in superior cleaning, delicate handling, better efficiency, and flexible installation.

To promote postpurchase satisfaction, a Use and Care video was issued with every purchased front-loading washing machine to educate the buyer and to prevent service calls related to the installation and/or use of the product. The Watch & Win contest provided an incentive to purchasers to watch the video if they had not done so prior to purchase. Also, a 1-800 customer line was established to address customer complaints, concerns, or comments.

An After-Sales Call program would be established, although not until 1998. This would be a continuation of the earlier experiment that allowed customers to talk directly to the manufacturing personnel who had actually built their washing machine. The management team believed that this interaction not only would result in satisfied customers but also would pinpoint product problems and areas for product improvement.

EARLY SALES PERFORMANCE AND CONCERNS

The front-loading washer was released to the public on October 1, 1996. The initial project release date had been May 1995; however, due to several late design changes and some unanticipated component failures, the introduction was delayed. The development of the washer had taken considerably longer to complete than any other machine Frigidaire had ever produced. The primary reason for the delay was that the front-loader represented a much more complex design than the top-loading machine, and it was mandatory that this machine be "perfect"—it could not have the problems that so many of the early front-loading machines had. Despite these setbacks, the front-loader was a design success—it met initial design specifications and, more important, met the high quality and reliability standards established during the infant stages of the development process.

Unfortunately, initial sales volumes for the horizontal-axis machine were sluggish. Based on the target market analysis, previous sales, industry projections, brand positioning factors, and future DOE

EXHIBIT F

Sales Volume Forecast—Horizontal-Axis Washer (000s of units)

Brand	1996	1997	1998	1999
Frigidaire	60	70	100	120
Kenmore	20	30	30	30
Private Label	10	10	10	10
International	8	12	20	30
TOTAL	98	122	160	190

Source: Frigidaire Marketing Department, Webster City, Iowa.

regulations, Bill Topper and his team had developed a sales volume forecast for the front-loading washer for 1996 through 1999. The forecast incorporated Frigidaire's plans to sell the washer not only under its own brand name but also under Sears' Kenmore label and other private-label agreements being negotiated; international sales also were projected. However, because the forecast was based on several market variables that were not yet truly understood, Topper believed sales tracking would be critical to the determination of market reaction. Details of the forecast are located in Exhibit F.

Sales for October, November, and December of 1996, the first three months that the front-loading machine was on the market, were up to 30 percent below projected levels (see Exhibit G). In fact, sales projections for the first year had been decreased from 98,000 units to 60,000 units because Frigidaire had been unable to finalize negotiations with Sears to manufacture the horizontal-axis washer under the Kenmore name.

The reasons for this unanticipated dismal performance were unclear. Some managers believed the retail price was to blame for slow sales; as a result of the delayed introduction (delayed from May 1995 to October 1996), the target retail price had been increased from $799 to $999. The delay, everyone agreed, had been necessary to correct quality and reliability problems. However, costs increased, driving the retail price higher. In addition, it was speculated that Maytag's competing front-loading washer, due out in 1997, would be priced in the range of $1200 to $1300. Because of Maytag's high association with quality, Frigidaire managers worried that their washer priced at $799

EXHIBIT G

Horizontal-Axis Front-Loading Washing Machine Sales, October 1, 1996–December 27, 1996

Month	Monthly Production Budget	Monthly Sales Forecast	Monthly Sales	Sold/ Forecast (%)
October	5750	4503	4876	108.28
November	4750	3456	2433	70.40
December	4500	2483	1894	76.28
TOTAL	15,000	10,442	9203	88.13

Notes: (1) Production budget = (units produced/day) × (# of available work days per month). Current production schedule is to build 250 units/day (equivalent to 60,000 units/year). (2) Monthly sales forecast is the original forecast.
Source: Frigidaire Marketing Department, Webster City, Iowa.

would be perceived as inferior relative to Maytag. Consequently, the price was increased to $999 in order to still be competitive with Maytag's product and at the same time to be close enough to Maytag's price that consumers would perceive Frigidaire as a quality washing machine. Managers reasoned that if a price adjustment was necessary, it would be easier to decrease the price than to increase it. However, other factors also may have been responsible for the lackluster sales. For example, managers questioned the decision to limit mass-media advertising, especially in light of the fact that Maytag was known to effectively use television and print media to mass advertise its products. It also was possible that demand for the front-loading washer had been overestimated.

In response to the initial sales volumes, the management team began to review its marketing strategies and objectives. The dominant question on their minds was, "How do we develop a market that has failed to take off for over 50 years?" Bill Topper knew they had to do something quickly to create a market for the front-loading washer if Frigidaire wanted to establish itself as the dominant player and industry leader in this new sector of the laundry market.

America Online

This case was prepared by Natalya V. Delcoure, Lawrence R. Jauch, and John L. Scott of Northeast Louisiana University.

America Online, Inc. (NYSE: AOL), was founded in 1985. This media company, with headquarters in Dulles, Virginia, has more than 10 million members and currently operates in the United States, Canada, the United Kingdom, France, and Germany. AOL provides on-line services including electronic mail, on-line conferencing, Internet access, news, magazines, sports, weather, stock quotes, mutual fund transactions, software files, games, computing support, and on-line classes.

According to the company, its mission is "to lead the development of a new interactive medium that eliminates traditional boundaries between people and places to create a new kind of interactive global community that holds the potential to change the way people obtain information, communicate with one another, buy products and services, and learn."

To accomplish this mission, the company's strategy is to continue investment in the growth of its subscriber base, pursue related business opportunities often through joint ventures and acquisitions, provide a full range of interactive services, and maintain technological flexibility.

AOL's rapid growth and community orientation have made it the most popular, easiest, and well-known way for consumers to get on-line. In December 1996, AOL had 8.5 million member sessions a day, 7 million e-mails sent to 12 million recipients a day, and it accounted for approximately $750,000 per day in merchandise transactions.

However, AOL has not been trouble-free. On August 7, 1996, AOL threw 6 million subscribers off line for 19 hours due to software problems. America Online revealed that the glitch resulted from an error made by its working subsidiary, ANS Co., in reconfiguring software and from a bug in router software. The error cost AOL $3 million in rebates. On January 8, 1997, America Online suffered a partial outage that forced it to shut down half its system for 4 hours to find a problem. The problem was with an interface in a router device, which manages the flow of data in the network. The outage drew front-page headlines around the world, as millions of users were unable to access electronic mail, the Internet, and a variety of services and publications on-line for nearly a day.

AMERICA ONLINE COMPANY PROFILE

America Online emerged from a firm founded in the early 1980s as Control Video Corp., aimed to create an on-line service that specialized in games.

It failed to meet strong competition from the Apple II and Commodore 64. Control Video was reorganized as Quantum Computer Services and became a custom developer of online services for other companies. Over time, Quantum managed to persuade Tandy Corp. and Apple Computers to offer a new service called Applelink Personal Edition. At the last minute, Apple withdrew from the deal and left Quantum holding a lot of software it had developed expressly for Applelink. In 1989, Quantum was only scraping by, and it did not have much money for splashy ad campaigns to attract computer users to its new service—America Online. So it came on the market with a unique approach, which was to blanket the countryside with diskettes containing America Online software. As the years went by, the company changed the way it accounted for the costs of acquiring subscribers and its pricing plans, but America Online, Inc., had never actually made any money in its entire history. At the same time, America Online had positioned itself apart from traditional print and television companies as the first "digital media company." Similar to television, the company produces digital content and distributes it digitally and allows a customer to interact digitally.

AOL Organization

AOL Corporation now oversees the operations of several subsidiaries and three divisions: AOL Networks, ANS Access, and AOL Studios. The corporation comprises the core business functions of finance, human resources, legal affairs, corporate communications, corporate development, and technology. AOL Technologies is responsible for delivering research, development, network/data-center operations, and member support to the other America Online divisions, technology licensees, and joint-venture partners. The group is also responsible for support functions—including technical support, billing, and sales.

AOL Networks is responsible for extending the AOL brand into the market, developing new revenue streams, advertising, and online transactions. AOL Networks is led by Robert Pittman, president, formerly managing partner and CEO of Century 21 and cofounder of MTV Network.

ANS Access is responsible for the telecommunications network. The network consists of more than 160,000 modems connecting 472 cities in the United States and 152 cities internationally. Nearly 85 percent of the American population can dial into AOLNet on a local number. For America Online's members who travel, GlobalNet offers access in approximately 230 additional cities in 83 countries. The ANS technical team is responsible for architecture, design, development, installation, management, and maintenance of hardware and software for the nationwide corporate data networks and Internet backbone by which communications take place.

AOL Studios, formerly AOL Productions, runs AOL's innovative chat (iChatco), games (INN), local (Digital City), and independent (Greenhouse) programming properties. AOL Studios is the newest division in AOL. It is working on development of leading-edge technology for broadband and mid-band distribution, interactive brands that can be extended into other media properties such as TV and radio, and managing joint ventures with companies including Time-Warner and CapCities/ABC. World-Play, built from ImagiNation Network entertainment, is the provider of computer on-line games for AOL. ImagiNation Network was founded in 1991 and became an independent subsidiary of AOL in 1996.

Digital City provides local programming, news, services, chat rooms, and commerce to AOL members as well as to the Internet at large. To date, Digital City has been launched nationally in Washington, D.C., Boston, Philadelphia, Atlanta, San Francisco, and Los Angeles. Digital City planned to expand to over 40 cities in 1997. Digital City, Inc., is owned by Digital City LP. AOL owns a majority interest in that entity, and the Tribune Company owns the remaining interest.

Advanced CO+RE Systems, Inc., a wholly owned subsidiary of America Online, provides network services for AOLnet, together with Sprint Corporation and BBN Corporation. Through this subsidiary, America Online designs, develops, and operates high-performance wide-area networks for business, research, education, and government organizations.

In February 1996, AOL merged with the Johnson-Grace Company, a leading developer of compression technology and multimedia development and delivery tools. Using the Johnson-Grace technology, America Online is able to deliver the data-intensive graphics and audio and video capabilities using narrow-band technologies, even over the slower-speed modems currently used by most AOL members.

2Market, Inc., is a joint venture of America Online, Apple Computer, and Medior. It provides retail catalog shopping CD-ROMs that include on-line ordering capabilities. In 1997, America Online, along with Netscape Communications and Disney's ABC unit, announced plans to launch ABCNEWS.com, a 24-hour news service.

Since the beginning of 1995, the company also acquired Advanced Network and Services, Inc. (ANS), Ubique, Ltd., Navisoft, Inc., Global Network Navigator, Inc. (GNN), BookLink Technologies, Inc., and Redgate Communications Corporation. ANS was used to build the AOLNet telephone network and has now been traded to WorldCom in return for CompuServe. (This transaction is discussed more fully later.) Ubique, Ltd., was an Israeli company that developed unique and personable ways to interact over the Internet, notably Virtual Places. Navisoft, Inc., made software such as that which allowed AOL's users to author Web pages. GNN was AOL's flat-rate full Web service provider. However, AOL's flat-rate pricing scheme rendered GNN redundant. BookLink Technologies, Inc., produced software to browse the Web. Redgate Communications Corporation was a multimedia services corporation with a specialization in using multimedia in marketing.

AOL is also planning to go in to the bookselling business in a joint venture with Barnes & Noble, but the timing is still uncertain.

AOL Marketing

The goals of the firm's consumer marketing programs are to increase the general visibility of America Online and to make it easy for customers to experiment with and subscribe to its services. AOL attracts new subscribers through independent marketing programs such as direct mail, disk inserts and inserts in publications, advertising, and a variety of comarketing efforts. The company has entered into comarketing agreements with numerous personal computer hardware, software, and peripheral production companies, as well as with certain of its media partners. These companies bundle America Online software with their products and cater to the needs of a specific audience.

America Online also has been expanding into business-to-business markets, using AOL's network to provide customized network solutions to both individual businesses and professional communities and industries. These private AOLs (the PAOLs) offer the ease of use America Online is known for, as well as customized features and functionality accessible only by preauthorized users, access to the fleet of AOL distribution platforms, secure communications, and information. The company offers these products using a direct salesforce and direct marketing and through resellers and system integrators.

America Online uses specialized retention programs designed to increase customer loyalty and satisfaction and to maximize customer subscription life. These retention programs include regularly scheduled on-line events and conferences; the regular addition of new content, services, and software programs; and on-line promotions of upcoming on-line events and new features. The firm also provides a variety of support mechanisms such as on-line technical support and telephone support services.

In May 1995, America Online introduced its Web browser, which provides integrated World Wide Web access within the AOL services. The integrated approach allows the user to seamlessly use the full suite of America Online features, including chat room, e-mail gateways and mailing lists, File Transfer Protocol, USENET newsgroups, WAIS, and Gopher.

In the summer of 1997, America Online planned to offer its 8 million members a three-dimensional gaming world, CyberPark. The company will try to compete with such heavyweights as Microsoft, the Internet Gaming Zone site, and MCI, which will launch a service in 1997 that allows computer users to play their favorite CD-ROM games. The projected earnings are expected to reach $127 million in 1997, but there are still some technical problems to overcome and the uncertainty of how much to charge future users.

America Online has included international market expansion in its strategy to gain competitive advantage. In April 1995, AOL entered into a joint venture with Bertelsmann, one of the world's largest media companies, to offer interactive services in Europe: Germany (November 1995), the United Kingdom (January 1996), and France (March 1996). Bertelsmann agreed to contribute up to $100 million to fund the launch of the European services, provided access to its book and music club membership base of over 30 million, and offered its publishing content to the joint venture on a most favored customer basis. In addition, Bertelsmann acquired approximately a 5 percent interest in America Online and designated a member of the company's board of directors. AOL contributed interactive technology and management expertise, proprietary software licenses and development services, and staff training and technical support in order to develop, test, and launch the interactive services in Europe. Subscribers to the European services enjoy access to America Online's services in the United States, and U.S. subscribers enjoy access to the European services.

AOL Canada, launched in January 1996, features local content and services. In Ocober 1996, AOL Canada offered Canadian members software, thirteen local channels, billing in Canadian dollars, e-mail, message boards, and easy access to the Internet through a Web browser. AOL Canada's key partners include Citytv, an internationally renowned broadcaster and program producer; MuchMusic, Canada's first national music television channel; *Shift Magazine,* Canada's hottest publication in media; Intuit Canada, makers of the world's leading personal finance software, Quicken; and Southam New Media, a wholly owned subsidiary of Southam, Inc., Canada's largest news organization.

In May 1996, America Online announced a partnership with Mitsui & Co., one of the world's largest international trading companies, and Nikkei, one of Japan's leading media companies with respected business and computer publications. The joint venture consists of Mitsui & Co. owning 40 percent, Nikkei 10 percent, and AOL 50 percent. Japanese partners contributed more than 120 years of experience and credibility in the Japanese market, a strong management team, and $56 million to fund the launch of the Japanese service. America Online brings to the venture its ability to develop, manage, and execute interactive on-line services in the United States, Europe, and Canada.

America Online's wildly successful marketing ploy of flat-rate pricing in the United States turned out to contribute to AOL's latest problem. About 75 percent of AOL's customers took the flat-rate offer. As a result, total daily AOL customer use soared from 1.6 million hours on-line in October 1996 to more than 4 million hours in January 1997. (These problems are described more fully later in this case.)

Meeting Customer Needs

The company provides tools to its members so that they can control their child's or teen's experience on-line without cramping the adults who enjoy using AOL's services to talk to other adults. Parental controls can block or limit the use of chat, instant messages, e-mail, binary files, newsgroups, or the Web. Different on-line areas support different values. For instance:

- *ACLU Forum:* This encourages lively yet responsible debate. Illegal activities (harassment, distribution of illegal materials) are not permitted in this area.
- *Womens' Network:* This is a women-friendly and safe space for chatting, learning, teaching, and networking, but men are still welcome to join the communication.
- *Christian Chat Room:* This allows fellowship among Christian members. In this space, proselytizing is forbidden.
- *Kids Only:* This gives children their own space on-line for searching help with homework, sending e-mail, and hanging out in chat rooms. Parental control can be set up in this area.

The average adult spends about an hour on-line, but the average kid spends three. Currently, there are 4.1 million kids surfing the Net. By 2000, it is expected that there will be 19.2 million. Kids, who spent $307 million in 1996 on on-line services, will spend $1.8 billion by 2002, and this is why media and Web giants are scrambling to offer new kid-friendly sites. Fox TV features cartoons and kid shows. Disney gave AOL first crack at hosting Daily Blast, which offers kids games, comics, and stories for $4.95 per month or $39.95 per year. "But," says Rob Jennings, vice president for programming for AOL networks, "We felt we had a good mix already." Yahooligans! offers kids-friendly Web sites for free. AOL still has partnerships with other media giants such as Disney rival Viacom, Inc.'s Nickelodeon unit for other offerings.

Since 1994, AOL has offered a Kids Only area featuring homework help, games, and on-line magazines, as well as the usual fare of software, games, and chat rooms. The area gets about 1 million 8- to 12-year-old visitors monthly.

In April 1996, America Online began to see the effect of seasonality in both member acquisitions and in the amount of time spent by customers using its services. The company expects that member acquisition is to be highest in the second and third fiscal quarters, when sales of new computers and computer software are highest due to holiday seasons (AOL's fiscal year ends June 30.) Customer usage is expected to be lower in the summer months, due largely to extended daylight hours and competing outdoor leisure activities.

AOL Employees

As of June 30, 1996, America Online had 5828 employees, including 1058 in software and content development, 3271 in customer support, 199 in marketing, 1099 in operations, and 291 in corporate operations. None of AOL's employees is represented by a labor union, and America Online has never experienced a work stoppage.

AOL employs numerous part-time workers around the world known as "remote staff." These are volunteer staff who develop content and provide both marketing and operations functions. Remote staff write informational articles, produce graphics, host chat rooms, provide technical assistance, and fulfill various support functions. Remote staff duties vary. Some may work as little as 10 hours per week or more than 40 hours per week. AOL's remote staff is compensated for these services with "community leader accounts"—a membership for which the staff members are not charged. Relatively few remote staff members are paid as independent contractors.

AOL's flat-rate pricing plan had a serious impact on its remote staff. Prior to the flat rate, members paid about $3 per hour of on-line access. Hence a "free" account would have a monthly value of approximately $300 for a staff member who spent 3 hours per day online.

After the flat-rate pricing plan, this account's value fell to $20. This enormous decrease in incentives led many remote staff members to resign their positions. The positions hardest hit were those for which the job pressures were highest, including AOL's guides and Techlive. Guides served to police AOL's chat rooms and to assist users with whom they came in contact. Techlive assisted users with computer problems, computer use, and navigation of AOL. Techlive is now buried beneath menu options that do not hint that real-time online help is available.

AOL Finance

Exhibits A and B present the financial statements for fiscal years 1995 and 1996. About 90 percent of the firm's revenues are generated from on-line subscription fees. AOL's other revenues are generated from sales of merchandise, data network services, online transactions and advertising, marketing and production services, and development and licensing fees. The increase of over $600 million in service revenues from 1995 to 1996 was attributed primarily to a 93 percent increase in AOL subscribers.

This is expected to undergo radical change, due to the flat rate pricing, with much less revenue coming from subscriber fees, which AOL hopes to make up by increases in the other revenue streams.

Cost of revenue, which includes network-related costs, consists of data and voice communication costs and costs associated with operating the data centers and providing customer support. These increased almost $400 million from 1995 to 1996. This increase was related to a growth of data communication costs, customer support costs, and royalties paid to information and service providers.

For fiscal year 1996, marketing expenses increased 176 percent over fiscal year 1995. This was attributed primarily to an increase in the size and number of marketing programs designed to expand the subscriber base.

Product development costs include research and development, other product development, and the amortization of software. For fiscal year 1996, these costs increased 277 percent over fiscal year 1995 and increased as a percentage of total revenues from 3.6 to 4.9 percent. The increases in product development costs were attributable primarily to an increase in the number of technical employees. Product development costs, before capitalization and amortization, increased by 242 percent.

For fiscal year 1996, general and administrative costs increased 159 percent over fiscal year 1995 and decreased as a percentage of total revenues from 10.8 to 10.1 percent. The increase in general and administrative costs was related to higher personnel, office, and travel expenses related to an increase in the number of employees. The decrease in general and administrative costs as a percentage of total revenues was a result of the substantial growth in revenues, which more than offset the

EXHIBIT A

Income Statement (Year Ended June 30; Amounts in Thousands, Except per Share Data)

	1997	1996	1995
Revenues			
On-line service revenues	$1,429,445	$991,656	$344,309
Other revenues	255,783	102,198	49,981
Total revenues	1,685,228	1,093,854	394,290
Costs and expenses			
Cost of revenues	1,040,762	638,025	232,318
Marketing	409,260	212,710	77,064
Write-off of deferred subscriber acquisition costs	385,221	—	—
Product development	58,208	43,164	11,669
General and administrative	193,537	110,653	42,700
Acquired research and development	—	16,981	50,335
Amortization of goodwill	6,549	7,078	1,653
Restructuring charge	48,627	—	—
Contract termination charge	24,506	—	—
Settlement charge	24,204	—	—
Total costs and expenses	2,190,874	1,028,611	415,739
Income (loss) from operations	(505,646)	65,243	(21,449)
Other income (expense), net	6,299	(2,056)	3,074
Merger expenses	—	(848)	(2,207)
Income (loss) before provision for income taxes	(499,347)	62,339	(20,582)
Provision for income taxes	—	(32,523)	(15,169)
Net income (loss)	$ (499,347)	$ 29,816	$ (35,751)
Earnings (loss) per share			
Net income (loss)	$(5.22)	$0.28	$(0.51)
Weighted average shares outstanding	95,607	108,097	69,550

additional general and administrative costs, combined with the semivariable nature of many of the general and administrative costs.

Acquired research and development costs relate to in-process research and development purchased with the acquisition of Ubique, Ltd., in September 1995. Acquired research and development costs relate to in-process research and development purchased as part of the acquisitions of BookLink Technologies, Inc. (Booklink), and Navisoft, Inc. (Navisoft).

The amortization of goodwill increase relates primarily to America Online's fiscal 1995 acquisitions of Advanced Network & Services, Inc., and Global Network Navigator, Inc., which resulted in approximately $56 million of goodwill. The goodwill related to these acquisitions is being amortized on a straight-line basis over periods ranging from 5 to 10 years. The increase in amortization of goodwill results from a full year of goodwill recognized in fiscal year 1996 compared with only a partial year of goodwill recognized in fiscal year 1995.

Other income (expenses) consists of interest expense and nonoperating charges net of investment income and nonoperating gains. The change in other income (expenses) was attributed to the $8 million settlement of a class action lawsuit partially offset by an increase in investment income.

Nonrecurring merger expenses totaling $848,000 were recognized in fiscal year 1996 in connection with the merger of America Online with Johnson-Grace Company. Nonrecurring merger expenses totaling $2,207,000 were recognized in fiscal year 1995 in connection with the mergers of AOL with Redgate Communications Corporation, Wide Area Information Servers, Inc., and Medior, Inc.

EXHIBIT B

Consolidated Balance Sheet (June 30; Amounts in Thousands; Except per Share Data)

	1997	1996	1995
Assets			
Current assets			
Cash and cash equivalents	$124,340	$118,421	$ 45,877
Short-term investments	268	10,712	18,672
Trade accounts receivable	65,306	49,342	32,176
Other receivables	26,093	23,271	11,381
Prepaid expenses and other current assets	107,466	65,290	25,527
Total current assets	323,473	267,036	133,633
Property and equipment at cost, net	233,129	111,090	70,919
Other assets			
Restricted cash	50,000	—	—
Product development costs, net	72,498	44,330	18,949
Deferred subscriber acquisition costs, net	—	314,181	77,229
License rights, net	16,777	4,947	5,579
Other assets	84,618	29,607	9,121
Deferred income taxes	24,410	135,872	35,627
Goodwill, net	41,783	51,691	54,356
Total assets	$846,688	$958,754	$405,413
Liabilities and stockholders' equity			
Current liabilities			
Trade accounts payable	$ 69,703	$105,904	$ 84,640
Other accrued expenses and liabilities	297,298	127,876	23,509
Deferred revenue	166,007	37,950	20,021
Accrued personnel costs	20,008	15,719	2,863
Current portion of long-term debt	1,454	2,435	2,329
Total current liabilities	554,470	289,884	133,362
Long-term liabilities			
Notes payable	50,000	19,306	17,369
Deferred income taxes	24,410	135,872	35,627
Deferred revenue	86,040	—	—
Minority interests	2,674	22	—
Other liabilities	1,060	1,168	2,243
Total liabilities	$718,654	$446,252	$188,601
Stockholders' equity			
Preferred stock, $.01 par value; 5,000,000 shares authorized, 1,000 shares issued and outstanding at June 30, 1997 and 1996	1	1	—
Common stock, $.01 par value; 300,000,000 and 100,000,000 shares authorized, 100,188,971 and 92,626,000 shares issued and outstanding at June 30, 1997 and 1996, respectively	1,002	926	767
Unrealized gain on available-for-sale securities	16,924	—	—
Additional paid-in capital	617,221	519,342	252,668
Accumulated deficit	(507,114)	(7,767)	(36,623)
Total stockholders' equity	128,034	512,502	216,812
Total liabilities and equity	$846,688	$958,754	$405,413

In December 1993, the company completed a public stock offering of 8 million shares of common stock, which generated net cash proceeds of approximately $62.7 million. In April 1995, the joint venture with Bertelsmann AG to offer interactive on-line services in Europe, netted approximately $54 million through the sale of approximately 5 percent of its common stock to Bertelsmann. In October 1995, AOL completed a public offering of 4,963,266 shares of common stock, which generated net cash proceeds of approximately $139.5 million. In May 1996, America Online received approximately $28 million through the sale of convertible preferred stock to Mitsui in its joint venture with Mitsui & Co., Ltd., and Nohon Keizai Shimbun, Inc., to offer interactive on-line services in Japan. The preferred stock has an aggregate liquidation preference of approximately $28 million and accrues dividends at a rate of 4 percent per annum. Accrued dividends can be paid in the form of additional shares of preferred stock. Exhibit C shows the history of share prices of AOL's common stock.

America Online has financed its operations through cash generated from operations and the sale of its capital stock. AOL has financed its investments in facilities and telecommunications equipment principally through leasing. American Online leases the majority of its facilities and equipment under noncancelable operating leases. The communications network requires a substantial investment in telecommunications equipment, which America Online plans to finance principally through leasing. The company has never declared, nor has it paid, any cash dividends on its common stock. AOL currently intends to retain its earnings to finance future growth.

The company uses its working capital to finance ongoing operations and to fund marketing and content programs and the development of its products and services. America Online plans to continue to invest in computing and support infrastructure. Additionally, AOL expects to use a portion of its cash for the acquisition and subsequent funding of technologies, products, or businesses complementary to the company's current business.

For example, America Online is investing in the development of alternative technologies to deliver its services. AOL has entered into agreements with several manufacturers of personal digital assistants (PDAs are low-powered, hand-held computers), including Sony, Motorola, Tandy, and Casio, to bundle a palmtop edition of America Online's client software with their PDAs. AOL is participating in early cable trials using cable as the conduit into PCs and has announced future support of ISDN, which allows digital transmission, as opposed to the analog transmission of telephones, and wireless, similar to cell phone and satellite transmission. By the time that cable modems are poised for market penetration, a new generation of competitive telephone modems may be available. In the paging market, AOL has entered into agreements with AT&T Wireless Services and MobileMedia to provide their paging customers who subscribe to AOL with mobile access to certain America Online services.

EXHIBIT C

Market Price of Common Stock

For the Quarter Ended	High	Low
September 30, 1994	$10.28	$ 6.88
December 31, 1994	14.63	7.47
March 31, 1995	23.69	12.31
June 30, 1995	24.06	16.75
September 30, 1995	37.25	21.38
December 31, 1995	46.25	28.25
March 31, 1996	60.00	32.75
June 30, 1996	71.00	36.63
September 30, 1996	37.75	34.65
December 31, 1996	33.38	32.25

AOL'S ENVIRONMENT

AOL is subject to federal and state regulations applicable to business in general. However, America Online must keep up with changes in the regulatory environment relating to telecommunications and the media. Additional legislative proposals from international, federal, and state government bodies in the areas of content regulations, intellectual property, privacy rights, and state tax issues could impose additional regulations and obligations on all online service providers. For a long time, such companies as AT&T, Western Union, and RCA dominated the telecommunications industry.

The courts deregulated the telephone industry in the 1980s. Although technology and market development made passage of new telecommunications legislation inevitable, it took about 10 years to frame it. Even though the Telecommunications Reform Act of 1996 meant to remove many of the regulatory barriers and make it easier for telecom companies to invest in the information superhighway, so far it has made little difference.

The Department of Commerce and the U.S. Trade Representative have pushed the World Trade Organization to open up the telecom sector to more service and equipment competition. As a result of trade negotiations in Singapore, tariffs on many telecommunications products and services will be reduced, with great potential benefit to U.S. firms. Additional talks were under way in Switzerland in 1997 that may permit U.S. telecommunications companies to compete on equal footing with providers in Europe and elsewhere.

Telephone companies are collecting high revenues as computer and on-line services expand. One study found that local carriers collected revenues totaling $1.4 billion in 1995 from second phone lines used mainly for Net links while spending only $245 million to upgrade their networks for the additional usage. Phone companies experienced 8 to 9 percent profit growth in 1996 since second phone line installations at homes grew 25 percent. Both local carriers and on-line service providers agree that there is a necessity to build higher-capacity networks to satisfy the increasing demand for public phone networks to meet the growing trend in cybersurfing.

The future of technology is difficult to predict but can affect AOL's future strategy. Some speculate that interactive TV is going to be replaced by network computers (such as those from Sun). Some argue that Internet connections should be available to people who want to use them and that public monies should be provided to ensure access for all. There is a growing place for satellite and fiber in the new communication system. Technology trends are sometimes born of social change. Here are some of the most important trends to watch for the next 5 years:

- The world phone could be a satellite wireless phone that uses digital technology. A combination of Global System for Mobilization (GSM) and satellite technologies could be the model for the world phone. Pioneers such as Wildfire Communications, Lucent Technologies, Dialogic, and VDOnet are among hundreds of alternative carriers that try to unite PCs, phone, e-mail, fax, and video into a seamless fabric. They are designing software that sends phone calls around the world on the Internet very cheaply. The line dividing computers and telephones, voice and data is blurring. Building on the union of data networks and computers, the Internet has become the new global communications infrastructure for businesses.

- Personal communication systems (PCSs) could broadside local telecom carriers. Projections are that local exchange carriers must brace for a loss of 35 percent of high-margin business customers and 25 percent or more of their residential shares to PCS providers. Mobile subscribers could represent 17 percent of traditional wireline carrier business by 2010. VocalTec, Ltd., leading maker of Internet telephony products, recently broadened the appeal by introducing gateways that connect the Internet to standard phone systems—allowing PC users to call non-PC users on their phones, and vice versa. VocalTec claims it saves $10,000 a month on phone bills between the company's New Jersey and Israeli offices.

- Wireless convergence. Commercial mobile wireless will include mobile satellite, and satellite communication will overlap coverage and mobility with cellular/PCS. Cordless telephony will play major roles. Several years ago, Microsoft Corp. and Novell, Inc., tried to apply computer-telephony integration technology to any desktop by creating competing standards for connecting phone systems to PC networks. But the products, TAPI and TSAPI, which allowed desktop computer users to receive and manage phone calls through their PCs, went nowhere. Now, a wave of products built on TAPI and TSAPI that work with standard telecom equipment is hitting the market. Users can select a handful of names from a database and command the phone switch to set up a conference call with all of them. Pacific Bell is testing a sophisticated messaging service on 300 wireless-phone customers in San Diego. It answers incoming phone calls, screens them, and automatically routes them to wherever you are—a conference room, your home office, or a shopping mall. For a richer media experience, many companies are concentrating on desktop video-conferencing products from Intel, C-Phone, and VDOnet, among others. These products are very cost-efficient and price-compatible.

- Asynchronous transfer mode. ATM carrier services are still expensive. Originally developed by Bell Laboratories for high-speed voice networks, ATM has now been adapted for data applications. They are able to move data at 155 mb/s, whereas advanced modems top out at 56 kb/s. The Defense Department uses a fiberoptic ATM network between the United States and Germany. The Mayo Clinic in Rochester, Minnesota, uses ATM for "telemedicine"—doctors can videoconference with patients. ATM switches account for an estimated savings of $200,000 per month for the American Petroleum Institution, which uses this tool to transmit drilling-site data over satellite. This technology is moving quickly into the public phone network, which increases the speed of the global communications network.

- Residential gateways will let customers plug in telecom carriers and cable companies' networks and give users more control.

Increased competition makes it hard to make money by selling unlimited online access. Service providers have to upgrade their equipment to handle higher modem speeds and install separate equipment and phone lines for rival technologies. Sales of new modems are expected to be huge, driven by the Internet boom. AOL signed a deal with U.S. Robotics, which was scheduled to start turning on telephone access numbers on February 27, 1997, to give subscribers log-on access at a faster speed. Currently, the only high-speed (56 kb/s) modems that America Online customers can use are made by U.S. Robotics, which now controls a quarter of the market. Modems from the Open 56K Forum Group—available in March 1997—cannot talk to those of U.S. Robotics. Most of the Open 56K Group will have modems out in March 1997. U.S. Robotics has dominated the market; thus it appears that AOL chose well. The number 2 modem maker, Hayes Microcomputer Products, Inc., registered more than 40,000 people for a deal it offered on the company's Web page: Customers can get their high-speed modems

for $99 by sending in any brand modem. U.S. Robotics sells its superfast modems for $199 for a version that is installed into the computer or $239 for an external model.

Use of the Net has increased dramatically the demand for techies. An estimated 760,000 people are working for Net-related companies alone. The Internet is full of companies' ads wanting programmers. A new study by the Information Technology Association of America estimates that 190,000 "infotech" jobs stand vacant in U.S. companies—half in the information industry. The situation can get worse, because the number of college students in computer science has fallen 43 percent in the past decade. Net-related companies are spending millions of dollars recruiting employees. In 1996, pay for infotech workers rose by 12 percent to 20 percent, while average annual pay for software architects rose to $85,600.

The on-line services market is highly competitive. Major direct competitors include Prodigy Services Company, a joint venture of International Business Machines Corp. and Sears, Roebuck and Co.; e-World, a service of Apple Computer, Inc.; GEnie, a division of General Electric Information Services; Delphi Internet Services Corporation, a division of News Corp.; Interchange, a service of AT&T Corp.; and Microsoft Corp., which launched its on-line service under the name Microsoft Network. Microsoft has been devoting considerable resources and energy to focus the firm and its products squarely on the Internet. The Internet directory services are another source of competition, including NETCOM On-Line Communication Services, Inc., Bolt, Beranek & Newman, Inc., Performance System International, UUNET Technologies with Internet MCI, Yahoo, Inc., Excite, Inc., Infoseek Corporation, and Lycos, Inc. Finally, software providers such as Intuit, Inc., and Netscape Communication Corporation are another category of competitors.

America Online is by far the largest on-line service, with 10 million American members as of 1997. CompuServe was the second largest service prior to AOL acquiring it. The Microsoft Network is the second largest online service, with 2.3 million subscribers. But a great deal of the competition comes from the small local Internet providers, who were the catalyst that drove AOL to the flat-rate pricing plan.

The imperatives for global communications look very promising. Telecom and data networks should become a lifeline for nations, businesses, and individuals. The Internet is pushing world financial markets and the flow of goods and services. The Net has the potential to revolutionize business and human lives, but it also has the danger that the network can be a vehicle of isolation. Communication by fax, modem, wireless handset, videoconferencing, or telecommuting can create personal isolation. A high-tech world may need to be counterbalanced by community, family, and person-to-person contacts.

The Internet and more advanced computing, plus training for people to understand and participate in the network, have obvious educational potential.

THE FLAT-RATE DEBACLE

Through December 31, 1994, America Online's standard monthly membership fee for its service, which included 5 hours of services, was $9.95, with a $3.50 hourly fee for usage in excess of 5 hours per month. Effective January 1, 1995, the hourly fee for usage in excess of 5 hours per month decreased from $3.50 to $2.95, while the monthly membership fee remained the same.

In October 1995, AOL launched its Internet Service, Global Network Navigator (GNN), which was aimed at consumers who wanted a full-featured Internet-based service but without the full-service quality of AOL. The monthly fee for GNN was $14.95. This fee included 20 hours of service per month with a $1.95 hourly fee for usage in excess of 20 hours per month. In May 1996, AOL announced an additional pricing plan, which was oriented to its heavier users and called Value Plan. It became

effective July 1, 1966, and included 20 hours of services for $19.95 per month with a $2.95 hourly fee for usage in excess of 20 hours per month.

AOL usage increased dramatically when the company announced its plans to offer flat-rate unlimited pricing in October 1996. AOL switched its more than 7 million members to unlimited access for $19.95 a month. Its network was deluged by subscribers, many of whom could not log onto the system during peak evening hours or on weekends. Exhibit D shows comparative data before and after this new pricing policy.

Following the second shutdown of its system in January 1997, the company's chairman and CEO, Steve Case, emphasized that AOL took full responsibility for the "busy signals":

> When we decided . . . to introduce unlimited use pricing, we were well aware that usage would increase substantially. We did some consumer testing and operations modeling to generate usage forecasts, and we began building extra capacity in advance of the December launch of unlimited pricing. We thought that there would be some problems with busy signals during our peak periods in some cities. . . . But we expected those problems to be modest, and not too long in duration.

AOL has tried to decrease the "busy signal" by increasing the size and pace of the system capacity expansion by bringing in new hardware, installing circuits, adding 150,000 new modems, increasing the number of customer service representatives to 4000, offering a toll-free line, and reducing marketing efforts. Mr. Case even asked the customers for help by moderating their own use of AOL during peak hours.

EXHIBIT D

AOL System Use Before and After Flat-Rate Pricing

Average AOL	January 1997	September 1996
Member daily usage	32 minutes	14 minutes
Daily sessions	10 million	6 million
Total hours daily	4.2 million	1.5 million
Total hours per month	125 million (est.), (Dec.: 102 million)	45 million
Peak simultaneous usage	260,000	140,000
Average minutes per session	26 minutes	16 minutes

Even so, AOL became fodder for comics and lawsuits. In one comic strip, the customer is shown on the telephone conversing with "customer service":

Caller: "I am not getting my money's worth with your online service."

Service: "Good news, sir! We have just cut our rates."

Caller: "Your lines are always busy. . . . I can't get online!"

Service: "Don't forget you get unlimited time online for no extra charge."

A number of AOL customers filed lawsuits against the company in more than 37 states, charging the firm with civil fraud, breach of contract, negligence, and violation of state consumer-protection statutes. The negative publicity from the "busy signals" allowed other online providers the opportunity to expand their number of subscribers and increase their revenues from advertising and merchandising fees.

America Online began a refund offer to its members, and the attorneys general in several states agreed to support its proposed plan to members. The plan involved the following refund policy: Customers had a choice of a free month online or up to $39.90—the cost of 2 months of its unlimited service. In addition, AOL increased customer service staffing to handle member cancellations so that calls were answered within 2 minutes. Also, AOL gave customers the opportunity to cancel their membership through mail, fax, or toll-free number.

In the meantime America Online was facing another legal problem, this time from its shareholders. On February 24, 1997, shareholders sued in U.S. District Court in Virginia alleging that AOL directors and outside accountants violated securities laws in the way the company did its accounting. The online giant took a $385 million charge in October 1996, for marketing expenses it had capitalized.

The various problems facing America Online raised serious doubts among analysts about its ability to meet its goal to earn $60 million in fiscal year 1998 (ending in June) without more revenues from sources outside of operations. An analyst with Smith, Barney & Company believed that the $1.7 billion company had a cash flow problem that could force AOL to raise cash through bank loans or another stock offering—which would be the company's fourth. "The worst time to go to the market is when you need to," notes Abe Mastbaum, money manager of American Securities.

Prior to 1997, AOL was able to maintain its positive cash flow through the addition of new members. Due to overload of the system, brought on by flat-rate pricing, new members cannot be added as aggressively as needed. The company will have to develop new sources of revenue, such as on-line advertising and fees on electronic transfers, or charge additional fees for premium channels. AOL launched its first premium channel in July of 1997. Its premium games channel allows people from around the world to play both traditional games, such as hearts, and new games against each other. It charges $2 per hour for the premium games channel.

Since AOL did not have the infrastructure in place to handle the increased usage that came with the revised pricing structure, America Online planned to hold its membership at 8 million and spend $350 million to expand system capacity and customer support. Then a large acquisition substantially changed system capacity.

In April 1997, rumors were heard about AOL acquiring CompuServe from WorldCom. America Online declined to comment. CompuServe said the company is in "external discussions" regarding a deal. Buying CompuServe would add much-needed network capacity to AOL's strained system. These speculations gave a boost to both companies' stock: CompuServe's shares jumped 12 percent to $11; AOL's stock was up 7.6 percent to $45.75. A month before, CompuServe Corp. had quietly cut 500 jobs, or 14 percent of its workforce, which was the latest evidence of the on-line company's troubles as it lost members in an intense competition with America Online and other rivals. The cuts left CompuServe's home office in Columbus, Ohio, with about 3200 employees who were primarily on-line content and service specialists. At the same time, CompuServe posted a $14 million quarterly loss, and 3 days later the company's president and chief executive, Robert J. Massey, resigned. In September 1997, AOL bought CompuServe.

CompuServe was acquired in exchange for AOL's ANS Communications Subsidiary. AOL also received $175 million in cash. This added 100,000 modems to AOL's system for the short term. AOL also received long-term network commitments from WorldCom. AOL expected that the exchange would allow it to focus on its core assets—AOL Networks and AOL Studios. CompuServe would be retained as a brand name with continued marketing to small business and professional markets but with AOL's expanded content and ease of use. The companies plan to collaborate on the future development of a broadband communications network, as opposed to the current narrow-band network that consists mainly of telephone lines.

Philip Morris, Inc. ("Big Mo"): The Consumer Brand Powerhouse Plans Its Future (2001)

This case was prepared by Carol H. Anderson, Crummer Graduate School of Business, Rollins College, and Alexander T. Wood, Educational Foundations, College of Education, University of Central Florida.

Abstract: This case describes the challenges faced by a successful multi-national leading consumer products company when its lawfully marketed adult products are met with legal, ethical, and social responsibility concerns by the public. Philip Morris Companies Inc. must develop strategies for profitable long-term corporate growth across all subsidiaries, while dealing with tobacco litigation and anti-smoking sentiments.

Hal, a hypothetical college student, is feeling hungry and is ready to take a break from studying. He looks in his refrigerator and kitchen cabinets for a likely repast. What do you think he sees? In his refrigerator he finds Cracker Barrel cheese, Oscar Mayer wieners, Claussen pickles, and Miracle Whip salad dressing. There are also several bottles of Icehouse, Red Dog, and Miller High Life beer. Hal's freezer contains a DiGiorno pizza with pepperoni. In his kitchen cabinet he spots Jell-O pudding mix, a package of Kool-Aid drink mix, and an open can of Maxwell House coffee. He finds a Toblerone chocolate bar hidden behind a box of Grape-Nuts cereal, and notices a Taco Bell dinner kit and a box of Kraft macaroni and cheese. Finally, he spies a half-empty pack of Marlboro cigarettes on the kitchen table.

This case was prepared as a basis for class discussion rather than as an illustration of either effective or ineffective handling of the situation. The case study is based on company communications and publications, published documents, and public sources, without direct input from management. All rights reserved to the authors. Reprinted by permission of the authors.

We are not sure which food or beverage will appeal to Hal in this situation, or what his attitude toward smoking might be. However, we do know that all of these products and many more are among the extensive food, beverage, and tobacco products offered to the consumer market by the multinational corporation that is the focus of this case study: The Philip Morris Companies Inc.

PHILIP MORRIS COMPANIES, INC.

Geoffrey Bible, chairman of the board and CEO of Philip Morris Companies Inc., told shareholders at the company's annual meeting on April 26, 2001:[1]

> "...Philip Morris entered 2001 with momentum and expects 'solid results again this year.' Our strategies have served us well, and we intend to stay the course and adhere to them as our guideposts for the future.... Our corporate infrastructure is powerful and sound, and we are successfully managing our litigation challenges

EXHIBIT I

Philip Morris Companies Inc.

Delivering on Our Promise...
...to Be the Most Successful Consumer Products Company in the World

Philip Morris has been guided for many years by a number of fundamental strategies that drive our growth, our profitability and our vision for the future. Together, these strategies enable us to continue delivering on our promise:

✓ To invest in the development, retention and motivation of our talented employees, and to provide a workplace where creativity, respect and diversity are valued and encouraged.

✓ To conduct our businesses as a responsible manufacturer and marketer of consumer products, including those intended for adults.

✓ To profitably grow our worldwide tobacco, food and beer businesses.

✓ To reinvest in our businesses and brands and meet the changing demands of consumers through innovation and new product development.

✓ To pursue a disciplined program of acquisitions, while pruning businesses that no longer offer a strategic fit.

✓ To enhance shareholder value through a balanced program of dividends and share repurchases.

✓ To steadfastly safeguard our credit rating.

✓ To successfully manage our litigation challenges and play an active and constructive role in regulatory issues.

Source: Philip Morris Companies Inc., *2000 Annual Report*, Inside front cover.

and we are changing the way we conduct our businesses in concert with societal expectations."

Mr. Bible expressed confidence in the future, with growth coming from adherence to a set of fundamental strategies. (See Exhibit 1.) He also stated "that both Philip Morris Incorporated (PM USA) and Philip Morris International (PMI) are reaching out to critics and others regarding regulation of tobacco products. Mr. Bible also said that the company is looking forward to taking part in the process of creating a new and rational regulatory environment for the manufacture, sale, and marketing of cigarettes— one that addresses health issues while respecting the principle of freedom of choice among adults."

The big question on the minds of many shareholders, financial analysts, and others is whether Philip Morris Companies Inc. can continue its history of growth across all divisions in the face of tobacco litigation and a growing anti-smoking culture.

Philip Morris Companies Inc. (or "Big MO" as it is known on Wall Street) is the world's largest manufacturer and marketer of consumer packaged goods, and is ranked in the top ten in net income in the *Fortune* 500 listing of U.S. companies. This corporate powerhouse has one of the most valuable portfolios of premium brands in the entire consumer packaged goods industry. Although many people associate the Philip Morris name with only the tobacco industry (and with the issues faced by the tobacco industry over the past several decades), this is but one of the company's major product lines. The company's extensive food (Kraft) and beer (Miller) businesses also consist of an impressive array of leading global brands. In 2000, revenues for the combined tobacco, food, and beer subsidiaries exceeded $80 billion, compared to $78 billion in 1999. Ninety-one of the company's brands (including 16 acquired from Nabisco) each generated over $100 million in revenues. Fifteen "mega-brands" each exceeded $1 billion. Among these were: Marlboro, Kraft, Oscar Mayer, Miller Lite, Basic, L&M, Virginia Slims, Post, Parliament, Jacobs, Maxwell House, Philip Morris,

EXHIBIT 2

Philip Morris Brands (2001)

List of Products

Tobacco

- Marlboro
- Virginia Slims
- Parliament
- Merit
- Benson & Hedges
- Basic
- L&M
- Chesterfield
- Lark
- Cambridge

Selected International Brands
- Apollo Soyuz
- Bond Street
- Caro
- Diana

- f6
- Kazakstan
- Klubowe
- Longbeach
- Multifilter
- Muratti

- Peter Jackson
- Petra
- Philip Morris
- Polyot
- SG
- Vatra

Food

Chinese, Meals and Enhancers

Cheese
- Athenos
- Cheez Whiz
- Churny
- Cracker Barrel
- Deli Deluxe
- DiGiorno
- Easy Cheese
- Hoffman's
- Kraft
- Philadelphia
- Polly-O
- Velveeta

Dairy Products
- Breakstone's sour cream, cottage cheese
- Knudsen sour cream, cottage cheese
- Kraft dips
- Light n' Lively lowfat cottage cheese

Meals
- Kraft macaroni & cheese and other dinners
- Minute
- Stove Top
- Taco Bell†
- Velveeta shells & cheese

Enhancers
- A.1.
- Bull's-Eye
- Good Seasons
- Grey Poupon
- Kraft barbecue sauce, mayonnaise, salad dressings
- Miracle Whip
- Oven Fry
- Sauceworks
- Seven Seas
- Shake 'N Bake

Biscuits, Snacks and Confectionery

Cookies & Crackers
- Better Cheddars
- Cheese Nips
- Chips Ahoy!
- Handi-Snacks
- Honey Maid
- Newtons
- Nilla
- Nutter Butter
- Oreo
- Premium
- Ritz
- SnackWell's
- Stella D'oro
- Teddy Grahams
- Triscuit
- Wheat Thins

Snacks
- Cornnuts
- Planters

Pet Snacks
- Milk-Bone

Confectionery
- Altoids
- Callard & Bowser**
- Creme Savers
- Farley's
- Gummi Savers
- Jet-Puffed
- Life Savers
- Milka L'il Scoops
- Now and Later
- Sather's
- Terry's
- Tobler
- Toblerone
- Trolli

Beverages, Desserts and Cereals
Beverages
- Capri Sun†
- Country Time
- Crystal Light
- Kool-Aid
- Tang

Coffee
- General Foods
- International Coffees
- Gevalia
- Maxwell House

- Sanka
- Starbucks†
- Yuban

Desserts
- Baker's
- Balance Bar
- Breyers yogurt†
- Calumet
- Certo
- Cool Whip
- Dream Whip
- Ever-Fresh
- Handi-Snacks
- Jell-O
- Knox
- Light n' Lively lowfat yogurt
- Minute
- Sure-Jell

Cereals
- Alpha-Bits
- Banana Nut Crunch
- Blueberry Morning
- Cranberry Almond Crunch
- Cream of Wheat
- Cream of Rice
- Fruit & Fibre
- Golden Crisp
- Grape-Nuts
- Great Grains
- Honey Bunches of Oats
- Honeycomb
- Oreo O's
- Pebbles†
- Raisin Bran
- Shredded Wheat
- Toasties
- Waffle Crisp

Oscar Mayer and Pizza
Meats
- Louis Rich
- Louis Rich Carving Board
- Lunchables
- Oscar Mayer

Meat Alternatives
- Boca

Pickles and Sauerkraut
- Claussen

Pizza
- California Pizza Kitchen†
- DiGiorno
- Jack's
- Tombstone

Selected International Brands*
Snacks
- Aladdin
- Artic
- Cerealitas
- Chips Ahoy!
- Club Social
- Côte d'Or
- Daim
- Diamante Negro
- Estrella
- Express
- Figaro
- Freia
- Guayabita
- Korono
- Lacta
- Laka
- Lucky
- Maarud
- Marbu
- Marabou
- Merries
- Milan
- Milka
- Oreo
- Ouro Branco
- Pacific Soda
- Peanøtt
- Planters
- Poiana
- Prince Polo
- Rhodesia
- Ritz
- Royal
- Shot
- Sonho de Valsa
- Suchard
- Sugus
- Tapita
- Terrabusi
- Terry's
- Trakinas
- Toblerone
- Tita

Coffee
- Blendy
- Carte Noire
- Dadak
- Gevalia
- Grand' Mère
- Kaffee HAG
- Jacobs Krönung
- Jacobs Milea
- Jacobs Monarch
- Jacques Vabre
- Kenco
- Maxim
- Maxwell
- Nabob
- Onko
- Saimaza
- Splendid

Powdered Soft Drinks
- Clight
- Fresh
- Frisco
- Kool-Aid
- Mañanita
- Q-Refres-Ko
- Ki-Suco
- Royal
- Tang
- Verao

Cheese
- Dairylea
- Eden
- El Caserio
- Invernizzi
- Kraft Cracker Barrel
- Kraft Lindenberger
- Kraft Singles
- Kraft Sottilette
- Mama Luise
- Philadelphia
- P'tit Québec

Convenient Meals and Grocery
- Dairylea Lunchables
- Fleischmann's
- Kraft Delissiopizza
- Kraft Lunchables
- Kraft ketchup
- Kraft peanut butter
- Kraft pourables
- Magic Moments
- Miracle Whip
- Mirácoli
- Simmenthal
- Vegemite

Beer

- Miller Lite
- Miller Genuine Draft
- Miller Genuine Draft Light
- Miller High Life
- Miller High Life Light
- Milwaukee's Best
- Milwaukee's Best Light
- Icehouse
- Foster's†
- Red Dog
- Southpaw Light
- Leinenkugel's
- Henry Weinhard's
- Henry's Hard Lemonade
- Hamm's
- Mickey's
- Olde English 800
- Magnum
- Presidente
- Sharp's non-alcohol brew

*Not generally available in the U.S.   **International products available in some specialty stores and supermarkets.   †Licensed trademark.
Source: Philip Morris Companies, Inc., *2001 Fact Book.*

Philadelphia, and Merit. Marlboro, one of the world's best-selling consumer packaged products, had sales of $30 billion in 1999.[2] (See Exhibit 2 for a listing of major Philip Morris brands.)

The company's production and marketing efforts are supported by an extensive network of manufacturing plants and distribution channels throughout the world, thus enabling it to meet consumer demand quickly in each of the markets in which it operates. Philip Morris subsidiaries operate in nearly 200 countries, and employ 137,000 people worldwide.[3]

Philip Morris has a major impact on many aspects of the global economy. The company is the largest purchaser of U.S.-grown tobacco, and leads all other consumer packaged goods companies in the world in the purchase of dairy products, grains, wheat, poultry, coffee, cocoa, and sugar. The company's economic impact is felt in other areas as well. Philip Morris is a major U.S. taxpayer, and a major contributor to profitable business transactions in other industries. In 2000, the company generated nearly $15 billion in taxes,[4] making it one of the largest taxpayers in the U.S. A recent study indicates that the total combined economic impact of Philip Morris and its thousands of U.S. business partners reached over $55 billion in the U.S. (in addition to its overseas economic impact). The company and its business partners in agriculture, construction, wholesale and retail trade, transportation, utilities, insurance and real estate, and other industries together generated over 490,000 jobs in the U.S., and $11 billion in wages, benefits and other compensation.[5]

PHILIP MORRIS 2000 ANNUAL MEETING OF STOCKHOLDERS

Geoffrey C. Bible, Chairman of the Board and Chief Executive Officer of Philip Morris Companies Inc. opened the 2000 Annual Meeting of Stockholders on April 27, 2000, with this statement[6] (see Exhibit 3 for company press release concerning this meeting):

> ...First I would like to make it clear that while 1999 was a year of transition, our businesses came through the year in very good shape and we are beginning 2000 with strong momentum across all our operating companies.

Unfortunately, the performance of our stock has not reflected this strength. I know that you are all deeply concerned about this situation. The Board and I share your concern.

Clearly, the primary reason for the low stock price is investor concern about the legal challenges and societal perceptions surrounding the domestic tobacco industry. I am convinced that these concerns are based on an extremely pessimistic reading of our company's situation. When you examine the facts, the story is quite compelling. Yes, we are facing a lot of litigation. However, the litigation environment has improved in significant ways since we last met.

Mr. Bible cited a number of reasons for his optimism regarding the litigation that plagued the company's tobacco business during the previous year:[7]

- A positive trend in class-action suit dismissals, for a total of 23 cases brought against Philip Morris in the U.S.—representing the overwhelming majority of decisions in these cases.

- Juries found in favor of the defense in six individual smoking and health lawsuits tried in 1999.

- The jury voted unanimously in favor of the Company in the Ohio *Iron Workers* case. (As of the date of the Stockholders Meeting, this is the only case concerning a third-party payor to proceed to a jury verdict.)

- Lawsuits brought by other third-party payors of healthcare costs were rejected by five federal circuit courts of appeal, and numerous cases were dismissed at the trial court level. The U.S. Supreme Court turned down a request by labor funds to review three of these decisions, and rejected the FDA's attempt to regulate tobacco.

- An important source of litigation risk to Philip Morris was removed with the Tobacco Settlement reached with the State Attorneys General in 1998.

Counteracting these successes, the *Engle* class-action case in Florida dominated the attention of investment analysts and others at the time of the 2000 Annual Stockholders Meeting, because of the magnitude of potential punitive damage awards and their impact on industry stocks.[8] In addition, Mr. Bible noted that another source of investor concern is a lawsuit brought by the Clinton

EXHIBIT 3

Philip Morris Annual Shareholders Meeting (2000)

Philip Morris Companies, Inc., Press Release (April 27, 2000)

PHILIP MORRIS
COMPANIES INC.
120 PARK AVENUE, NEW YORK, NY. 10017

FOR IMMEDIATE RELEASE

PHILIP MORRIS HOLDS 2000 ANNUAL MEETING

Chairman Says Company Has Strong Business Momentum Going Forward Notes

Improved Litigation Environment

Notes Improved Litigation Environment

Reaffirms Commitment To "Constructive Engagement" With The Public

RICHMOND, Va., April 27, 2000

Geoffrey C. Bible, chairman of the board and chief executive officer of Philip Morris Companies Inc. (NYSE: MO), told an audience of approximately 1,100 shareholders at the company's annual meeting today that Philip Morris "came through the year in very good shape" in a "litigation environment that has improved in significant ways." He also reaffirmed the company's commitment to "engage in a constructive dialogue" with the company's critics as well as the general public.

Mr. Bible opened the meeting by noting that "while 1999 was a year of transition," the company performed well during the year and "we are beginning 2000 with strong momentum across all of our operating companies." He acknowledged that "unfortunately, the performance of our stock has not reflected this strength."

Mr. Bible attributed the company's low stock price primarily to "investor concern about the legal challenges and societal perceptions surrounding the domestic tobacco industry. Highlighting improvements in the litigation environment, he cited a number of favorable legal developments during the year, as well as the 1998 Tobacco Settlement Agreement with the State Attorneys General, which removed a significant source of litigation risk to the company.

Despite these successes, Mr. Bible said that two lawsuits, the Engle class-action case in Florida and the Department of Justice suit to recover health care costs, have "added to investor concerns." He noted that the Engle case is now proceeding to the next phase, and that the Department of Justice suit is one in which "we believe we have a good chance of prevailing" if the case proceeds to trial.

Mr. Bible emphasized that Philip Morris is "ready and eager to engage in a constructive dialogue about strong, meaningful and reasonable regulation of cigarettes." He said that the company wants to be "at the table and part of the process of creating a regulatory framework that is fair for smokers, the general public and for the industry."

Administration's Department of Justice. The purpose of this lawsuit is to recover Medicare costs paid out by the U.S. government for alleged tobacco-related illnesses.

PHILIP MORRIS 2001 ANNUAL MEETING OF STOCKHOLDERS

Mr. Geoffrey Bible reported positive financial and strategic results for the year 2000. In addition to portions of this speech that were included at the beginning of the case, Mr. Bible discussed (among other topics) the following themes that underlie expectations of growth in 2001 and beyond:[9]

- Continued development of talented employees around the world.
- People of Philip Morris work to make a difference in their communities.
- Continued growth in businesses and increased earning per share.
- Completed acquisition of Nabisco, and integration of Nabisco with Kraft worldwide.
- IPO of common stock for Kraft Foods, reinvestment in businesses and brands.
- Progress in aligning global businesses to meet high expectations of society (including "reasonable and practical" positions regarding tobacco regulation, and leadership in food safety).
- Favorable actions concerning the litigation environment (Engle verdict appeal, dismissed cases, and other legal actions).
- Continued social responsibility emphasis.

HISTORICAL HIGHLIGHTS OF A GROWING FAMILY OF BRANDS

The corporate timeline of the Philip Morris Company's business growth began in 1847 when Philip Morris, Esq., a tobacconist and importer of fine cigars, opened a shop on Bond Street in London. The histories of many other companies that eventually became part of Philip Morris' consumer brands in the tobacco, food, and beer industries have evolved simultaneously over the past century and

a half. As stated in the Corporate Timeline published by the Company, "The key to our past has been the power of our brands and the energy and creativity of our people. Our success in the years ahead will depend on continuing that legacy."[10] This legacy includes the following selected corporate highlights:

- Mid-1800s—Philip Morris establishes Bond Street shop in London.
- 1902—Philip Morris & Co., Ltd. is incorporated in New York.
- 1919—The U.S. Philip Morris Company is acquired by a new company owned by U.S. stockholders, and incorporated in Virginia under the name of Philip Morris & Co. Ltd., Inc.
- 1929—Philip Morris begins manufacturing its own cigarettes by purchasing a factory in Richmond, Virginia.
- Mid-1950s—Philip Morris & Co. Ltd, Inc. acquires Benson & Hedges, sets up first affiliate outside U.S. (Australia), sets up an overseas division, introduces the Marlboro brand with a special filter in a flip-top box.
- 1960s—Organizes as three operating companies to manage the business of Philip Morris Incorporated; 1968 operating revenues top $1 billion.
  - The Surgeon General issues report on Smoking and Health.
  - Tobacco industry creates advertising code (voluntary agreement not to promote cigarettes to young people, and to avoid implying that cigarettes have health or social benefits).
  - U.S. Federal Cigarette Labeling Act (1966) takes effect to require warning label on all cigarette packages.
- 1970s—Acquires 100% each of Miller Brewing Company, Mission Viejo Company, and the Seven-Up Company, and the international cigarette business of the Liggett Group Inc.
  - TV and radio cigarette advertising ban takes effect in 1971.
  - Miller Brewing Company introduces Miller Lite nationally to create a new beer category.
- 1980s—In 1980 Philip Morris celebrates its 125th anniversary; revenues are nearly $10

billion, and grow to nearly $45 billion by 1989, largely through acquisitions.

- More changes in the corporate structure, and Philip Morris Credit Corporation is incorporated.

- Philip Morris acquires General Foods Corporation (1985) and Kraft (1988)—later to be renamed Kraft General Foods (KGF), the largest U.S. food company; sells most of Philip Morris Industrial, Seven-Up International and Seven-Up Canada, and the U.S. franchise business of Seven-Up.

- General Foods forms three separate operating companies: General Foods, USA; General Foods, Coffee & International; and Oscar Mayer Foods; also buys Freihofer Baking Company.

- Miller Brewing Company introduces Miller Genuine Draft and Sharp's (nonalcoholic), and acquires Jacob Leinenkugel Brewing Company.

- 1990s—Philip Morris acquires Jacobs Suchard AG, Swiss-based coffee and confectionery company.

  - KGF introduces seven categories of fat-free products; acquires Capri Sun, Inc. and Jack's Frozen Pizza; completes purchase of U.S. and Canadian ready-to-eat cold cereal businesses of RJR Nabisco; and acquires foreign confectionery manufacturers while expanding existing brands.

- 1998—U.S. tobacco industry settlement with the Attorney Generals of 46 states—payout of $206 billion over 25 years for tobacco-related claims and lawsuits; agreement includes advertising and marketing restrictions.

- 1999—Corporate communications initiatives include launching of corporate online website at http://www.philipmorris.com.

  - 1999 revenues are over $78 billion, and operating companies income reaches $15.2 billion.

- 2000—Kraft Foods acquires Balance Bar and Boca Burger.

  - Litigation issues continue in the tobacco industry.

  - August 2000—World Health Organization investigators claim that for many years Philip Morris and other multinational cigarette

manufacturers have systematically attempted to discredit the agency and undermine its global anti-smoking efforts.[11]

- December 2000—Philip Morris acquires all outstanding shares of Nabisco Group Holdings Corp. for $19.2 billion (to be combined with Kraft Foods, Inc.).[12]

- June 2000—Philip Morris Companies Inc. and Kraft Foods, Inc. issued an initial public offering (IPO) of 280 million shares of Kraft Foods Inc. stock. (This financial move was designed to help the company pay down the debt incurred with the purchase of Nabisco, and to overcome some of the investors' negative sentiment due to ongoing liability in tobacco lawsuits.)[13]

CURRENT SITUATION AT PHILIP MORRIS: CIRCA 2000

Litigation

Philip Morris Companies Inc.'s food and beer industry businesses are enjoying tremendous growth and success. However, litigation and health and social concerns related to smoking plague the financial and marketing successes of the tobacco business. Legal battles against the tobacco industry started in 1954 with a tobacco liability lawsuit brought by a lung cancer victim (case was dropped 13 years later). In 1964 the Surgeon General released reports stating that smoking causes lung cancer. The pace and pressure of lawsuits escalated in the 1990s, along with tighter restrictions on the marketing of cigarettes—particularly to the nation's youth. Tobacco companies face legal battles in the form of class action suits, suits by individuals, federal claims, and insurer and third-party claims.[14]

Perhaps the most famous tobacco litigation is the Engle case in Florida, which was appealed by Philip Morris. In June 2001, a Los Angeles jury awarded a $3 billion verdict to a 56-year-old man with lung cancer. Philip Morris said it would appeal the verdict if the trial judge did not overturn it. Many other claims have been rejected in favor of the company and the industry. While there are legal challenges against tobacco companies throughout the world (including actions by the World Health Organization), Philip Morris believes it has shown that litigation is manageable over time, and that the company can remain profitable.

Corporate Communications

Philip Morris Companies Inc. launched a new long-term corporate communications initiative in 1999. This ongoing program, entitled *Working to Make a Difference: The People of Philip Morris,* is designed to tell the public "who we are and what we do." As stated in the 1999 Annual Report: "This domestic communications program is reinforced by a policy of 'constructive engagement' worldwide, which commits us to engaging the media, government, the public and our critics to seek constructive solutions to the issues surrounding our businesses." This includes advertising, education and community partnership and outreach, and active participation with governments, schools, parents, civic groups, and distributors, wholesalers, retailers and suppliers. A major part of the initiative is the Philip Morris Web site, launched in 1999, to enable the company to communicate with the public about its company and products over the Internet.[15] This site includes links to a number of national and worldwide health organizations, such as the World Health Organization, the American Cancer Society, the U.S. Centers for Disease Control and Prevention, and the U.S. Surgeon General.[16]

Social Responsibility

Philip Morris Companies Inc. is actively involved in philanthropy, and has been one of the world's most generous corporate philanthropists for more than four decades. The company has supported programs in the areas of food and hunger; AIDS awareness and treatment; prevention of domestic violence and shelter for victims, humanitarian aid, and the arts. In response to concerns related to smoking, the company has committed major resources to youth smoking prevention (over 100 programs in 60 countries), and is addressing drunk driving and underage drinking issues through education and community involvement.

The company follows a set of environmental principles that are designed to reduce a negative impact on the environment and sustain the world's natural resources, while providing quality products for consumers. For example, Miller Brewing Company has used resources more efficiently by reducing the consumption of water and electricity, and lowering wastewater discharge. Kraft Foods North America recycles or reuses more than 90 percent of its total solid waste and by-products. Packaging has been improved for the company's brands through reduced package size and the use of recycled materials. Performance is measured regularly for these and other environmental efforts.[17]

For many consumers, social responsibility issues related to the tobacco and beer industries include both corporate and individual responsibility. The dilemma is magnified when a company sells legal products in a quasi-regulated environment. In the Philip Morris Companies Inc. 2000 Annual Report, CEO Geoffrey Bible describes the company's proactive programs for prevention of youth smoking, underage drinking, and drunk driving. Mr. Bible states: "Let me make it clear that we do not want youth to smoke, we do not market our products to youth and we are fully committed to making a difference on this issue." He further states: "It is a fact, however, that a large part of our business involves selling adult products. And we continue to believe very strongly that adults have a right to choose to use tobacco and beer products, just as they have the freedom to make a range of choices in their lives."[18]

FINANCIAL CONDITION: CONSOLIDATED AND BY SUBSIDIARIES

Philip Morris Companies Inc. has enjoyed steady growth for over 150 years, primarily through strategic acquisitions in growth categories, and strong brand equity throughout the world. In spite of legal issues in the tobacco industry, all company subsidiaries have prospered. Although the company met its earnings-per-share growth target for 1999 and 2000, stock performance was a disappointment—primarily attributable to litigation. Year 1999 and 2000 financial results are presented in Exhibits 4 and 5, including both a consolidated statement and results by business segment.

EXHIBIT 4

2000 Financial Highlights

Philip Morris Companies, Inc. 2000 Annual Report

(in millions of dollars, except per share data)

Consolidated Results

	Reported			Underlying		
	2000	1999	% Change	2000	1999	% Change
Operating revenues	$80,356	$78,596	2.2%	$80,316	$77,829	3.2%
Operating companies income	16,228	14,825	9.5%	16,045	15,144	5.9%
Net earnings	8,510	7,675	10.9%	8,427	7,926	6.3%
Basic earnings per share	3.77	3.21	17.4%	3.73	3.31	12.7%
Diluted earnings per share	3.75	3.19	17.6%	3.71	3.30	12.4%
Dividends declared per share	2.02	1.84	9.8%	2.02	1.84	9.8%

Compounded Average Annual Growth Rates

	2000–1995	2000–1990	2000–1985	2000–1995	2000–1990	2000–1985
Operating revenues	4.0%	4.6%	11.3%	4.0%	4.6%	11.3%
Net earnings	9.3%	9.2%	13.6%	9.0%	9.1%	13.5%
Basic earnings per share	11.7%	11.4%	15.4%	11.3%	11.3%	15.3%
Diluted earnings per share	11.8%	11.4%	15.4%	11.4%	11.3%	15.3%

Results by Business Segment

	Reported			Underlying		
	2000	1999	% Change	2000	1999	% Change
Tobacco						
Domestic						
Operating revenues	$22,658	$19,596	15.6%	$22,658	$19,596	15.6%
Operating companies income	5,350	4,865	10.0%	5,350	5,048	6.0%
International						
Operating revenues	26,374	27,506	(4.1%)	26,503	27,377	(3.2%)
Operating companies income	5,211	4,968	4.9%	5,270	5,045	4.5%
Food						
North American						
Operating revenues	$18,461	$17,897	3.2%	$18,522	$17,801	4.1%
Operating companies income	3,547	3,190	11.2%	3,570	3,312	7.8%

(continued)

EXHIBIT 4 *(continued)*

2000 Financial Highlights
Philip Morris Companies, Inc. 2000 Annual Report

	Reported			Underlying		
	2000	**1999**	**% Change**	**2000**	**1999**	**% Change**
International						
Operating revenues	8,071	8,900	(9.3%)	7,966	8,547	(6.8%)
Operating companies income	1,208	1,063	13.6%	1,050	996	5.4%
Beer						
Operating revenues	$4,375	$4,342	0.8%	$4,250	$4,153	2.3%
Operating companies income	650	511	27.2%	543	515	5.4%
Financial Services						
Operating revenues	$417	$355	17.5%	$417	$355	17.5%
Operating companies income	262	228	14.9%	262	228	14.9%
Total						
Operating revenues	$80,356	$78,596	2.2%	$80,316	$77,829	3.2%
Operating companies income	16,228	14,825	9.5%	16,045	15,144	5.9%

Notes:
Underlying results reflect the results of our business operations, excluding significant one-time items for employee separation programs, write-downs of property, plant and equipment, sales made in advance of the century date change and gains on sales of businesses. Underlying operating revenues and operating companies income also exclude the results of businesses that have been sold.
Operating revenues and operating companies income for 1999 have been restated to reflect the transfer of managerial responsibility for Mexico and Puerto Rico to North American food from international food.
Source: Philip Morris Companies Inc., *2000 Annual Report,* p.1.

In August, 2000, Goldman Sachs analysts predicted that shares of Philip Morris "could 'nearly triple in two years' if the company follows through with the 2001 partial spin-off of its Kraft foods operations, and if aggravated claims cases disappear."[19] The success of the Kraft IPO and acquisition of Nabisco should help this prediction become a reality.

PHILIP MORRIS MANAGEMENT FACES THE CHALLENGE OF THE FUTURE WHILE DEALING WITH THE PAST

Philip Morris plans to drive future growth by taking advantage of its strengths and key business strategies, including:[20]

1. Developing new products consistent with emerging consumer trends.

2. Building leadership position in key categories.

3. Creating opportunities in new, high-growth categories through strategic acquisitions and partnerships.

4. Driving businesses at retail through superior marketing expertise and sales execution.

5. Improving margins by lowering costs.

6. Generating growth and enhancing efficiency by capitalizing on new technology.

Senior management of Philip Morris Companies Inc. and its major subsidiaries in the food, beer, and tobacco industries are faced with a number of related decisions. They must determine both short- and long-term strategies that will help the company achieve the six corporate objectives listed above, as well as the expectations of financial analysts and stockholders for higher stock prices. The outcomes of these

EXHIBIT 5

Philip Morris, Inc. 2001 Second Quarter Fact Sheet

Consolidated Financial Review
(in millions, except per share data)

	Second Quarter	
Reported Selected Earnings Highlights	2001	2000
Operating revenues	$23,188	$20,844
Cost of sales	8,599	7,517
Excise taxes on products	4,319	4,421
Operating companies income[A]	4,626	4,131
Earnings before income taxes and minority interest	3,766	3,587
Net earnings	2,288	2,171
Basic EPS	1.04	0.96
Diluted EPS	1.03	0.95

[A]Operating companies income is income before amortization of goodwill, general corporate expenses, minority interest, interest and other debt expense, net, and income taxes.

	Operating Revenues		Operating Companies Income	
	Second Quarter		Second Quarter	
Underlying Earnings Highlights	2001	2000	2001	2000
Consolidated Totals	$23,188	$20,744	$4,626	$4,116
% of Total: Tobacco	57%	60%	59%	63%
Food	37%	33%	36%	31%
Beer	5%	6%	4%	5%
Financial Services	1%	1%	1%	1%

	2001	2000
Net earnings	$2,288	$2,171
Basic EPS	$1.04	$0.96
Diluted EPS	$1.03	$0.95

Underlying operating revenues and operating companies income exclude the results of businesses that have been sold.

	June 30,	December 31,
Balance Sheet Highlights and Ratios	2001	2000
Property, plant and equipment, net (consumer products)	$15,064	$15,303
Inventories (consumer products)	8,724	8,765
Total assets	79,467	79,067
Total debt (consumer products)	18,623	27,196
Total debt (financial services)	1,809	1,926
Stockholders' equity	19,535	15,005
Ratio of total debt to stockholders' equity	1.05 to 1	1.94 to 1
Ratio of consumer products debt to stockholders' equity	0.95 to 1	1.81 to 1
Net return on average stockholders' equity	48.5%	56.2%

(continued)

EXHIBIT 5 *(continued)*

Philip Morris, Inc. 2001 Second Quarter Fact Sheet

Cash Flow Statement Highlights	Six Months Ended June 30,	
	2001	2000
Net cash provided by operating activities	$4,626	$5,849
Capital expenditures (consumer products)	790	700
Dividends paid	2,342	2,229

Domestic Tobacco

(in millions, with % change vs. prior year)

Philip Morris Inc. (Philip Morris U.S.A.)	Second Quarter	
	2001	2000
Operating revenues	$6,425, up 12.6%	$5,706, up 20.5%
Operating companies income	$1,383, up 8.6%	$1,274, up 6.5%

International Tobacco

(in millions, with % change vs. prior year)

Philip Morris International Inc.	Second Quarter	
	2001	2000
Operating revenues	$6,753, down 0.7%	$6,801, down 1.8%
Operating companies income	$1,348, up 2.9%	$1,310, up 4.6%

North American Food

(in millions, with % change vs. prior year)

Kraft Foods North America, Inc.	Second Quarter	
	2001	2000
Operating revenues—underlying*	$6,518, up 32.9%	$4,906, up 4.1%
Operating companies income—underlying*	$1,353, up 31.6%	$1,028, up 5.9%

*Underlying operating revenues and operating companies income exclude the results of businesses that have been sold since the beginning of 2000.

During the fourth quarter of 2000, managerial responsibility for the Company's food operations in Mexico and Puerto Rico was transferred from the international food segment to the North American food segment. Prior period amounts have been reclassified to reflect the transfer.

International Food

(in millions, with % change vs. prior year)

Kraft Foods International, Inc.	Second Quarter	
	2001	2000
Operating revenues—underlying*	$2,174, up 8.2%	$2,009, down 0.4%
Operating companies income—underlying*	$ 298, up 21.6%	$ 245, up 2.9%

*Underlying operating revenues and operating companies income exclude the results of businesses that have been sold since the beginning of 2000.

During the fourth quarter of 2000, managerial responsibility for the Company's food operations in Mexico and Puerto Rico was transferred from the international food segment to the North American food segment. Prior period amounts have been reclassified to reflect the transfer.

EXHIBIT 5 *(continued)*

Philip Morris, Inc. 2001 Second Quarter Fact Sheet

Beer

(in millions, with % change vs. prior year)

	Second Quarter	
Miller Brewing Company	2001	2000
Operating revenues—underlying*	$1,207, down 0.7%	$1,215, up 4.7%
Operating companies income—underlying*	$168, down 11.6%	$190, up 14.5%

*Underlying operating revenues and operating companies income exclude the results of businesses that have been sold since the beginning of 2000.

Financial Services

(in millions, with % change vs. prior year)

	Second Quarter	
Philip Morris Capital Corporation	2001	2000
Operating revenues	$111, up 3.7%	$107, up 10.3%
Operating companies income	$ 76, up 10.1%	$ 69, up 15.0%

Source: Philip Morris Companies Inc., *2001 Fact Book.*

corporate strategies will have a significant effect on consumers, employees, stockholders, suppliers, government entities, and all other constituencies of the company.

Assuming that you are in the position of Mr. Geoffrey Bible, CEO of Philip Morris Companies Inc., what will you be prepared to say to stockholders about the company's strategies and performance at the next Annual Meeting of Stockholders?

Endnotes

1. Transcript of speech: "Remarks of Geoffrey C. Bible, Chairman of the Board and Chief Executive Officer, Philip Morris Companies, Inc., 2001 Annual Meeting of Stockholders" (April 26, 2001), Richmond, VA.
2. *Philip Morris Companies, Inc., 2000 Fact Book; Philip Morris Companies Inc., 1999 Annual Report* (February 22, 2000); *Philip Morris Companies, Inc., 2001 Fact Book; Philip Morris Companies Inc., 2000 Annual Report* (February 27, 2001).
3. *Ibid.*
4. Taxes include federal and state excise taxes; federal and state income taxes; and sales, property, payroll and other taxes.
5. Transcript of speech: "Remarks of Geoffrey C. Bible, Chairman of the Board and Chief Executive Officer, Philip Morris Companies, Inc., 2000 Annual Meeting of Stockholders" (April 27, 2000), Richmond, VA.
6. *Ibid.*
7. *Ibid.*
8. On Friday, July 14, 2000, a six-member state-court jury in Miami, Florida, ordered the tobacco industry to pay $145 billion in punitive damages to plaintiffs who sued the industry for their tobacco-related illnesses. (Geyelin, Milo and Gordon Fairclough, "Taking a Hit: Yes, $145 Billion Deals Tobacco a Huge Blow, but Not a Killing One," *Wall Street Journal* (July 17, 2000), pp. A1, A8; "Damage Award in Florida Case Took the Wind Out of Big Tobacco's New Repentance Tactic," New York Times News Service, *St. Louis Post-Dispatch* (July 16, 2000), pp. A1, A3; "$145 Billion Award Doesn't Mean End of Tobacco Industry," Associated Press, *The Southern Illinoisan* (July 16, 2000), pp. 1C, 3C.)
9. *Ibid,* 2001 Annual Meeting to Shareholders.
10. "Philip Morris Through the Years," *Corporate Timeline,* http://philipmorris.com/corporate/corp_over/timeline/index.html, and "The Philip Morris History," (1765–1987), Philip Morris Companies Inc. publication.
11. Fairclough, Gordon, "Philip Morris and Other Cigarette Firms Tried to Foil WHO, Agency's Staff Says," *Wall Street Journal* (August 2, 2000), pp. A3, A6.
12. "Philip Morris Acquires Nabisco for $55.00 Per Share in Cash and Plans for IPO of Kraft," Philip Morris Companies Inc, Press Release (June 25, 2000); *Philip Morris Companies Inc. 2001 Fact Book.*
13. Schoen, John W., "Big Appetite for Kraft Foods IPO," http://msnbc.com/news/585852.asp.
14. Geyelin, Milo and Gordon Fairclough, "Taking a Hit: Yes, $145 Billion Deals Tobacco a Huge Blow, but Not a Killing One," *Wall Street Journal* (July 17, 2000), pp. A1, A8.

15. *Philip Morris Companies Inc., 1999 Annual Report* (February 22, 2000), p. 4.

16. *Working to Make a Difference: The People of Philip Morris,* Corporate Pamphlet (More Than a Tobacco Company), Philip Morris Companies, Inc., p. 20.

17. *Working to Make a Difference: The People of Philip Morris,* Corporate Pamphlet (Environmental Principles), Philip Morris Companies, Inc.

18. *Philip Morris Companies Inc., 2000 Annual Report*, p. 4.

19. "Goldman: Tobacco Stock Valuations to Improve, MO Could Triple," *Newstraders* (August 11, 2000), Hoovers Online, http:/www.hoovers.com.

20. Letter to Shareholders from Geoffrey C. Bible, Chairman of the Board and CEO, *Philip Morris Companies Inc: 1999 Annual Report* (February 22, 2000), p. 5.

Kellogg Company

This case was prepared by Craig A. Hollingshead, W. Blaker Bolling, Richard L. Jones, and Ashli White of Marshall University.

From a news item in the *New York Times:*

> Battle Creek, January 25, 1995—Since the Kellogg Company posted fourth-quarter earnings on Friday, investors and analysts have become concerned that the company might be forced to adopt discounting measures to defend market share, weakening its profit margins. Last spring, Kellogg significantly cut back on discounting measures such as "buy one—get one free" offers on some of its best-selling cereals to lower costs and raise profits. The strategy succeeded at first, but then sales in Kellogg's core domestic cereal business fell, continuing a decline in market share that has seen Kellogg's brands go from over 40 percent of the $8 billion market in the late 1980s to 35 percent today.[1] Kellogg has assured investors that it will not reintroduce promotions. However, in response to Kellogg chairman and chief executive officer Arnold Langbo's remark that Kellogg is "extremely sensitive toward further volume decline," Kellogg shares dropped by $2.75 on Friday to close at $54.25 on the New York Stock Exchange.

Reprinted by permission of Craig A. Hollingshead.

In Battle Creek, Michigan, headquarters of Kellogg Company, Chief Executive Officer and Chairman of the Board Arnold G. Langbo reflected back on the company's performance in 1994. Although Kellogg's sales increased for the fiftieth consecutive year and earnings increased for the forty-first time in 42 years, the company did not meet its growth objectives for the year. Kellogg remained the world's leading producer of ready-to-eat cereal products and controlled 43 percent of the global market. Even though Kellogg continued to lead the industry in 1994, it faced many challenges. Langbo was concerned with how the company would reach its marketing objectives and continue leading the industry, how it could maintain profit margin, and how it might increase its stock price, which was near a 3-year low in early 1995.

THE CEREAL INDUSTRY

Cereal grains milled into breakfast cereal is an $8 billion business worldwide. The worldwide demand for ready-to-eat cereal is in a long-term upward trend. Annual per capita cereal consumption in North America is 10.3 pounds, while the world's leading consumer of cereal, Ireland, topped at 17 pounds. However, cereal for breakfast is not part of the cultural tradition in many parts of the world. For example, in Africa and Asia, per capita cereal consumption runs well below 1 pound per year, offering a great opportunity for market development. In North America and Europe, an increasing consciousness of healthy diet and nutrition needs drives increased demand among adults. U.S. annual growth is estimated at 2 to 3 percent, with worldwide growth in the 5 to 7 percent range.

Competition within the industry centers around several companies. Kellogg Company is the worldwide leader with a 35 percent U.S. market share, 43 percent worldwide. Of the 10 most popular breakfast cereals in the world, six wear a Kellogg label. The number two player, and Kellogg's primary competitor, is General Mills, with a 25 percent U.S. market share. General Mills was a messy conglomerate in the early 1980s. Since 1985, however, it has sought to focus more on cereal products. Worldwide, General Mills formed joint ventures with Nestlé (Cereal Partners Worldwide) and PepsiCo (Snack Ventures Europe). Both are relatively new, and neither of these enterprises has scored significant success. General Mills' recent performance has been marred by disappointing returns from its Big G cereal business and violations of Food and Drug Administration (FDA) regulations. Unregistered pesticide traces were found in the company's raw oat supply. Although not a particular health hazard, this disrupted General Mills' production and marketing plans. Traditionally more broadly diversified than Kellogg, General Mills had recently sold off its three restaurant chains: Red Lobster, Olive Garden, and China Coast. The company retained Betty Crocker, Gold Medal, and Yoplait Products Divisions.

Other companies seeking market share were Quaker Oats, Ralston Purina, Kraft, General Foods, and Nabisco. With a growing worldwide demand, these companies had a chance to build markets and increase profits.

KELLOGG COMPANY

Kellogg Company and its subsidiaries are involved primarily in the manufacture and marketing of con-venience foods. The main products of the company are ready-to-eat cereals, including Frosted Flakes, Corn Flakes, Apple Jacks, Frosted Mini-Wheats, Rice Krispies, Raisin Bran, Cracklin' Oat Bran, and Nut & Honey Crunch. These products are manufactured in 18 countries and distributed in more than 150. These cereals are sold primarily to grocery stores for resale to consumers and are marketed globally. In addition to ready-to-eat cereals, Kellogg produces or processes and distributes frozen dessert pies, toaster pastries, waffles, snacks, and other convenience foods in the United States, Canada, and other limited areas outside the United States. Some of these products include Pop-Tarts, Eggo waffles, Nutri-Grain Bars, Croutettes, and Corn Flake Crumbs.

The corporate culture at Kellogg is focused on the long-term well-being of the business. Management's primary objective is to increase share-holders' value over time. In order to reach this objective, the Kellogg Strategy was formed:

> Continued aggressive investment in new cereal markets, increased returns on existing investments, maximizing cash flows, and minimizing the cost of capital through appropriate financial policies.

At Kellogg, it was believed that the 16,000 employees were the company's most important competitive advantage.

Kellogg Company History

Kellogg Company's worldwide leadership came from the accidental invention of flaked cereal at the Battle Creek Sanitarium in 1894. The sanitarium was a famous Seventh Day Adventist hospital and health spa where exercise, fresh air, and a strict diet were offered. Sanitarium Superintendent Dr. John Harvey Kellogg and Will Keith Kellogg, his younger brother and business manager, invented many grain-based foods served at the facility.

The sanitarium served hard and tasteless bread. The Kellogg brothers conducted experiments to develop a better-tasting alternative. Wheat was cooked, forced through granola rollers, and then rolled into long sheets of dough.

One day the brothers experienced a fortunate accident. A batch of wheat was cooked but then set aside, neglected. Later, the brothers decided to process the stale dough. Instead of producing long sheets of dough, the rollers flattened the wheat mixture into small, thin flakes. Toasted, these flakes tasted light and crispy.

The patients at the sanitarium liked these new flakes so well that they wanted to eat them at home. To satisfy that demand, the Kellogg brothers started the Sanitas Nut Food Company, selling the toasted wheat flakes by mail order. In 1898, Will Keith Kellogg extended the process to flaking corn. Seeing his brother's lack of interest in expanding the food company, W. K. Kellogg went into business for himself.

On April 1, 1906, the Battle Creek Toasted Corn Flake Company started production. W. K. Kellogg used his manufacturing and marketing ideas to promote his product. He added malt flavoring to the corn flakes to make them unique. He advertised to healthy people the benefits of a product with flavor, freshness, value, and convenience. Kellogg used most of his working capital to buy a full-page ad in *The Ladies Home Journal* in 1906. Results were amazing. Sales quickly went from 33 cases to 2900 cases per day. With continued advertising, the company's annual sales surged to more than a million cases by 1909. W. K. Kellogg became known for his innovative sales promotions, which included free samples and premiums. The company was renamed Kellogg Company in 1922.

Effective marketing led to the company's success. In addition, Kellogg constantly sought ways to improve the product. He was committed to providing consumers with information about diet and nutrition. Kellogg was the first company to print nutrition messages, recipes, and product information on cereal packages in the 1930s. By that time, products such as All-Bran and Rice Krispies had been introduced. Kellogg became an international business when it built facilities in Canada, Australia, and England. In 1930, the W. K. Kellogg Foundation was established. Today, it is one of the largest philanthropic institutions in the world, funding projects in health, education, agriculture, leadership, and youth.

During the 1950s, products such as Corn Pops, Frosted Flakes, and Honey Smacks were introduced. Television also became an important part of advertising in the 1950s. As the mid-1960s approached, Pop Tarts and Product 19 were added.

Consumers began showing more interest in health and nutrition in the 1960s. So Kellogg Company provided information programs for schools, health organizations, and consumers. During the 1970s, Kellogg provided more detailed package labels, including amounts of sodium and dietary fiber. By the mid-1980s, packages included cholesterol, potassium, and nutrient information. New product introductions included Nutri-Grain, Crispix, Just Right, and Mueslix.

In Kellogg's continued commitment to health, the company led an All-Bran/National Cancer Institute campaign that produced more than 80,000 contacts to the National Cancer Institute (NCI) for information about the role of diet in reducing the risk of some kinds of cancers. Recently, Kellogg took pride in providing information to consumers about healthy lifestyles, cholesterol, and heart disease.

Production

Kellogg Company traditionally sought market leadership through production efficiency and product quality control, product innovation, and marketing effectiveness. The company spent considerable capital to maintain high-tech, high-capacity production capability. The result was low production costs but considerable excess capacity. To take advantage of possible economies of scale in production, there was constant pressure to build and maintain markets. New product innovations were an important part of this strategy. Kellogg moved Nutri-Grain from the health food store to the supermarket in 1981 and modified the production process to gain extended shelf life for the product.

Kellogg practiced Japanese-style total quality management (TQM) principles. The company strictly monitored product quality control. It made sure that new automated manufacturing machinery was thoroughly tested before it went on-line to serve a market. Worker teams monitored quality, controlled costs, and suggested improvements. Kellogg sought to improve inbound logistics by developing stronger relations with a limited number of suppliers.

Marketing

One of the roots of Kellogg's success was a strong marketing program. This was logical considering that the company marketed a low-priced, convenience good and that high volumes of repeat sales were necessary to maintain market share. The foundation of Kellogg's marketing strategy had been to offer a good product backed with high-performance promotion. The company used a mix of price and sales promotion to build and maintain market share. It believed that money spent to introduce good products would build market share. This was a successful strategy until the early 1990s. Success, for Kellogg, traditionally had been measured by market share.

The primary consumers of breakfast cereal products in the United States were children. Kellogg sought to serve this target market with its mainstay brands: Corn Flakes, Rice Krispies, Corn Pops, Honey Smacks, Froot Loops, Apple Jacks, and Raisin Bran had heavy consumption by kids. These products were in the maturity stage of their product lifecycle, but the market constantly renewed itself as younger children moved into the school-age years. Kellogg sought to maintain brand loyalty with a good-tasting product, vigorously promoted through advertising and coupon offers. In the past, Kellogg was known for new product innovation, rolling out four or five brand extensions a year. This rate of introduction was reduced recently to one, maybe two, per year.

One high-potential market niche was health-conscious adults. In the late 1980s, oat-bran products offered the promise of minimizing blood cholesterol and reducing the chances of heart attack. Oat bran was "by far the most dramatic thing that has ever happened to the cereal industry," said one high-level industry executive. Oat

bran and oat products doubled their market share to 18 percent in 1989, while the ready-to-eat cereal market grew only 1 to 2 percent. Kellogg, with only about 20 percent of its product line based on oats, was late to market with an acceptable brand. The company never really caught up. When it did offer a product, it cannibalized share from its existing offerings. Then the balloon burst. The health benefits of oat bran were placed in doubt. Consumers rebelled. Sales plummeted. Oat bran tasted like cattle feed—if it wasn't *really* good for you, people wouldn't eat it. Kellogg's Common Sense Oat Bran dropped from a 2 percent share to 0.7 percent. Cracklin' Oat Bran fell from 1.4 percent in 1990 to 0.4 percent in 1991.

Market share for Kellogg's domestic products had been slipping for a decade (see Table below). Kellogg's declining market share was the result of two factors: (1) product price increases accompanied by a heavy reliance on price-promotion spending and (2) increased competition. Kellogg raised prices six times, accompanied by heavy couponing in the 3 years preceding 1994. In 1994, the company cut back on coupons, maintained restraint on pricing, and spent money on increased advertising. Kellogg was concerned about the effect on its strategy when General Mills decreased prices. Low-priced private-label cereals, mostly from Ralston Purina, also were a concern. Kellogg's choice: Keep prices high and risk a further loss of market share or lower prices at the expense of profits—with no assurance that market share would increase. For the meantime, the focus was on profitability. Arnold Langbo calculated that price maintenance and selective couponing would increase profits more than simply cutting prices across the board. He thought that Kellogg's brand equity and consumer loyalty were great enough that the public would tolerate price increases with no added value to the product. Langbo told a meeting of Wall Street analysts:

Kellogg Company Domestic Market Share

Year	1986	1987	1988	1989	1990	1991	1992	1993	1994
%	42	41	42	40	37	39	37	37	35

"There are 140 brands of cereal being bought by very loyal consumers. Some of the fastest-growing brands are the most expensive, so it's not all about price."

In the early 1990s, Kellogg and its major U.S. competitors sought to maintain higher pricing and profitability by steadily increasing their use of price-promotion spending, including lots of buy-one-get-one-free offers, known as "bogos." However, this strategy failed to stop Kellogg's continued slide in U.S. market share. In 1994, Kellogg CEO Arnold Langbo said: "In the long run, bogos don't work. They borrow share. They don't earn share."

Kellogg also was hurt by its lack of appealing new cereal products that were needed to pull up U.S. volume. Kellogg's Healthy Choice cereals, introduced in early 1994, have performed well, but the overall new-product performance by Kellogg and its competitors since the early 1980s has been, at best, unspectacular.

Kellogg's Global Markets

Unlike some companies that sought product diversification to build profits, Kellogg concentrated on marketing cereal and other food products. Eighty percent of its worldwide sales came from cereal. The company's market development took the form of expanding to foreign markets. The company entered Canada in 1914 and by 1991 had 17 cereal plants located in 15 foreign countries. Since then, the company has added Argentina, Latvia, India, and China. In 1994, Kellogg controlled 43 percent of worldwide cereal sales.

Kellogg North America led its market with a 37 percent share in 1993. It enjoyed both good product quality control and high labor productivity. It also led the market in advertising expenditures. In addition to ready-to-eat cereals, Kellogg North America offered other grain-based convenience foods: frozen dessert pies, toaster pastries, waffles, granola bars, and snacks. In 1993, new product rollouts included Low Fat Granola Bars, Nutri-Grain Bars, new Eggo versions, Mini Eggos, and new flavors of Pop Tarts.

The best of the overseas beachheads seemed to be in the old British Empire (Britain, Ireland, Australia), where eating breakfast cereal was culturally accepted. Kellogg Europe controlled 50 percent of

the market, six times the share of its nearest competitor. During 1993, the company was selected first in customer service among all British manufacturers for the fourth year in a row. Ireland was the world's top cereal consumer, but market growth potential was still great. Kellogg gained 5 percent in sales volume in Ireland during 1993. A promising new market in this division was the Republic of Latvia. In a joint venture with Adazi Food Products, Kellogg opened a new cereal plant in 1993. This was the first Western cereal enterprise in the former Soviet Union. Cereal for breakfast was not a tradition in this region, so market potential could be great. Initially, demand would be low, but competition would be zero. Kellogg was substantially increasing advertising expenditures throughout Europe, trying to interest younger people in testing the convenience of cereal for breakfast or a snack instead of a croissant or *schwartzbrot*. This strategy was successful, resulting in a strong growth in the cereal business in continental Europe in the late 1980s and early 1990s.

So far as market potential was concerned, some countries had a very low market penetration rate. Worldwide cereal consumption averaged around 2 pounds per year, compared with North America's 10 pounds. Cereal for breakfast was not yet culturally accepted in certain areas. Kellogg marketing people thought it was merely a matter of education to get these consumers turned on to eating breakfast cereal. In some countries, there also was the matter of obtaining dairy products for topping. Some countries didn't drink a lot of milk and/or have an established dairy industry or an established channel of distribution that offered refrigeration. People did not have facilities to keep milk to pour over their Corn Flakes. Kellogg had a few cultural and infrastructure problems to solve before its market potential estimates could be realized.

Kellogg Asia Pacific controlled a 47 percent market share. New plants in India and China would serve millions of potential customers, more than one-third of the world's population. Here again, market development would require effecting significant changes in the traditional tastes and preferences of local consumers. Kellogg developed specific cereal products for niche foreign markets. A high-mineral multigrain cereal was developed for the health-conscious Australians, while in Japan, where fish and rice made a traditional breakfast,

Kellogg was offering Genmai Flakes, made from whole-grain rice.

Operations in the Latin America Division covered Mexico, Central America, and South America, and Kellogg dominated this market with 78 percent market share. This market share placed Kellogg in control of the developing markets as well. A new plant was under construction near Buenos Aires, Argentina, and capacity increases occurred at the plants in Bogota, Colombia; Maracay, Venezuela; and São Paulo, Brazil. Performance for the year in Latin America was favorable for the most part. However, disappointing results in Mexico had a negative impact on the overall performance of the division.

Opportunities for future growth were quite favorable with the increased interest in health and nutrition in Latin America. Kellogg had performed many different activities in order to make consumers more aware of the importance of nutrition. Some of the activities included school nutrition education programs, which covered 300,000 children in Mexico alone, fiber symposia, and nutritional newsletters to health professionals.

In an attempt to provide consumers with additional value in its products, Kellogg added extra vitamins to the cereals in Latin Americans' diets and added zinc to products in other selected countries. This adaptation of products to the culture was one of Kellogg's ways to boost cereal consumption.

THE COMPANY TODAY

Even with intense competition and many challenges faced by Kellogg during 1993, worldwide revenues increased by 2 percent. This was the forty-ninth consecutive year for increases. In the United States alone, sales rose by 6 percent. There were 24 new product introductions worldwide. Kellogg received 40 percent of its revenues from outside the United States.

In Europe, sales decreased 8 percent due to unfavorable foreign currency exchange rates. If this problem had not occurred, sales would have been up by 4 percent. Dividends increased for the thirty-seventh consecutive year, with 10 percent growth in 1993. Price-earnings multiple remained at one of the highest levels in the food industry. However, the performance of stock was disappointing.

In 1993, Kellogg decided to divest units that did not fit with long-term strategic plans. So the British carton container and Argentinian snack food businesses were sold for a total pretax gain of $65.9 million. (Other results of operations may be found in the financial statements provided at the end of the case.)

In 1994, Kellogg followed a price-maintenance policy to provide value to consumers. The company also cut back on coupons. Since then, the company's market share has been steady.

THE FUTURE

The future for Kellogg and the ready-to-eat cereal industry looked quite favorable at the end of 1995. Demand continued in a long-term upward trend, with growth estimated at 2 to 3 percent in the United States and 5 to 7 percent overseas. This continued growth would come with the increasing recognition by consumers of the nutritional value of cereal. Domestic growth also would come with the increasing ages of Baby-Boomers from young adulthood to middle age, where cereal consumption had grown steadily.

It also appeared that the trend among competitors in the industry was to cut promotional spending. These competitors could have unbounded opportunities to establish a position in the new markets that were being entered, such as India and China.

CEO Langbo has come to the conclusion: "If this business was ever easy, it isn't anymore."

EXHIBIT A

Kellogg Company and Subsidiaries: Consolidated Balance Sheet (At December 31, in millions)

	1993	1992
Current assets		
Cash and temporary investments	$ 98.1	$ 126.3
Accounts receivable, less allowances of $6.0 and $6.2	536.8	519.1
Inventories:		
Raw materials and supplies	148.5	167.7
Finished goods and materials in process	254.6	248.7
Deferred income taxes	85.5	66.2
Prepaid expenses	121.6	108.6
Total current assets	1,245.1	1,236.6
Property		
Land	40.6	40.5
Buildings	1,065.7	1,021.2
Machinery and equipment	2,857.6	2,629.4
Construction in progress	308.6	302.6
Accumulated depreciation	(1,504.1)	(1,331.0)
Property, net	2,768.4	2,662.7
Intangible assets	59.1	53.3
Other assets	164.5	62.4
Total assets	$4,237.1	$4,015.0
Current liabilities		
Current maturities of long-term debt	$ 1.5	$ 1.9
Notes payable	386.7	210.0
Accounts payable	308.8	313.8
Accrued liabilities:		
Income taxes	65.9	104.1
Salaries and wages	76.5	78.0
Advertising and promotion	233.8	228.0
Other	141.4	135.2
Total current liabilities	1,214.6	1,071.0
Long-term debt	521.6	314.9
Nonpension postretirement benefits	450.9	407.6
Deferred income taxes	188.9	184.6
Other liabilities	147.7	91.7
Shareholders' equity		
Common stock, $.25 par value		
Authorized: 330,000,000 shares		
Issued: 310,292,753 shares in 1993 and 310,193,228 in 1992	77.6	77.5
Capital in excess of par value	72.0	69.2
Retained earnings	3,409.4	3,033.9
Treasury stock, at cost: 82,372,409 and 72,874,738 shares	(1,653.1)	(1,105.0)
Minimum pension liability adjustment	(25.3)	
Currency translation adjustment	(167.2)	(130.4)
Total shareholders' equity	1,713.4	1,945.2
Total liabilities and shareholders' equity	$4,237.1	$4,015.0

EXHIBIT B

Kellogg Company and Subsidiaries: Consolidated Earnings and Retained Earnings
(Year ended December 31, in millions, except per share amounts)

	1993	1992	1991
Net Sales	$6,295.4	$6,190.6	$5,786.6
Other revenue (deductions), net	(1.5)	36.8	14.6
	6,293.9	6,227.4	5,801.2
Cost of goods sold	2,989.0	2,987.7	2,828.7
Selling and administrative expense	2,237.5	2,140.1	1,930.0
Interest expense	33.3	29.2	58.3
	5,259.8	5,157.0	4,817.0
Earnings before income taxes and cumulative effect of accounting change	1,034.1	1,070.4	984.2
Income taxes	353.4	387.6	378.2
Earnings before cumulative effect of accounting change	680.7	682.8	606.0
Cumulative effect of change in method of accounting for postretirement benefits other than pensions—$1.05 a share (net of income tax benefit of $144.6)		(251.6)	
Net earnings—$2.94, $1.81, $2.51 a share	680.7	431.2	606.0
Retained earnings, beginning of year	3,033.9	2,889.1	2,542.4
Dividends paid—$1.32, $1.20, $1.075 a share	(305.2)	(286.4)	(259.3)
Retained earnings, end of year	$3,409.4	$3,033.9	$2,889.1

Bibliography

Cohen, Waren, "A Crunch for Cereal Makers," *U.S. News & World Report*, March 28, 1994.

Elliott, Stuart, "Consumers Take Center Stage in a Campaign to Promote the Value of a Kellogg Breakfast," *New York Times*, July 20, 1994.

Erickson, Julie Liesse, "Schroeder: Kellogg Is Popping," *Advertising Age*, August 14, 1989, p. 3.

Erickson, Julie Liesse, "Why Schroeder Is Leaving Kellogg," *Advertising Age*, September 25, 1989, p. 6.

General Mills 1994 Annual Report.

Gibson, Richard, "Head of Kellogg's U.S. Cereal Business Resigns as Part of Management Shuffle," *Wall Street Journal*, July 5, 1994, p. B7.

Gibson, Richard, "Kellogg Tries to Keep Cereal Sales Crisp as Rivals Nibble Away at Market Share," *Wall Street Journal*, November 9, 1993, p. A5B.

Gibson, Richard, "Kellogg Earnings Increased 3.5% in Third Quarter," *Wall Street Journal*, October 24, 1994, p. A9A.

Kahn, Mir Maqbool Alam, "Kellogg Reports Brisk Cereal Sales in India," *Advertising Age*, November 14, 1994, p. 60.

"Kellogg Says It Plans to Further Cut Use of Discount Programs," *Wall Street Journal*, November 14, 1994, p. B5A.

Kellogg Company 1993 Annual Report.

Kellogg Company, Value Line, Edition 10, August 1994, pp. 1468, 1476, 1485.

Liesse, Julie, "Kellogg, Alpo Top Hot New Product List," *Advertising Age*, January 4, 1993, p. 66.

Liesse, Julia, and Judann Degnoll, "Kellogg's Golden Era Flakes Away," *Advertising Age*, August 31, 1990, p. 4.

Liesse, Julia, "Gen. Mills 1, Kellogg 0," *Advertising Age*, September 20, 1993, p. 2.

Liesse, Julie, "Kellogg's Prices Go Up, Up, Up," *Advertising Age*, August 9, 1993, p. 1.

Mitchell, Russell, "Big G Is Growing Fat on Oat Cuisine," *Business Week*, September 18, 1989, p. 29.

Mitchell, Russell, "The Health Craze Has Kellogg Feeling G-R-R-Reat," *Business Week*, March 30, 1987, pp. 52–53.

Moody's Industrial Manual, Vol. 2 (New York: Moody's Investors Service, Inc., 1993), pp. 4001–4004.

"The History of Kellogg Company," Kellogg Company pamphlet, 1992.

"¿Tiene usted los Corn Flakes?" *Forbes,* January 4, 1991, p. 168.

Sellers, Patricia, "How King Kellogg Beat the Blahs," *Fortune,* August 29, 1988, pp. 55–64.

Serwer, Andrew E., "What Price Brand Loyalty," *Fortune,* January 10, 1994, pp. 103–104.

Treece, James B., and Greg Burns, "The Nervous Faces Around Kellogg's Breakfast Table," *Business Week,* July 18, 1994, p. 33.

Woodruff, David, "Winning the War of Battle Creek," *Business Week,* May 31, 1991, p. 80.

Endnote

1. A conversation with Richard E. Lovell, manager, corporate communications, Kellogg's Company Corporate Headquarters, indicated a factual error in the news item. Kellogg's strategy of reducing price-promotion spending resulted in a 1 percent market share drop at first. This leveled off at 35 percent and has remained constant since then. The authors appreciate the great assistance provided by Mr. Lovell in the preparation of this case.

Kentucky Fried Chicken and the Global Fast-Food Industry

This case was prepared by Jeffrey A. Krug of the Department of Business Administration, University of Illinois at Urbana-Champaign.

Kentucky Fried Chicken Corporation (KFC) was the world's largest chicken restaurant chain and third largest fast-food chain. KFC held over 55 percent of the U.S. market in terms of sales and operated over 10,200 restaurants worldwide in 1998. It opened 376 new restaurants in 1997 (more than one restaurant a day) and operated in 79 countries. One of the first fast-food chains to go international during the late 1960s, KFC has developed one of the world's most recognizable brands.

Japan, Australia, and the United Kingdom accounted for the greatest share of KFC's international expansion during the 1970s and 1980s. During the 1990s, KFC turned its attention to other international markets that offered significant opportunities for growth. China, with a population of over one billion, and Europe, with a population roughly equal to the United States, offered such opportunities. Latin America also offered a unique opportunity because of the size of its markets, its common language and culture, and its geographic proximity to the United States. Mexico was of particular interest because of the North American Free Trade Agreement (NAFTA), a free-trade zone between Canada, the United States, and Mexico that went into effect in 1994.

Reprinted by permission of the author, Jeffrey A. Krug, University of Illinois at Urbana-Champaign.

Prior to 1990, KFC expanded into Latin America primarily through company-owned restaurants in Mexico and Puerto Rico. Company-owned restaurants gave KFC greater control over its operations than franchised or licensed restaurants. By 1995, KFC also had established company-owned restaurants in Venezuela and Brazil. In addition, it had established franchised units in numerous Caribbean countries. During the early 1990s, KFC shifted to a two-tiered strategy in Latin America. First, it established 29 franchised restaurants in Mexico following enactment of Mexico's new franchise law in 1990. This allowed KFC to expand outside its company restaurant base in Mexico City, Guadalajara, and Monterrey. KFC was one of many U.S. fast-food, retail, and hotel chains to begin franchising in Mexico following the new franchise law. Second, KFC began an aggressive franchise building program in South America. By 1998, it was operating franchised restaurants in 32 Latin American countries. Much of this growth was in Brazil, Chile, Colombia, Ecuador, and Peru.

COMPANY HISTORY

Fast-food franchising was still in its infancy in 1952 when Harland Sanders began his travels across the United States to speak with prospective franchisees about his "Colonel Sanders Recipe Kentucky Fried

Chicken." By 1960, "Colonel" Sanders had granted KFC franchises to over 200 take-home retail outlets and restaurants across the United States. He had also succeeded in establishing a number of franchises in Canada. By 1963, the number of KFC franchises had risen to over 300, and revenues had reached $500 million.

By 1964, at the age of 74, the Colonel had tired of running the day-to-day operations of his business and was eager to concentrate on public relations issues. Therefore, he sought out potential buyers, eventually deciding to sell the business to two Louisville businessmen—Jack Massey and John Young Brown, Jr.—for $2 million. The Colonel stayed on as a public relations man and goodwill ambassador for the company.

During the next 5 years, Massey and Brown concentrated on growing KFC's franchise system across the United States. In 1966, they took KFC public, and the company was listed on the New York Stock Exchange. By the late 1960s, a strong foothold had been established in the United States, and Massey and Brown turned their attention to international markets. In 1969, a joint venture was signed with Mitsuoishi Shoji Kaisha, Ltd., in Japan, and the rights to operate 14 existing KFC franchises in England were acquired. Subsidiaries also were established in Hong Kong, South Africa, Australia, New Zealand, and Mexico. By 1971, KFC had 2450 franchises and 600 company-owned restaurants worldwide and was operating in 48 countries.

Heublein, Inc.

In 1971, KFC entered negotiations with Heublein, Inc., to discuss a possible merger. The decision to seek a merger candidate was partially driven by Brown's desire to pursue other interests, including a political career (Brown was elected governor of Kentucky in 1977). Several months later, Heublein acquired KFC. Heublein was in the business of producing vodka, mixed cocktails, dry gin, cordials, beer, and other alcoholic beverages. However, Heublein had little experience in the restaurant business. Conflicts quickly erupted between Colonel Sanders, who continued to act in a public relations capacity, and Heublein management. Colonel Sanders became increasingly distraught over quality control issues and restaurant cleanliness. By 1977, new restaurant openings had slowed to about 20 per year. Few restaurants were

being remodeled, and service quality had declined.

In 1977, Heublein sent in a new management team to redirect KFC's strategy. A "back-to-the-basics" strategy was immediately implemented. New unit construction was discontinued until existing restaurants could be upgraded and operating problems eliminated. Restaurants were refurbished, an emphasis was placed on cleanliness and service, marginal products were eliminated, and product consistency was reestablished. By 1982, KFC had succeeded in establishing a successful strategic focus and was again aggressively building new units.

R. J. Reynolds Industries, Inc.

In 1982, R. J. Reynolds Industries, Inc. (RJR), merged Heublein into a wholly owned subsidiary. The merger with Heublein represented part of RJR's overall corporate strategy of diversifying into unrelated businesses, including energy, transportation, food, and restaurants. RJR's objective was to reduce its dependence on the tobacco industry, which had driven RJR sales since its founding in North Carolina in 1875. Sales of cigarettes and tobacco products, while profitable, were declining because of reduced consumption in the United States. This was mainly the result of an increased awareness among Americans about the negative health consequences of smoking.

RJR had no more experience in the restaurant business than did Heublein. However, it decided to take a hands-off approach to managing KFC. Whereas Heublein had installed its own top management at KFC headquarters, RJR left KFC management largely intact, believing that existing KFC managers were better qualified to operate KFC's businesses than were its own managers. In doing so, RJR avoided many of the operating problems that plagued Heublein. This strategy paid off for RJR as KFC continued to expand aggressively and profitably under RJR ownership. In 1985, RJR acquired Nabisco Corporation for $4.9 billion. Nabisco sold a variety of well-known cookies, crackers, cereals, confectioneries, snacks, and other grocery products. The merger with Nabisco represented a decision by RJR to concentrate its diversification efforts on the consumer foods industry. It subsequently divested many of its nonconsumer food businesses. RJR sold KFC to PepsiCo, Inc., one year later.

PEPSICO, INC.

Corporate Strategy

PepsiCo, Inc., was formed in 1965 with the merger of the Pepsi-Cola Co. and Frito-Lay, Inc. The merger of these companies created one of the largest consumer products companies in the United States. Pepsi-Cola's traditional business was the sale of soft drink concentrates to licensed independent and company-owned bottlers that manufactured, sold, and distributed Pepsi-Cola soft drinks. Pepsi-Cola's best known trademarks were Pepsi-Cola, Diet Pepsi, Mountain Dew, and Slice. Frito-Lay manufactured and sold a variety of snack foods, including Fritos Corn Chips, Lay's Potato Chips, Ruffles Potato Chips, Doritos, Tostitos Tortilla Chips, and Chee-tos Cheese Flavored Snacks. PepsiCo quickly embarked on an aggressive acquisition program similar to that pursued by RJR during the 1980s, buying a number of companies in areas unrelated to its major businesses. Acquisitions included North American Van Lines, Wilson Sporting Goods, and Lee Way Motor Freight. However, success in operating these businesses failed to live up to expectations, mainly because the management skills required to operate these businesses lay outside of PepsiCo's area of expertise.

Poor performance in these businesses led then-chairman and chief executive officer Don Kendall to restructure PepsiCo's operations in 1984. First, businesses that did not support Pepsi-Co's consumer product orientation, such as North American Van Lines, Wilson Sporting Goods, and Lee Way Motor Freight, were divested. Second, PepsiCo's foreign bottling operations were sold to local businesspeople who better understood the culture and business environment in their respective countries. Third, Kendall reorganized PepsiCo along three lines: soft drinks, snack foods, and restaurants.

Restaurant Business and Acquisition of KFC

PepsiCo first entered the restaurant business in 1977 when it acquired Pizza Hut's 3200-unit restaurant system. Taco Bell was merged into a division of PepsiCo in 1978. The restaurant business completed PepsiCo's consumer product orientation. The marketing of fast food followed many of the same patterns as the marketing of soft drinks and snack foods. Therefore, PepsiCo believed that its management skills could be easily transferred among its three business segments. This was compatible with PepsiCo's practice of frequently moving managers among its business units as a way of developing future top executives. PepsiCo's restaurant chains also provided an additional outlet for the sale of Pepsi soft drinks. Pepsi-Cola soft drinks and fast-food products also could be marketed together in the same television and radio segments, thereby providing higher returns for each advertising dollar. To complete its diversification into the restaurant segment, PepsiCo acquired Kentucky Fried Chicken Corporation from RJR-Nabisco for $841 million in 1986. The acquisition of KFC gave PepsiCo the leading market share in chicken (KFC), pizza (Pizza Hut), and Mexican food (Taco Bell), three of the four largest and fastest-growing segments within the U.S. fast-food industry.

Management

Following the acquisition by PepsiCo, KFC's relationship with its parent company underwent dramatic changes. RJR had operated KFC as a semiautonomous unit, satisfied that KFC management understood the fast-food business better than they. In contrast, PepsiCo acquired KFC in order to complement its already strong presence in the fast-food market. Rather than allowing KFC to operate autonomously, PepsiCo undertook sweeping changes. These changes included negotiating a new franchise contract to give PepsiCo more control over its franchisees, reducing staff in order to cut costs, and replacing KFC managers with its own. In 1987, a rumor spread through KFC's headquarters in Louisville that the new personnel manager, who had just relocated from PepsiCo's headquarters in New York, was overheard saying that "there will be no more home grown tomatoes in this organization."

Such statements by PepsiCo personnel, uncertainties created by several restructurings that led to layoffs throughout the KFC organization, the replacement of KFC personnel with PepsiCo managers, and conflicts between KFC and PepsiCo's corporate cultures created a morale problem within KFC. KFC's culture was built largely on Colonel Sanders' laid-back approach to management. Employees enjoyed relatively good employment stability and security. Over the years, a strong loyalty had been created among KFC employees and franchisees, mainly because of the efforts of Colonel Sanders to provide for his employees' benefits, pension, and other non-income needs. In addition, the southern environment of Louisville resulted in a friendly, relaxed atmosphere at KFC's corporate offices. This corporate culture was left essentially unchanged during the Heublein and RJR years.

In stark contrast to KFC, Pepsi-Co's culture was characterized by a strong emphasis on performance. Top performers expected to move up through the ranks quickly. PepsiCo used its KFC, Pizza Hut, Taco Bell, Frito Lay, and Pepsi-Cola divisions as training grounds for its top managers, rotating its best managers through its five divisions on average every 2 years. This practice created immense pressure on managers to continuously demonstrate their managerial prowess within short periods, in order to maximize their potential for promotion. This practice also left many KFC managers with the feeling that they had few career opportunities with the new company. One PepsiCo manager commented, "You may have performed well last year, but if you don't perform well this year, you're gone, and there are 100 ambitious guys with Ivy League MBAs at PepsiCo who would love to take your position." An unwanted effect of this performance-driven culture was that employee loyalty often was lost, and turnover tended to be higher than in other companies.

Kyle Craig, president of KFC's U.S. operations, was asked about KFC's relationship with its corporate parent. He commented:

> The KFC culture is an interesting one because I think it was dominated by a lot of KFC folks, many of whom have been around since the days of the Colonel. Many of those people were very intimidated by the PepsiCo culture, which is a very high performance, high accountability, highly driven culture. People were concerned about whether they would succeed in the new culture. Like many companies, we have had a couple of downsizings which further made people nervous. Today, there are fewer old KFC people around and I think to some degree people have seen that the PepsiCo culture can drive some pretty positive results. I also think the PepsiCo people who have worked with KFC have modified their cultural values somewhat and they can see that there were a lot of benefits in the old KFC culture.

PepsiCo pushes its companies to perform strongly, but whenever there is a slip in performance, it increases the culture gap between PepsiCo and KFC. I have been involved in two downsizings over which I have been the chief architect. They have been probably the two most gut-wrenching experiences of my career. Because you know you're dealing with peoples' lives and their families, these changes can be emotional if you care about the people in your organization. However, I do fundamentally believe that your first obligation is to the entire organization.

A second problem for PepsiCo was its poor relationship with KFC franchisees. A month after becoming president and chief executive officer in 1989, John Cranor addressed KFC's franchisees in Louisville in order to explain the details of the new franchise contract. This was the first contract change in 13 years. It gave PepsiCo greater power to take over weak franchises, relocate restaurants, and make changes in existing restaurants. In addition, restaurants would no longer be protected from competition from new KFC units, and it gave PepsiCo the right to raise royalty fees on existing restaurants as contracts came up for renewal. After Cranor finished his address, there was an uproar among the attending franchisees, who jumped to their feet to protest the changes. The franchisees had long been accustomed to relatively little interference from management in their day-to-day operations (a tradition begun by Colonel Sanders). This type of interference, of course, was a strong part of PepsiCo's philosophy of demanding change. KFC's franchise association later sued PepsiCo over the new contract. The contract remained unresolved until 1996, when the most objectionable parts of the contract were removed by KFC's new president and CEO, David Novak. A new contract was ratified by KFC's franchisees in 1997.

PepsiCo's Divestiture of KFC, Pizza Hut, and Taco Bell

PepsiCo's strategy of diversifying into three distinct but related markets—soft drinks, snack foods, and fast-food restaurants—created one of the world's largest consumer products companies and a portfolio of some of the world's most recognizable brands. Between 1990 and 1996, PepsiCo grew at an annual rate of over 10 percent, surpassing $31 billion in sales in 1996. However, PepsiCo's sales

EXHIBIT A

Tricon Global Restaurants, Inc.—Organizational Chart (1998)

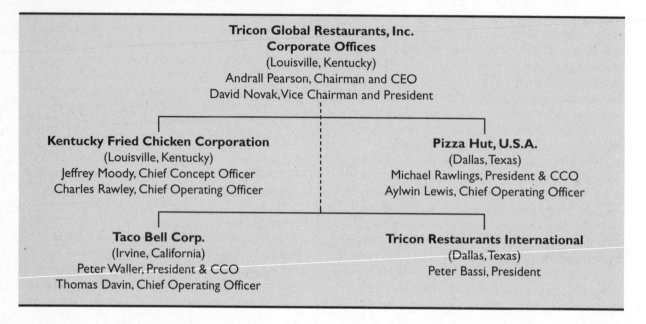

growth masked troubles in its fast-food businesses. Operating margins (profit as a percent of sales) at Pepsi-Cola and Frito Lay averaged 12 and 17 percent between 1990 and 1996, respectively. During the same period, margins at KFC, Pizza Hut, and Taco Bell fell from an average of over 8 percent in 1990 to a little more than 4 percent in 1996. Declining margins in the fast-food chains reflected increasing maturity in the U.S. fast-food industry, more intense competition among U.S. fast-food competitors, and the aging of KFC and Pizza Hut's restaurant base. As a result, PepsiCo's restaurant chains absorbed nearly one-half of PepsiCo's annual capital spending during the 1990s. However, they generated less than one-third of PepsiCo's cash flows. Therefore, cash was diverted from PepsiCo's soft drink and snack food businesses to its restaurant businesses. This reduced PepsiCo's return on assets, made it more difficult to compete effectively with Coca-Cola, and hurt its stock price. In 1997, PepsiCo spun off its restaurant businesses into a new company called Tricon Global Restaurants, Inc. (see Exhibit A). The new company was based in KFC's headquarters in Louisville, Kentucky. PepsiCo's objective was to reposition itself as a packaged goods company, to strengthen its balance sheet, and to create more consistent earning growth. PepsiCo received a one-time distribution from Tricon of $4.7 billion, $3.7 billion of which was used to pay off short-term debt. The balance was earmarked for stock repurchases.

FAST-FOOD INDUSTRY

According to the National Restaurant Association (NRA), food-service sales topped $320 billion for the approximately 500,000 restaurants and other food outlets making up the U.S. restaurant industry in 1997. The NRA estimated that sales in the fast-food segment of the food service industry grew 5.2 percent to $104 billion, up from $98 billion in 1996. This marked the fourth consecutive year that fast-food sales either matched or exceeded sales in full-service restaurants, which grew 4.1 percent to $104 billion in 1997. The growth in fast-food sales reflected the long, gradual change in the restaurant industry from an industry once dominated by independently operated sit-down restaurants to an industry fast becoming dominated by fast-food restaurant chains. The U.S. restaurant industry as a whole grew by approximately 4.2 percent in 1997.

Major Fast-Food Segments

Six major business segments made up the fast-food segment of the food service industry. Sales data for the leading restaurant chains in each segment are shown in Exhibit B. Most striking is the dominance of McDonald's, which had sales of over $16 billion in 1996. This represented 16.6 percent of U.S. fast-food sales, or nearly 22 percent of sales among the nation's top 30 fast-food chains. Sales at McDonald's restaurants average $1.3 million per year, compared with about $820,000 for the average U.S. fast-food restaurant. Tricon Global Restaurants (KFC, Pizza Hut, and Taco Bell) had U.S. sales of $13.4 billion in 1996. This represented 13.6 percent of U.S. fast-food sales and 17.9 percent of the top 30 fast-food chains.

Sandwich chains made up the largest segment of the fast-food market. McDonald's controlled 35 percent of the sandwich segment, while Burger King ran a distant second with a 15.6 percent market share. Competition had become particularly intense within the sandwich segment as the U.S. fast-food market became more saturated. In order to increase sales, chains turned to new products to win customers away from other sandwich chains, introduced products traditionally offered by nonsandwich chains (such as pizzas, fried chicken, and tacos), streamlined their menus, and upgraded product quality. Burger King recently introduced its Big King, a direct clone of the Big Mac. McDonald's quickly retaliated by introducing its Big 'n Tasty, a direct clone of the Whopper. Wendy's introduced chicken pita sandwiches, and Taco Bell introduced sandwiches called "wraps," breads stuffed with various fillings. Hardee's successfully introduced fried chicken in most of its restaurants. In addition to new products, chains lowered pricing, improved customer service, cobranded with other fast-food chains, and established restaurants in nontraditional locations (e.g., McDonald's installed restaurants in Wal-Mart stores across the country) to beef up sales.

The second largest fast-food segment was dinner houses, dominated by Red Lobster, Applebee's, Olive Garden, and Chili's. Between 1988 and 1996, dinner houses increased their share of the fast-food market from 8 to over 13 percent. This increase came mainly at the expense of grilled buffet chains, such as Ponderosa, Sizzler, and Western Sizzlin'. The market share of steak houses fell from 6 percent in 1988 to under 4 percent in 1996. The rise of dinner houses during the 1990s was partially the result of an aging and wealthier population that increasingly demanded higher-quality food in more upscale settings. However, rapid construction of new restaurants, especially among relative newcomers, such as Romano's Macaroni Grill, Lone Star Steakhouse, and Outback Steakhouse, resulted in overcapacity within the dinner house segment. This reduced per-restaurant sales and further intensified competition. Eight of the sixteen largest dinner houses posted growth rates in excess of 10 percent in 1996. Romano's Macaroni Grill, Lone Star Steakhouse, Chili's, Outback Steakhouse, Applebee's, Red Robin, Fuddruckers, and Ruby Tuesday grew at rates of 82, 41, 32, 27, 23, 14, 11, and 10 percent, respectively.

The third largest fast-food segment was pizza, long dominated by Pizza Hut. While Pizza Hut controlled over 46 percent of the pizza segment in 1996, its market share has slowly eroded because of intense competition and its aging restaurant base. Domino's Pizza and Papa John's Pizza have been particularly successful. Little Caesars is the only pizza chain to remain predominantly a take-out chain, although it recently began home delivery. However, its policy of charging customers $1 per delivery damaged its perception among consumers as a high-value pizza chain. Home delivery, successfully introduced by Domino's and Pizza Hut, was a driving force for success among the market leaders during the 1970s and 1980s. However, the success of home delivery drove competitors to look for new methods of increasing their customer bases. Pizza chains diversified into nonpizza items (e.g., chicken wings at Domino's, Italian cheese bread at Little Caesars, and stuffed crust pizza at Pizza Hut), developed nontraditional items (e.g., airport kiosks and college campuses), offered special promotions, and offered new pizza variations with an emphasis on high-quality ingredients (e.g., Roma Herb and Garlic Crunch pizza at Domino's and Buffalo Chicken Pizza at Round Table Pizza).

Chicken Segment

KFC continued to dominate the chicken segment, with 1997 sales of $4 billion (see Exhibit C). Its nearest competitor, Boston Market, was second with sales of $1.2 billion. KFC operated 5120 restaurants in the United States in 1998, eight fewer restaurants than in 1993. Rather than building new restaurants

EXHIBIT B

Leading U.S. Fast-Food Chains (Ranked by 1996 Sales, $000s)

Sandwich Chains	Sales	Share	Family Restaurants	Sales	Share
McDonald's	16,370	35.0%	Denny's	1,850	21.2%
Burger King	7,300	15.6%	Shoney's	1,220	14.0%
Taco Bell	4,575	9.8%	Big Boy	945	10.8%
Wendy's	4,360	9.3%	Int'l House of Pancakes	797	9.1%
Hardee's	3,055	6.5%	Cracker Barrel	734	8.4%
Subway	2,700	5.8%	Perkins	678	7.8%
Arby's	1,867	4.0%	Friendly's	597	6.8%
Dairy Queen	1,225	2.6%	Bob Evans	575	6.6%
Jack-in-the-Box	1,207	2.6%	Waffle House	525	6.0%
Sonic Drive-In	985	2.1%	Coco's	278	3.2%
Carl's Jr.	648	1.4%	Steak 'n Shake	275	3.2%
Other chains	2,454	5.2%	Village Inn	246	2.8%
Total	46,745	100.0%	Total	8,719	100.0%

Dinner Houses	Sales	Share	Pizza Chains	Sales	Share
Red Lobster	1,810	15.7%	Pizza Hut	4,927	46.4%
Applebee's	1,523	13.2%	Domino's Pizza	2,300	21.7%
Olive Garden	1,280	11.1%	Little Caesars	1,425	13.4%
Chili's	1,242	10.7%	Papa John's	619	5.8%
Outback Steakhouse	1,017	8.8%	Sbarros	400	3.8%
T.G.I. Friday's	935	8.1%	Round Table Pizza	385	3.6%
Ruby Tuesday	545	4.7%	Chuck E. Cheese's	293	2.8%
Lone Star Steakhouse	460	4.0%	Godfather's Pizza	266	2.5%
Bennigan's	458	4.0%	Total	10,614	100.0%
Romano's Macaroni Grill	344	3.0%			
Other dinner houses	1,942	16.8%			
Total	11,557	100.0%			

Grilled Buffet Chains	Sales	Share	Chicken Chains	Sales	Share
Golden Corral	711	22.8%	KFC	3,900	57.1%
Ponderosa	680	21.8%	Boston Market	1,167	17.1%
Ryan's	604	19.4%	Popeye's Chicken	666	9.7%
Sizzler	540	17.3%	Chick-fil-A	570	8.3%
Western Sizzlin'	332	10.3%	Church's Chicken	529	7.7%
Quincy's	259	8.3%	Total	6,832	100.0%
Total	3,116	100.0%			

Source: Nation's Restaurant News.

EXHIBIT C

Top U.S. Chicken Chains

Sales ($ M)	1992	1993	1994	1995	1996	1997	Growth Rate (%)
KFC	3,400	3,400	3,500	3,700	3,900	4,000	3.3
Boston Market	43	147	371	754	1,100	1,197	94.5
Popeye's	545	569	614	660	677	727	5.9
Chick-fil-A	356	396	451	502	570	671	11.9
Church's	414	440	465	501	526	574	6.8
Total	4,758	4,952	5,401	6,118	6,772	7,170	8.5
U.S. restaurants							
KFC	5,089	5,128	5,149	5,142	5,108	5,120	0.1
Boston Market	83	217	534	829	1,087	1,166	69.6
Popeye's	769	769	853	889	894	949	4.3
Chick-fil-A	487	545	534	825	717	762	9.0
Church's	944	932	937	953	989	1,070	2.5
Total	7,372	7,591	8,007	8,638	8,795	9,067	4.2
Sales per unit ($000s)							
KFC	668	663	680	720	764	781	3.2
Boston Market	518	677	695	910	1,012	1,027	14.7
Popeye's	709	740	720	743	757	767	1.6
Chick-fil-A	731	727	845	608	795	881	3.8
Church's	439	472	496	526	531	537	4.1
Total	645	782	782	782	782	782	3.9

Source: Tricon Global Restaurants, Inc., *1997 Annual Report;* Boston Chicken, Inc., *1997 Annual Report;* Chick-fil-A, corporate headquarters, Atlanta; AFC Enterprises, Inc., *1997 Annual Report.*

in the already saturated U.S. market, KFC focused on building restaurants abroad. In the United States, KFC focused on closing unprofitable restaurants, upgrading existing restaurants with new exterior signage, and improving product quality. The strategy paid off. While overall U.S. sales during the last 10 years remained flat, annual sales per unit increased steadily in 8 of the last 9 years.

Despite KFC's continued dominance within the chicken segment, it has lost market share to Boston Market, a new restaurant chain emphasizing roasted rather than fried chicken. Boston Market has successfully created the image of an upscale deli offering healthy, "home style" alternatives to fried chicken and other "fast foods." It has broadened its menu beyond rotisserie chicken to include ham, turkey, meat loaf, chicken pot pie, and deli

sandwiches. In order to minimize its image as a fast-food restaurant, it has refused to put drive-thrus in its restaurants and has established most of its units in outside shopping malls rather than in freestanding units at intersections so characteristic of other fast-food restaurants.

In 1993, KFC introduced its own rotisserie chicken, called Rotisserie Gold, to combat Boston Market. However, it quickly learned that its customer base was considerably different from that of Boston Market's. KFC's customers liked KFC chicken despite the fact that it was fried. In addition, customers did not respond well to the concept of buying whole chickens for take-out. They preferred instead to buy chicken by the piece. KFC withdrew its rotisserie chicken in 1996 and introduced a new line of roasted chicken called Tender

Roast, which could be sold by the piece and mixed with its Original Recipe and Extra Crispy Chicken.

Other major competitors within the chicken segment included Popeye's Famous Fried Chicken and Church's Chicken (both subsidiaries of AFC Enterprises in Atlanta), Chick-fil-A, Bojangle's, El Pollo Loco, Grandy's, Kenny Rogers Roasters, Mrs. Winner's, and Pudgie's. Both Church's and Popeye's had similar strategies—to compete head on with other "fried chicken" chains. Unlike KFC, neither chain offered rotisserie chicken, and nonfried chicken products were limited. Chick-fil-A focused exclusively on pressure-cooked and char-grilled skinless chicken breast sandwiches, which it served to customers in sit-down restaurants located predominantly in shopping malls. As many malls added food courts, often consisting of up to 15 fast-food units competing side by side, shopping malls became less enthusiastic about allocating separate store space to food chains. Therefore, in order to complement its existing restaurant base in shopping malls, Chick-fil-A began to open smaller units in shopping mall food courts, hospitals, and colleges. It also opened free-standing units in selected locations.

Demographic Trends

A number of demographic and societal trends contributed to increased demand for food prepared away from home. Because of the high divorce rate in the United States and the fact that people married later in life, single-person households represented about 25 percent of all U.S. households, up from 17 percent in 1970. This increased the number of individuals choosing to eat out rather than eat at home. The number of married women working outside the home also has increased dramatically during the last 25 years. About 59 percent of all married women have careers. According to the Conference Board, 64 percent of all married households will be double-income families by 2000. About 80 percent of households headed by individuals between the ages of 25 and 44 (both married and unmarried) will be double-income. Greater numbers of working women increased family incomes. According to *Restaurants & Institutions* magazine, more than one-third of all households had incomes of at least $50,000 in 1996. About 8 percent of all households had annual incomes over $100,000. The combination of higher numbers of dual-career families and rising incomes meant that fewer families had time to prepare food at home. According to Standard & Poor's *Industry Surveys,* Americans spent 55 percent of their food dollars at restaurants in 1995, up from 34 percent in 1970.

Fast-food restaurant chains met these demographic and societal changes by expanding their restaurant bases. However, by the early 1990s, the growth of traditional free-standing restaurants slowed as the U.S. market became saturated. The major exception was dinner houses, which continued to proliferate in response to Americans' increased passion for beef. Since 1990, the U.S. population has grown at an average annual rate of about 1 percent and reached 270 million people in 1997. Rising immigration since 1990 dramatically altered the ethnic makeup of the U.S. population. According to the Bureau of the Census, Americans born outside the United States made up 10 percent of the population in 1997. About 40 percent were Hispanic, while 24 percent were Asian. Nearly 30 percent of Americans born outside the United States arrived since 1990. As a result of these trends, restaurant chains expanded their menus to appeal to the different ethnic tastes of consumers, expanded into nontraditional locations such as department stores and airports, and made food more available through home delivery and take-out service.

Industry Consolidation and Mergers and Acquisitions

Lower growth in the U.S. fast-food market intensified competition for market share among restaurant chains and led to consolidation, primarily through mergers and acquisitions, during the mid-1990s. Many restaurant chains found that market share could be increased more quickly and cheaply by acquiring an existing company rather than building new units. In addition, fixed costs could be spread across a larger number of restaurants. This raised operating margins and gave companies an opportunity to build market share by lowering prices. An expanded restaurant base also gave companies greater purchasing power over supplies. In 1990, Grand Metropolitan, a British company, purchased Pillsbury Co. for $5.7 billion. Included in the purchase was Pillsbury's Burger King chain. Grand Met strengthened the franchise by upgrading existing restaurants and eliminated several levels of management in order to cut costs. This gave Burger King a long-needed boost in improving its position against McDonald's, its largest competitor. In 1988, Grand Met had purchased Wienerwald, a West German chicken chain, and the Spaghetti Factory, a Swiss chain.

Perhaps most important to KFC was Hardee's acquisition of 600 Roy Rogers restaurants from Marriott Corporation in 1990. Hardee's converted a large number of these restaurants to Hardee's units and introduced "Roy Rogers" fried chicken to its menu. By 1993, Hardee's had introduced fried chicken into most of its U.S. restaurants. Hardee's was unlikely to destroy the customer loyalty that KFC long enjoyed. However, it did cut into KFC's sales, because it was able to offer consumers a widened menu selection that appealed to a variety of family eating preferences. In 1997, Hardee's parent company, Imasco, Ltd., sold Hardee's to CKE Restaurants, Inc. CKE owned Carl's Jr., Rally's Hamburgers, and Checker's Drive-In. Boston Chicken, Inc., acquired Harry's Farmers Market, an Atlanta grocer that sold fresh quality prepared meals. The acquisition was designed to help Boston Chicken develop distribution beyond its Boston Market restaurants. AFC Enterprises, which operated Popeye's and Church's, acquired Chesapeake Bagel Bakery of McLean, Virginia, in order to diversify away from fried chicken and to strengthen its balance sheet.

The effect of these and other recent mergers and acquisitions on the industry was powerful. The top 10 restaurant companies controlled almost 60 percent of fast-food sales in the United States. The consolidation of a number of fast-food chains within larger, financially more powerful parent companies gave restaurant chains strong financial and managerial resources that could be used to compete against small chains in the industry.

International Quick-Service Market

Because of the aggressive pace of new restaurant construction in the United States during the 1970s and 1980s, opportunities to expand domestically through new restaurant construction in the 1990s were limited. Restaurant chains that did build new restaurants found that the higher cost of purchasing prime locations resulted in immense pressure to increase annual per-restaurant sales in order to cover higher initial investment costs. Many restaurants began to expand into international markets as an alternative to continued domestic expansion. In contrast to the U.S. market, international markets offered large customer bases with comparatively little competition. However, only a few U.S. restaurant chains had defined aggressive strategies for penetrating international markets by 1998.

Three restaurant chains that had established aggressive international strategies were McDonald's, KFC, and Pizza Hut. McDonald's operated the largest number of restaurants. In 1998, it operated 23,132 restaurants in 109 countries (10,409 restaurants were located outside the United States). In comparison, KFC, Pizza Hut, and Taco Bell together operated 29,712 restaurants in 79, 88, and 17 countries, respectively (9126 restaurants were located outside the United States). Of these four chains, KFC operated the greatest percentage of its restaurants (50 percent) outside the United States. McDonald's, Pizza Hut, and Taco Bell operated 45, 31, and 2 percent of their units outside the United States. KFC opened its first restaurant outside the United States in the late 1950s. By the time PepsiCo acquired KFC in 1986, KFC was already operating restaurants in 55 countries. KFC's early expansion abroad, its strong brand name, and its managerial experience in international markets gave it a strong competitive advantage vis-à-vis other fast-food chains that were investing abroad for the first time.

Exhibit D shows *Hotels'* 1994 list of the world's 30 largest fast-food restaurant chains (*Hotels* discontinued reporting these data after 1994). Seventeen of the 30 largest restaurant chains (ranked by number of units) were headquartered in the United States. There were a number of possible explanations for the relative scarcity of fast-food restaurant chains outside the United States. First, the United States represented the largest consumer market in the world, accounting for over one-fifth of the world's gross domestic product (GDP). Therefore, the United States was the strategic focus of the largest restaurant chains. Second, Americans were more quick to accept the fast-food concept. Many other cultures had strong culinary traditions that were difficult to break down. Europeans, for example, had histories of frequenting more midscale restaurants, where they spent hours in a formal setting enjoying native dishes and beverages. While KFC was again building restaurants in Germany by the late 1980s, it previously failed to penetrate the German market, because Germans were not accustomed to take-out food or to ordering food over

EXHIBIT D

The World's 30 Largest Fast-Food Chains (Year-End 1993, Ranked by Number of Countries)

	Franchise	Location	Units	Countries
1	Pizza Hut	Dallas, Texas	10,433	80
2	McDonald's	Oakbrook, Illinois	23,132	70
3	KFC	Louisville, Kentucky	9,033	68
4	Burger King	Miami, Florida	7,121	50
5	Baskin Robbins	Glendale, California	3,557	49
6	Wendy's	Dublin, Ohio	4,168	38
7	Domino's Pizza	Ann Arbor, Michigan	5,238	36
8	TCBY	Little Rock, Arkansas	7,474	22
9	Dairy Queen	Minneapolis, Minnesota	5,471	21
10	Dunkin' Donuts	Randolph, Massachusetts	3,691	21
11	Taco Bell	Irvine, California	4,921	20
12	Arby's	Fort Lauderdale, Florida	2,670	18
13	Subway Sandwiches	Milford, Connecticut	8,477	15
14	Sizzler International	Los Angeles, California	681	14
15	Hardee's	Rocky Mount, North Carolina	4,060	12
16	Little Caesar's	Detroit, Michigan	4,600	12
17	Popeye's Chicken	Atlanta, Georgia	813	12
18	Denny's	Spartanburg, South Carolina	1,515	10
19	A&W Restaurants	Livonia, Michigan	707	9
20	T.G.I. Friday's	Minneapolis, Minnesota	273	8
21	Orange Julius	Minneapolis, Minnesota	480	7
22	Church's Fried Chicken	Atlanta, Georgia	1,079	6
23	Long John Silver's	Lexington, Kentucky	1,464	5
24	Carl's Jr.	Anaheim, California	649	4
25	Loterria	Tokyo, Japan	795	4
26	Mos Burger	Tokyo, Japan	1,263	4
27	Skylark	Tokyo, Japan	1,000	4
28	Jack in the Box	San Diego, California	1,172	3
29	Quick Restaurants	Berchem, Belgium	876	3
30	Taco Time	Eugene, Oregon	300	3

Source: Hotels, May 1994; 1994 PepsiCo, Inc., Annual Report.

the counter. McDonald's had greater success penetrating the German market because it made a number of changes in its menu and operating procedures in order to better appeal to German culture. For example, German beer was served in all of McDonald's German restaurants. KFC had more success in Asia and Latin America, where chicken was a traditional dish.

Aside from cultural factors, international business carried risks not present in the U.S. market.

Long distances between headquarters and foreign franchises often made it difficult to control the quality of individual restaurants. Large distances also caused servicing and support problems. Transportation and other resource costs were higher than in the domestic market. In addition, time, cultural, and language differences increased communication and operational problems. Therefore, it was reasonable to expect U.S. restaurant chains to expand domestically as long as they achieved corporate profit and growth objectives. As the U.S. market became saturated and companies gained expertise in international markets, more companies could be expected to turn to profitable international markets as a means of expanding restaurant bases and increasing sales, profits, and market share.

KENTUCKY FRIED CHICKEN CORPORATION

KFC's worldwide sales, which included sales of both company-owned and franchised restaurants, grew to $8.0 billion in 1997. U.S. sales grew 2.6 percent over 1996 and accounted for about one-half of KFC's sales worldwide. KFC's U.S. share of the chicken segment fell 1.8 points to 55.8 percent (see Exhibit E). This marked the sixth consecutive year that KFC sustained a decline in market share. KFC's market share has fallen by 16.3 points since 1988, when it held a 72.1 percent market share. Boston Market, which established its first restaurant in 1992, increased its market share from 0 to 16.7 percent over the same period. On the surface, it appeared as though Boston Market's market-share gain was achieved by taking customers away from KFC. However, KFC's sales growth has remained

fairly stable and constant over the last 10 years. Boston Market's success was largely a function of its appeal to consumers who did not regularly patronize KFC or other chicken chains that sold fried chicken. By appealing to a market niche that was previously unsatisfied, Boston Market was able to expand the existing consumer base within the chicken segment of the fast-food industry.

Refranchising Strategy

The relatively low growth rate in sales in KFC's domestic restaurants during the 1992–1997 period was largely the result of KFC's decision in 1993 to begin selling company-owned restaurants to franchisees. When Colonel Sanders began to expand the Kentucky Fried Chicken system in the late 1950s, he established KFC as a system of independent franchisees. This was done in order to minimize his involvement in the operations of individual restaurants and to concentrate on the things he enjoyed the most—cooking, product development, and public relations. This resulted in a fiercely loyal and independent group of franchisees. PepsiCo's strategy when it acquired KFC in 1986 was to integrate KFC's operations in the PepsiCo system, in order to take advantage of operational, financial, and marketing synergies. How-

EXHIBIT E

Top U.S. Chicken Chains—Market Share (%)

	KFC	Boston Market	Popeye's	Chick-fil-A	Church's	Total
1988	72.1	0.0	12.0	5.8	10.1	100.0
1989	70.8	0.0	12.0	6.2	11.0	100.0
1990	71.3	0.0	12.3	6.6	9.8	100.0
1991	72.7	0.0	11.4	7.0	8.9	100.0
1992	71.5	0.9	11.4	7.5	8.7	100.0
1993	68.7	3.0	11.4	8.0	8.9	100.0
1994	64.8	6.9	11.3	8.4	8.6	100.0
1995	60.5	12.3	10.8	8.2	8.2	100.0
1996	57.6	16.2	10.0	8.4	7.8	100.0
1997	55.8	16.7	10.1	9.4	8.0	100.0
Change	−16.3	16.7	−1.9	3.6	−2.1	0.0

Source: Nation's Restaurant News.

ever, such a strategy demanded that PepsiCo become more involved in decisions over franchise operations, menu offerings, restaurant management, finance, and marketing. This was met by resistance with KFC franchises, who fiercely opposed increased control by the corporate parent. One method for PepsiCo to deal with this conflict was to expand through company-owned restaurants rather than through franchising. PepsiCo also used its strong cash flows to buy back unprofitable franchised restaurants, which could then be converted into company-owned restaurants. In 1986, company-owned restaurants made up 26 percent of KFC's U.S. restaurant base. By 1993, they made up about 40 percent (see Exhibit F).

While company-owned restaurants were relatively easier to control compared with franchises, they also required higher levels of investment. This meant that high levels of cash were diverted from PepsiCo's soft drink and snack food businesses into its restaurant businesses. However, the fast-food industry delivered lower returns than the soft drink and snack foods industries. Consequently, increased investment in KFC, Pizza Hut, and Taco Bell had a negative effect on PepsiCo's consolidated return on assets. By 1993, investors became concerned that PepsiCo's return on assets did not match returns delivered by Coca-Cola. In order to shore up its return on assets, PepsiCo decided to reduce the number of company-owned restaurants by selling them back to franchisees. This strategy lowered overall company sales but also lowered the amount of cash tied up in fixed assets, provided PepsiCo with one-time cash flow benefits from initial fees charged to franchisees, and generated an annual stream of franchise royalties. Tricon Global continued this strategy after the spin off in 1997.

Marketing Strategy

During the 1980s, consumers began to demand healthier foods, greater variety, and better service in a variety of nontraditional locations such as grocery stores, restaurants, airports, and outdoor events. This forced fast-food chains to expand menu offerings and to investigate nontraditional distribution channels and restaurant designs. Families also demanded greater value in the food they

EXHIBIT F

KFC Restaurant Count (U.S.)

	Company-Owned	% Total	Franchised/Licensed	% Total	Total
1986	1,246	26.4	3,474	73.6	4,720
1987	1,250	26.0	3,564	74.0	4,814
1988	1,262	25.8	3,637	74.2	4,899
1989	1,364	27.5	3,597	72.5	4,961
1990	1,389	27.7	3,617	72.3	5,006
1991	1,836	36.6	3,186	63.4	5,022
1992	1,960	38.8	3,095	61.2	5,055
1993	2,014	39.5	3,080	60.5	5,094
1994	2,005	39.2	3,110	60.8	5,115
1995	2,026	39.4	3,111	60.6	5,137
1996	1,932	37.8	3,176	62.2	5,108
1997	1,850	36.1	3,270	63.9	5,120
1986–1993 Compounded annual growth rate					
	7.1%		−1.7%		1.1%
1993–1997 Compounded annual growth rate					
	−2.1%		1.5%		0.1%

Source: Tricon Global Restaurants, Inc., 1997 Annual Report; PepsiCo, Inc., Annual Reports, 1994, 1995, 1996, 1997.

bought away from home. This increased pressure on fast-food chains to reduce prices and to lower operating costs in order to maintain profit margins.

Many of KFC's problems during the late 1980s surrounded its limited menu and inability to quickly bring new products to market. The popularity of its Original Recipe Chicken allowed KFC to expand without significant competition from other chicken competitors through the 1980s. As a result, new product introductions were never an important element of KFC's overall strategy. One of the most serious setbacks suffered by KFC came in 1989 as KFC prepared to add a chicken sandwich to its menu. While KFC was still experimenting with its chicken sandwich, McDonald's test marketed its McChicken sandwich in the Louisville market. Shortly thereafter, it rolled out the McChicken sandwich nationally. By beating KFC to the market, McDonald's was able to develop strong consumer awareness for its sandwich. This significantly increased KFC's cost of developing awareness of its own sandwich, which KFC introduced several months later. KFC eventually withdrew its sandwich because of low sales.

In 1991, KFC changed its logo in the United States from Kentucky Fried Chicken to KFC in order to reduce its image as a fried chicken chain. It continued to use the Kentucky Fried Chicken name internationally. It then responded to consumer demands for greater variety by introducing several products that would serve as alternatives to its Original Recipe Chicken. These included Oriental Wings, Popcorn Chicken, and Honey BBQ Chicken. It also introduced a dessert menu that included a variety of pies and cookies. In 1993, it rolled out Rotisserie Chicken and began to promote its lunch and dinner buffet. The buffet, which included 30 items, was introduced into almost 1600 KFC restaurants in 27 states by year-end. In 1998, KFC sold three types of chicken—Original Recipe and Extra Crispy (fried chicken) and Tender Roast (roasted chicken).

One of KFC's most aggressive strategies was the introduction of its Neighborhood Program. By mid-1993, almost 500 company-owned restaurants in New York, Chicago, Philadelphia, Washington, D.C., St. Louis, Los Angeles, Houston, and Dallas had been outfitted with special menu offerings to appeal exclusively to the black community. Menus were beefed up with side dishes such as greens, macaroni and cheese, peach cobbler, sweet-potato pie, and red beans and rice. In addition, restaurant employees wore African-inspired uniforms. The introduction of the Neighborhood Program increased sales by 5 to 30 percent in restaurants appealing directly to the black community. KFC followed by testing Hispanic-oriented restaurants in the Miami area, offering side dishes such as fried plantains, flan, and tres leches.

One of KFC's most significant problems in the U.S. market was that overcapacity made expansion of free-standing restaurants difficult. Fewer sites were available for new construction, and those sites, because of their increased cost, were driving profit margins down. Therefore, KFC initiated a new three-pronged distribution strategy. First, it focused on building smaller restaurants in nontraditional outlets such as airports, shopping malls, universities, and hospitals. Second, it experimented with home delivery. Home delivery was introduced in the Nashville and Albuquerque markets in 1994. By 1998, home delivery was offered in 365 U.S. restaurants. Other nontraditional distribution outlets being tested included units offering drive-thru and carry-out service only, snack shops in cafeterias, scaled-down outlets for supermarkets, and mobile units that could be transported to outdoor concerts and fairs.

A third focus of KFC's distribution strategy was restaurant cobranding, primarily with its sister chain, Taco Bell. By 1997, 349 KFC restaurants had added Taco Bell to their menus and displayed both the KFC and Taco Bell logos outside their restaurants. Cobranding gave KFC the opportunity to expand its business dayparts. While about two-thirds of KFC's business was dinner, Taco Bell's primary business occurred at lunch. By combining the two concepts in the same unit, sales at individual restaurants could be increased significantly. KFC believed that there were opportunities to sell the Taco Bell concept in over 3900 of its U.S. restaurants.

Operating Efficiencies

As pressure continued to build on fast-food chains to limit price increases, restaurant chains searched for ways to reduce overhead and other operating costs in order to improve profit margins. In 1989, KFC reorganized its U.S. operations to eliminate overhead costs and increase efficiency. Included in this reorganization was a revision of KFC's crew training programs and operating standards. A renewed emphasis was placed on improving customer service, cleaner restaurants, faster and friendlier service, and continued high-quality products. In 1992, KFC reorganized its middle-management ranks, eliminating 250 of the 1500 management positions at KFC's corporate headquarters. More responsibility was assigned to restaurant franchisees and marketing managers and pay was more closely aligned with customer service and restaurant performance. In 1997, Tricon Global signed a 5-year agreement with PepsiCo Food Systems (which was later sold by PepsiCo to AmeriServe Food Distributors) to distribute food and supplies to Tricon's 29,712 KFC, Pizza Hut, and Taco Bell units. This provided KFC with significant opportunities to benefit from economies of scale in distribution.

INTERNATIONAL OPERATIONS

Much of the early success of the top 10 fast-food chains was the result of aggressive building strategies. Chains were able to discourage competition by building in low-population areas that could only support a single fast-food chain. McDonald's was particularly successful because it was able to quickly expand into small towns across the United States, thereby preempting other fast-food chains. It was equally important to beat a competitor into more largely populated areas where location was of prime importance. KFC's early entry into international markets placed it in a strong position to benefit from international expansion as the U.S. market became saturated. In 1997, 50 percent of KFC's restaurants were located outside the United States. While 364 new restaurants were opened outside the United States in 1997, only 12 new restaurants were added to the U.S. system. Most of KFC's international expansion was through franchises, although some restaurants were licensed to operators or jointly operated with a local partner. Expansion through franchising was an important strategy for penetrating international markets because franchises were owned and operated by local entrepreneurs with a deeper understanding of local language, culture, and customs, as well as local law, financial markets, and marketing characteristics. Franchising was particularly important for expansion into smaller countries such as the Dominican Republic, Grenada, Bermuda, and Suriname, which could only support a single restau-

rant. Costs were prohibitively high for KFC to operate company-owned restaurants in these smaller markets. Of the 5117 KFC restaurants located outside the United States in 1997, 68 percent were franchised, while 22 percent were company-owned, and 10 percent were licensed restaurants or joint ventures.

In larger markets such as Japan, China, and Mexico, there was a stronger emphasis on building company-owned restaurants. By coordinating purchasing, recruiting and training, financing, and advertising, fixed costs could be spread over a large number of restaurants, and lower prices on products and services could be negotiated. KFC also was better able to control product and service quality. In order to take advantage of economies of scale, Tricon Global Restaurants managed all the international units of its KFC, Pizza Hut, and Taco Bell chains through its Tricon International Division located in Dallas, Texas. This enabled Tricon Global Restaurants to leverage its strong advertising expertise, international experience, and restaurant management experience across all its KFC, Pizza Hut, and Taco Bell restaurants.

Latin-American Strategy

KFC's primary market presence in Latin America during the 1980s was in Mexico, Puerto Rico, and the Caribbean. KFC established subsidiaries in Mexico and Puerto Rico, from which it coordinated the construction and operation of company-owned restaurants. A third subsidiary in Venezuela was closed because of the high fixed costs associated with running the small subsidiary. Franchises were used to penetrate other countries in the Caribbean whose market size prevented KFC from profitably operating company restaurants. KFC relied exclusively on the operation of company-owned restaurants in Mexico through 1989. While franchising was popular in the United States, it was virtually unknown in Mexico until 1990, mainly because of the absence of a law protecting patents, information, and technology transferred to the Mexican franchise. In addition, royalties were limited. As a result, most fast-food chains opted to invest in Mexico using company-owned units.

In 1990, Mexico enacted a new law that provided for the protection of technology transferred into Mexico. Under the new legislation, the franchisor and franchisee were free to set their own terms. Royalties also were allowed under the new law. Royalties were taxed at a 15 percent rate on technology assistance and knowhow and 35 percent for other royalty categories. The advent of the new franchise law resulted in an explosion of franchises in fast-food, services, hotels, and retail outlets. In 1992, franchises had an estimated $750 million in sales in over 1200 outlets throughout Mexico. Prior to passage of Mexico's franchise law, KFC limited its Mexican operations primarily to Mexico City, Guadalajara, and Monterrey. This enabled KFC to better coordinate operations and minimize costs of distribution to individual restaurants. The new franchise law gave KFC and other fast-food chains the opportunity to expand their restaurant bases more quickly into more rural regions of Mexico, where responsibility for management could be handled by local franchisees.

After 1990, KFC altered its Latin American strategy in a number of ways. First, it opened 29 franchises in Mexico to complement its company-owned restaurant base. It then expanded its company-owned restaurants into the Virgin Islands and reestablished a subsidiary in Venezuela. Third, it expanded its franchise operations into South America. In 1990, a franchise was opened in Chile, and in 1993, a franchise was opened in Brazil. Franchises were subsequently established in Colombia, Ecuador, Panama, and Peru, among other South American countries. A fourth subsidiary was established in Brazil, in order to develop company-owned restaurants. Brazil was Latin America's largest economy and McDonald's primary Latin American investment location. By June 1998, KFC operated 438 restaurants in 32 Latin American countries. By comparison, McDonald's operated 1091 restaurants in 28 countries in Latin America.

Exhibit G shows the Latin American operations of KFC and McDonald's. KFC's early entry into Latin America during the 1970s gave it a leadership position in Mexico and the Caribbean. It also had gained an edge in Ecuador and Peru, countries where McDonald's had not yet devel-

EXHIBIT G

Latin American Restaurant Count: KFC and McDonald's (as of December 31, 1997)

	KFC Company Restaurants	KFC Franchised Restaurants	KFC Total Restaurants	McDonald's
Argentina	—	—	—	131
Bahamas	—	10	10	3
Barbados	—	7	7	—
Brazil	6	2	8	480
Chile	—	29	29	27
Columbia	—	19	19	18
Costa Rica	—	5	5	19
Ecuador	—	18	18	2
Jamaica	—	17	17	7
Mexico	128	29	157	131
Panama	—	21	21	20
Peru	—	17	17	5
Puerto Rico & Virgin Islands	67	—	67	115
Trinidad & Tobago	—	27	27	3
Uruguay	—	—	—	18
Venezuela	6	—	6	53
Other	—	30	30	59
Total	207	231	438	1,091

Source: Tricon Global Restaurants, Inc.; McDonald's, 1997 Annual Report.

oped a strong presence. McDonald's focused its Latin American investment in Brazil, Argentina, and Uruguay, countries where KFC had little or no presence. McDonald's also was strong in Venezuela. Both KFC and McDonald's were strong in Chile, Colombia, Panama, and Puerto Rico.

Economic Environment and the Mexican Market

Mexico was KFC's strongest market in Latin America. While McDonald's had aggressively established restaurants in Mexico since 1990, KFC retained the leading market share. Because of its close proximity to the United States, Mexico was an attractive location for U.S. trade and investment. Mexico's population of 98 million people was approximately one-third as large as the United States and represented a large market for U.S. companies. In comparison, Canada's population of 30.3 million people was only one-third as large as Mexico's. Mexico's close proximity to the United States meant that transportation costs between the United States and Mexico were significantly lower than to Europe or Asia. This increased the competitiveness of U.S. goods in comparison with European and Asian goods, which had to be transported to Mexico across the Atlantic or Pacific Ocean at substantial cost. The United States was, in fact, Mexico's largest

trading partner. Over 75 percent of Mexico's imports came from the United States, while 84 percent of its exports were to the United States (see Exhibit H). Many U.S. firms invested in Mexico in order to take advantage of lower wage rates. By producing goods in Mexico, U.S. goods could be shipped back into the United States for sale or shipped to third markets at lower cost.

While the U.S. market was critically important to Mexico, Mexico still represented a small percentage of overall U.S. trade and investment. Since the early 1900s, the portion of U.S. exports to Latin America had declined. Instead, U.S. exports to Canada and Asia, where economic growth outpaced growth in Mexico, increased more quickly. Canada was the largest importer of U.S. goods. Japan was the largest exporter of goods to the United States, with Canada a close second. U.S. investment in Mexico also was small, mainly because of past government restrictions on foreign investment. Most U.S. foreign investment was in Europe, Canada, and Asia.

The lack of U.S. investment in and trade with Mexico during this century was mainly the result of Mexico's long history of restricting trade and foreign direct investment. The Institutional Revolutionary Party (PRI), which came to power in Mexico during the 1930s, had historically pursued protectionist economic policies in order to shield Mexico's

EXHIBIT H

Mexico's Major Trading Partners—% Total Exports and Imports

	1992		1994		1996	
	Exports	*Imports*	*Exports*	*Imports*	*Exports*	*Imports*
U.S.	81.1	71.3	85.3	71.8	84.0	75.6
Japan	1.7	4.9	1.6	4.8	1.4	4.4
Germany	1.1	4.0	0.6	3.9	0.7	3.5
Canada	2.2	1.7	2.4	2.0	1.2	1.9
Italy	0.3	1.6	0.1	1.3	1.2	1.1
Brazil	0.9	1.8	0.6	1.5	0.9	0.8
Spain	2.7	1.4	1.4	1.7	1.0	0.7
Other	10.0	13.3	8.0	13.0	9.6	12.0
% Total	100.0	100.0	100.0	100.0	100.0	100.0
Value ($M)	46,196	62,129	60,882	79,346	95,991	89,464

Source: International Monetary Fund, *Direction of Trade Statistics Yearbook,* 1997.

economy from foreign competition. Many industries were government-owned or controlled, and many Mexican companies focused on producing goods for the domestic market without much attention to building export markets. High tariffs and other trade barriers restricted imports into Mexico, and foreign ownership of assets in Mexico was largely prohibited or heavily restricted.

Additionally, a dictatorial and entrenched government bureaucracy, corrupt labor unions, and a long tradition of anti-Americanism among many government officials and intellectuals reduced the motivation of U.S. firms for investing in Mexico. The nationalization of Mexico's banks in 1982 led to higher real interest rates and lower investor confidence. Afterward, the Mexican government battled high inflation, high interest rates, labor unrest, and lost consumer purchasing power. Investor confidence in Mexico, however, improved after 1988, when Carlos Salinas de Gortari was elected president. Following his election, Salinas embarked on an ambitious restructuring of the Mexican economy. He initiated policies to strengthen the free-market components of the economy, lowered top marginal tax rates to 36 percent (down from 60 percent in 1986), and eliminated many restrictions on foreign investment. Foreign firms can now buy up to 100 percent of the equity in many Mexican firms. Foreign ownership of Mexican firms was previously limited to 49 percent.

Privatization

The privatization of government-owned companies came to symbolize the restructuring of Mexico's economy. In 1990, legislation was passed to privatize all government-run banks. By the end of 1992, over 800 of some 1200 government-owned companies had been sold, including Mexicana and AeroMexico, the two largest airline companies in Mexico, and Mexico's 18 major banks. However, more than 350 companies remained under government ownership. These represented a significant portion of the assets owned by the state at the start of 1988. Therefore, the sale of government-owned companies, in terms of asset value, was moderate. A large percentage of the remaining government-owned assets were controlled by government-run companies in certain strategic industries such as steel, electricity, and petroleum. These industries had long been protected

by government ownership. As a result, additional privatization of government-owned enterprises until 1993 was limited. However, in 1993, President Salinas opened up the electricity sector to independent power producers, and Petroleos Mexicanos (Pemex), the state-run petrochemical monopoly, initiated a program to sell off many of its nonstrategic assets to private and foreign buyers.

North American Free Trade Agreement (NAFTA)

Prior to 1989, Mexico levied high tariffs on most imported goods. In addition, many other goods were subjected to quotas, licensing requirements, and other nontariff trade barriers. In 1986, Mexico joined the General Agreement on Tariffs and Trade (GATT), a world trade organization designed to eliminate barriers to trade among member nations. As a member of GATT, Mexico was obligated to apply its system of tariffs to all member nations equally. As a result of its membership in GATT, Mexico dropped tariff rates on a variety of imported goods. In addition, import license requirements were dropped for all but 300 imported items. During President Salinas' administration, tariffs were reduced from an average of 100 percent on most items to an average of 11 percent.

On January 1, 1994, the North American Free Trade Agreement (NAFTA) went into effect. The passage of NAFTA, which included Canada, the United States, and Mexico, created a trading bloc with a larger population and gross domestic product than the European Union. All tariffs on goods traded among the three countries were scheduled to be phased out. NAFTA was expected to be particularly beneficial for Mexican exporters because reduced tariffs made their goods more competitive in the United States compared with goods exported to the United States from other countries. In 1995, one year after NAFTA went into effect, Mexico posted its first balance of trade surplus in 6 years. Part of this surplus was attributed to reduced tariffs resulting from the NAFTA agreement. However, the peso crisis of 1995, which lowered the value of the peso against the dollar, increased the price of goods imported into Mexico and lowered the price of Mexican products exported to the United States. Therefore, it was still too early to

EXHIBIT I

Selected Economic Data for Canada, the United States, and Mexico

Annual Change (%)	1993	1994	1995	1996	1997
GDP growth					
Canada	3.3	4.8	5.5	4.1	—
United States	4.9	5.8	4.8	5.1	5.9
Mexico	21.4	13.3	29.4	38.2	—
Real GDP growth					
Canada	2.2	4.1	2.3	1.2	—
United States	2.2	3.5	2.0	2.8	3.8
Mexico	2.0	4.5	−6.2	5.1	—
Inflation					
Canada	1.9	0.2	2.2	1.5	1.6
United States	3.0	2.5	2.8	2.9	2.4
Mexico	9.7	6.9	35.0	34.4	20.6
Depreciation against $U.S.					
Canada (C$)	4.2	6.0	−2.7	0.3	4.3
Mexico (NP)	−0.3	71.4	43.5	2.7	3.6

Source: International Monetary Fund, *International Financial Statistics,* 1998.

assess the full effects of the NAFTA agreement. (See Exhibit I for further details.)

Foreign Exchange and the Mexican Peso Crisis of 1995

Between 1982 and 1991, a two-tiered exchange-rate system was in force in Mexico. The system consisted of a controlled rate and a free-market rate. A controlled rate was used for imports, foreign debt payments, and conversion of export proceeds. An estimated 70 percent of all foreign transactions were covered by the controlled rate. A free-market rate was used for other transactions. In 1989, President Salinas instituted a policy of allowing the peso to depreciate against the dollar by one peso per day. The result was a grossly overvalued peso. This lowered the price of imports and led to an increase in imports of over 23 percent in 1989. At the same time, Mexican exports became less competitive on world markets.

In 1991, the controlled rate was abolished and replaced with an official free rate. In order to limit the range of fluctuations in the value of the peso, the government fixed the rate at which it would buy or sell pesos. A floor (the maximum price at which pesos could be purchased) was established at Ps 3056.20 and remained fixed. A ceiling (the maximum price at which the peso could be sold) was established at Ps 3056.40 and allowed to move upward by Ps 0.20 per day. This was later revised to Ps 0.40 per day. In 1993, a new currency, called the *new peso,* was issued with three fewer zeros. The new currency was designed to simplify transactions and to reduce the cost of printing currency.

When Ernesto Zedillo became Mexico's president in December 1994, one of his objectives was to continue the stability of prices, wages, and exchange rates achieved by ex-President Carlos Salinas de Gortari during his 5-year tenure as president. However, Salinas had achieved stability largely on the basis of price, wage, and foreign-exchange controls. While giving the appearance of stability, an overvalued peso continued to encourage imports, which exacerbated Mexico's balance of trade deficit. Mexico's government continued to use foreign reserves to finance its balance of trade deficits. According to the Banco de Mexico, foreign currency reserves fell from $24 billion in January 1994 to $5.5 billion in January 1995. Anticipating a devaluation of the peso, investors began to move capital into U.S. dollar investments. In order to relieve pressure on the peso, Zedillo announced on December 19, 1994 that the peso would be allowed to depreciate by an additional 15 percent per year against the dollar compared with the maximum allowable depreciation of 4 percent per year established during the Salinas administration. Within 2 days, continued pressure on the peso forced Zedillo to allow the peso to float freely against the dollar. By mid-January 1995, the peso had lost 35 percent of its value against the dollar, and the Mexican stock market plunged 20 percent. By November 1995, the peso had depreciated from 3.1 pesos per dollar to 7.3 pesos per dollar.

The continued devaluation of the peso resulted in higher import prices, higher inflation, destabilization within the stock market, and higher interest rates. Mexico struggled to pay its dollar-based debts. In order to thwart a possible default by Mexico, the U.S. government, International Monetary Fund, and World Bank pledged $24.9 billion in emergency loans. Zedillo then announced an emergency economic package called the pacto that included reduced government spending, increased sales of government-run businesses, and a freeze on wage increases.

Labor Problems

One of KFC's primary concerns in Mexico was the stability of labor markets. Labor was relatively plentiful, and wages were low. However, much of the workforce was relatively unskilled. KFC benefited from lower labor costs, but labor unrest, low job retention, high absenteeism, and poor punctuality were significant problems. Absenteeism and punctuality were partially cultural. However, problems with worker retention and labor unrest also were the result of workers' frustration over the loss of their purchasing power due to inflation and government controls on wage increases. Absenteeism remained high at approximately 8 to 14 percent of the labor force, though it was declining because of job security fears. Turnover continued to be a problem and ran at between 5 and 12 percent per month. Therefore, employee screening and internal training were important issues for firms investing in Mexico.

Higher inflation and the government's freeze on wage increases led to a dramatic decline in disposable income after 1994. Further, a slowdown in business activity, brought about by higher interest rates and lower government spending, led many businesses to lay off workers. By the end of 1995, an estimated 1 million jobs had been lost as a result of the economic crisis sparked by the peso devaluation. As a result, industry groups within Mexico called for new labor laws giving them more freedom to hire and fire employees and increased flexibility to hire part-time rather than full-time workers.

RISKS AND OPPORTUNITIES

The peso crisis of 1995 and resulting recession in Mexico left KFC managers with a great deal of uncertainty regarding Mexico's economic and political future. KFC had benefited from economic stability between 1988 and 1994. Inflation was brought down, the peso was relatively stable, labor unrest was relatively calm, and Mexico's new franchise law had enabled KFC to expand into rural areas using franchises rather than company-owned restaurants. By the end of 1995, KFC had built 29 franchises in Mexico. The foreign-exchange crisis of 1995 had severe implications for U.S. firms operating in Mexico. The devaluation of the peso resulted in higher inflation and capital flight out of Mexico. Capital flight reduced the supply of capital and led to higher interest rates. In order to reduce inflation, Mexico's government instituted an austerity program that resulted in lower disposable income, higher unemployment, and lower demand for products and services.

Another problem was Mexico's failure to reduce restrictions on U.S. and Canadian investment in a timely fashion. Many U.S. firms experienced problems getting required approvals for new ventures from the Mexican government. A good example was United Parcel Service (UPS), which sought government approval to use large trucks for deliveries in Mexico. Approvals were delayed, forcing UPS to use smaller trucks. This put UPS at a competitive disadvantage vis-à-vis Mexican companies. In many cases, UPS was forced to subcontract delivery work to Mexican companies that were allowed to use larger, more cost-efficient trucks. Other U.S. companies such as Bell Atlantic and TRW faced similar problems. TRW, which signed a joint-venture agreement with a Mexican partner, had to wait 15 months longer than anticipated before the Mexican government released rules on how it could receive credit data from banks. TRW claimed that the Mexican government slowed the approval process in order to placate several large Mexican banks.

A final area of concern for KFC was increased political turmoil in Mexico during the last several years. On January 1, 1994, the day NAFTA went into effect, rebels (descendants of the Mayans) rioted in the southern Mexican province of Chiapas on the Guatemalan border. After 4 days of fighting, Mexican troops had driven the rebels out of several towns earlier seized by the rebels. Around 150—mostly rebels—were killed. The uprising symbolized many of the fears of the poor in Mexico. While ex-President Salinas' economic programs had increased economic growth and wealth in Mexico, many of Mexico's poorest felt that they had not benefited. Many of Mexico's farmers, faced with lower tariffs on imported agricultural goods from the United States, felt that they might be driven out of business because of lower-priced imports. Therefore, social unrest among Mexico's Indians, farmers, and the poor could potentially unravel much of the economic success achieved in Mexico during the last 5 years.

Further, ex-President Salinas' hand-picked successor for president was assassinated in early 1994 while campaigning in Tijuana. The assassin was a 23-year-old mechanic and migrant worker believed to be affiliated with a dissident group upset with the PRI's economic reforms. The possible existence of a dissident group raised fears of political violence in the future. The PRI quickly named Ernesto Zedillo, a 42-year-old economist with little political experience, as their new presidential candidate. Zedillo was elected president in December 1994. Political unrest was not limited to Mexican officials and companies. In October 1994, between 30 and 40 masked men attacked a McDonald's restaurant in the tourist section of Mexico City to show their opposition to California's Proposition 187, which would have curtailed benefits to illegal aliens (primarily from Mexico). The men threw cash registers to the floor, cracked them open, smashed windows, overturned tables, and spray-painted slogans on the walls such as "No to Fascism" and "Yankee Go Home."

KFC faced a variety of issues in Mexico and Latin America in 1998. Prior to 1995, few restaurants had been opened in South America. However, KFC was now aggressively building new restaurants in the region. KFC halted openings of franchised restaurants in Mexico, and all restaurants opened since 1995 were company-owned. KFC was more aggressively building restaurants in South America, which remained largely unpenetrated by KFC through 1995. Of greatest importance was Brazil, where McDonald's had already established a strong market-share position. Brazil was Latin America's largest economy and a largely untapped market for KFC. The danger in ignoring Mexico was that a conservative investment strategy could jeopardize its market-share lead over McDonald's in a large market where KFC long enjoyed enormous popularity.

Procter & Gamble Online: Tide and Pampers Hit the Web

This case was prepared by Andrew Herz, Richard Palmer, Jeffrey Prus, and Yuval Steiman, MBA students at the University of Michigan Business School, under the direction of Professor Allan Afuah.

"In the short term, it's unlikely that interactive media will make or break the marketing plans for very many traditional package goods brands. However, if you extend the timeline just a few years, we see the potential for a digital media disruption that will rapidly reshape not only our advertising and marketing efforts, but perhaps our entire business model."[1]

Denis Beausejour
VP Advertising, Procter & Gamble

PROCTER & GAMBLE BACKGROUND

Founded in 1837 by candlemaker William Procter and soapmaker James Gamble, Procter & Gamble (P&G) has grown to become the United States' largest maker of household products and the world's largest advertiser. Worldwide earnings in 1998 were $3.8 billion from sales of $37.2 billion. (See Appendix 1 for financial highlights.) P&G

holds a strong position in several categories including paper goods (diapers, facial tissue, etc.), laundry and cleaning (laundry detergent, dish soap, etc.), beauty care (shampoo, cosmetics, etc.), health care (toothpaste, mouthwash, etc.) and food and beverage (peanut butter, coffee, etc.). They have developed some of the world's best known brands including Tide, Ariel, Downy, Bounty, Pampers, Ivory, Head & Shoulders, Crisco, Jif, Pringles, Crest and Scope. (See Appendix 2 for list of major brands.)

P&G has been dedicated to innovation in both products and advertising throughout its history. Product innovations include Tide—the world's first heavy-duty synthetic detergent, Pert Plus—the world's first two-in-one shampoo, and Pampers—the brand which created the disposable diaper business. Leading the development of advertising, P&G's Ivory campaign in the late 1800s was the first to advertise directly to consumers. As new advertising media became available, P&G capitalized on them. The company was the first to sponsor daytime dramas beginning with radio shows in 1932. In the 1950s, P&G created and produced television soap operas in order to reach American housewives. In 1998, P&G continued to be a leader in advertising, spending over $3.7 billion worldwide.

APPENDIX 1

Procter & Gamble Five-Year Financial Highlights
(Millions of Dollars Except Per Share Amounts)

	1998	1997	1996	1995	1994
Net Sales	37,154	35,764	35,284	33,482	30,385
Operating Income	6,055	5,488	4,815	4,244	3,670
Net Earnings	3,780	3,415	3,046	2,645	2,211
Net Earnings Margin	10.2%	9.5%	8.6%	7.9%	7.3%
Basic Net Earnings Per Common Share	2.74	2.43	2.14	1.85	1.54
Diluted Net Earnings Per Common Share	2.56	2.28	2.01	1.74	1.45
Dividends Per Common Share	1.01	.90	.80	.70	.62
Research and Development Expense	1,546	1,469	1,399	1,304	1,162
Advertising Expense	3,704	3,466	3,254	3,284	2,996
Total Assets	30,966	27,544	27,730	28,125	25,535
Capital Expenditures	2,559	2,129	2,179	2,146	1,841
Long-Term Debt	5,765	4,143	4,670	5,161	4,980
Shareholders' Equity	12,236	12,046	11,722	10,589	8,832

Source: Procter & Gamble, 1998 Annual Report

ORGANIZATION 2005

On September 9, 1998, John Pepper, P&G Chairman and Chief Executive, announced a major restructuring of P&G called Organization 2005. Ideally, the change would enable P&G to "capture the global upside potential of our opportunities to lead innovation in our businesses and to move at the speed today's marketplace requires".[2] The company will be reorganized around seven global business units (Baby Care, Beauty Care, Fabric & Home Care, Feminine Protection, Food & Beverage, Health Care [&] Corporate New Ventures, and Tissue & Towel), which have full profit responsibility. Creating a new global organization will enable P&G to react more quickly to changes in the marketplace including the rapid development of information technology. In the past, "...maybe every year you have a new ad campaign; every year or 18 months you have a new product. And so the time zone of where we are...and the time zone of what's happening in the digital information development are just totally different,"[3] states Denis Beausejour. Durk Yager, P&G President and Chief Operating Officer commented, "People think of us as a marketing company, but we are really first and foremost a technology company."[4] This organizational change was designed to help P&G continue its history of innovation at an even greater speed in the future. (See Appendix 3 for organizational chart.)

IMPLICATIONS OF THE INTERNET

Growth

The 1998 data on projected Internet usage indicated that the medium would continue to accelerate in importance in the future. In the U.S., Internet usage was expected to increase to 85 million people by 2002 (vs. 47 million in 1998). Revenue expenditure statistics from consumer online

APPENDIX 2

Major Procter & Gamble Brands

Laundry & Cleaning Products	Paper Products
Ace Bleach	Always/Whisper
Ariel	Bounty
Cascade	Charmin
Cheer	Luvs
Dawn	Pampers
Downy	Pampers Wipes
Fairy	Puffs
Joy	Tampax
Lenor	Tempo
Mr. Clean	
Tide	

Beauty Care Products	Health Care Products	Food & Beverage Products
Cover Girl	Asacol	Crisco
Head & Shoulders	Blend-A-Med	Folgers
Ivory	Chloraseptic	Hawaiian Punch
Max Factor	Crest	Jif
Oil of Olay	Didronel	Millstone
Old Spice	Macrobid	Olean
Pantene Pro-V	NyQuil	Pringles
Pert Plus	Pepto-Bismol	Punica
Rejoice	Scope	Sunny Delight
Safeguard	Vicks Formula 44	
Secret	Vicks VapoRub	
SK-II		
Vidal Sassoon		
Zest		

Source: Procter & Gamble, 1998 Annual Report

purchases were even more dramatic: from a projected $4.5 billion worldwide in 1998 to over $35 billion in 2002.

Beyond sheer quantity, the *quality* of Internet users in 1998 was enough to make companies sit up and take notice. It was estimated the roughly two-thirds of Internet users were college graduates, with 37% having some post-graduate education. Median household income estimates ranged from $59K to just under $67K, and median age estimates ranged from the mid- to late-thirties. Internet users were young, smart, and had money to spend, making them prime targets as long-term brand-loyal customers. Additionally, it was predicted that by 2000, 48% of Internet users would be women (vs. 24% in 1995). This had tremendous implications for consumer goods manufacturers because women frequently made these purchase decisions. (See Appendix 4 for charts on Internet usage.)

Market Information

Beyond being strictly a sales and marketing channel, the Internet had the potential to provide companies with extremely detailed behavioral information about their users. In addition to simply gathering a consumer's name, address, and purchasing history, web servers could track a customer's "digital footprints" throughout a site.[5] Knowing what items specific customers had previously purchased, as well as what items they perused, could help the merchant logically predict future buying behavior and develop extremely targeted personalized marketing on future site visits, as well as enhance inventory management efficiency.

Amazon.com was frequently cited as the leader in using past online behavior to its advantage. Previously registered visitors were personally greeted when logging on, and purchase recommendations

APPENDIX 3

Organizational Structure Pre-1999 Organization

Chairman & Chief Executive (J.E. Pepper)				
President & COO (D.I. Jager)				**Senior Vice Presidents**
EVP P&G Europe, Middle East and Africa	EVP P&G Asia	EVP P&G Latin America	EVP P&G North America	Advertising/Market Research/Public Affairs (R.L. Wehling)
				Finance (E.G. Nelson)
(H. Einsmann)	(A.G. Lafley)	(J.P. Montoya)	(W.C. Berndt)	Human Resources (R.L. Antionne)
				Legal (J.J. Johnson)
				Product Supply (G.T. Martin)
				Management Systems (T.A. Garrett)
				Research & Development (G.F. Brunner)
				Customer Business Development (S.N. David)
North America Region				
COO (D.I. Jager) EVP (W.C. Bernt)				
Beauty Care	Food & Beverage	Health Care	Laundry & Cleaning	Paper

APPENDIX 3 *(continued)*

Organization 2005

Global Business Units

"Drive greater innovation and speed by centering strategy and profit responsibility globally on brands, rather than on geographies."

Unit	Leader
Baby Care (Cincinnati)	Mark Ketchum
Beauty Care (Cincinnati)	A.G. Lafley
Fabric & Home Care (Brussels)	Wolfgang Berndt
Feminine Protection (Kobe)	R. Kerry Clark
Food & Beverage (Caracas)	Jorge Montoya
Health Care & Corporate New Ventures (Cincinnati)	Bruce Byrnes
Tissue & Towel (Cincinnati)	Gary Martin

Market Development Organizations

"Maximize the business potential of P&G's entire portfolio in each local market by developing innovative local maket strategies, new strategic alliances and distribution channels, superior retail customer relationships and external relations programs."

Region	Leader
North America (ex. Mexico)	A.G. Lafley
Central & Eastern Europe	Herbert Schmitz
Middle East/Africa/General Export	Fuad Kuraytim
Western Europe	Toni Belloni
ASEAN/India/Australasia	Martin Nuechtern
Northeast Asia	Robert McDonald
Health Care & Corporate New Ventures	Bruce Byrnes
Greater China	Dimitri Panayotopoulos
Latin America	Jorge Montoya

Global Business Services

"Provide essential business services, such as accounting, employee benefits and payroll, order management, and information and technology services to the rest of the company."

Function	Leader
Global Business Services	Michael Power
Corporate Customer Business Development	Steve David
Central & Eastern Europe	Herbert Schmitz
Corporate Finance	Clayt Daley
Corporate Human Resources	Dick Antoine
Corporate Information Technology	Todd Garrett
Corporate Legal	Jim Johnson
Corporate Mktg./Mkt. Research/Gov. Relations	Bob Wehling
Corporate Product Supply	Gary Martin
Corporate Public Affairs	Charlotte Otto
Corporate Research & Development	Gordon Brunner

Source: P&G Corporate Press Release, September 9, 1998.

could be made easily based on buying history. Consumers could then use Amazon.com's complementary services to read book reviews and learn about an author before deciding to buy. Once they were ready to checkout, previously stored shipping addresses and credit card information resulted in a one-click purchasing process. These innovations helped Amazon.com maintain a higher purchase average than traditional bookstores.

Information gathering was also effective beyond the boundaries of a retailer's own web site. Consumer data collected on their site could help companies target additional marketing spending to drive future business. For example, Preview Travel Inc., an online travel agency based in San Francisco, used previous bookings to determine top vacation choice trends in the industry. The company then purchased "keywords" for these locations on Internet directory sites such as Yahoo!; whenever a search was performed using these words, a banner ad for Preview Travel would appear with the search results.[6]

Strategic Online Branding

The Internet promised to radically change the definition of strategic branding. For example, Internet start-ups with access to server space and minimal advertising expenditures could immediately generate excitement about their brands. These companies could undercut older, established companies who had spent millions of dollars and decades establishing their own brands through traditional advertising channels that were growing increasingly crowded and fragmented.[7]

The Internet also provided the opportunity to take a brand's emotional value to a new level. Brand-builders hoped that effective online interactivity would not only increase sales, but also enhance brand loyalty. For example, General Motors

APPENDIX 4

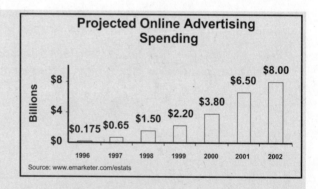

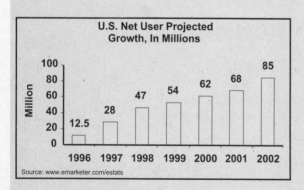

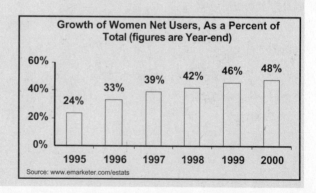

APPENDIX 4 (*continued*)

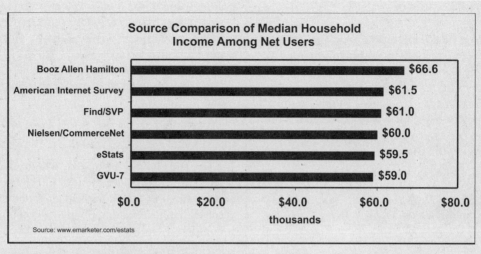

Source Comparison of Median Household Income Among Net Users

	thousands
Booz Allen Hamilton	$66.6
American Internet Survey	$61.5
Find/SVP	$61.0
Nielsen/CommerceNet	$60.0
eStats	$59.5
GVU-7	$59.0

Source: www.emarketer.com/estats

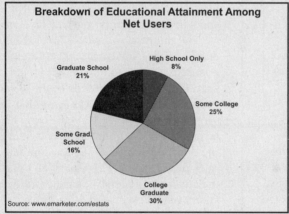

Breakdown of Educational Attainment Among Net Users

- High School Only 8%
- Some College 25%
- College Graduate 30%
- Some Grad School 16%
- Graduate School 21%

Source: www.emarketer.com/estats

APPENDIX 5

TV Ad Leaders Pale Online

Biggest Spenders on TV	Biggest Spenders Online
General Motors	Microsoft
Proter & Gamble	IBM
Johnson & Johnson	Excite
Philip Morris	Yahoo!
Ford Motor	Netscape

Source: Business Week, 11/9/98

Corp.'s Saturn division included on its web site a lease-price calculator, a design shop to choose and display vehicle options, and an online ordering form. This resulted in over 80% of Saturn's leads coming via the Internet in 1998. Mastercard went beyond simply mimicking a television commercial online to positioning itself as a seal of approval for secure E-commerce.[8] These traditional marketers followed the lead of online pioneers like Dell and Amazon.com, turning their online presence from extensions of television or print advertising into experienced-oriented destinations on the web. (See Appendix 5 for chart on television vs. online ad spenders.)

THE DEVELOPMENT OF THE WEB AS AN ADVERTISING MEDIUM

Advertising Expenditures

The population on the web had grown to 47 million people between 1996-98. Although the total number of televisions still dwarfed the total number of PCs, sales of PCs were expected to pass TV sales in 1998 with approximately 110 million units annually.[9] Growth in PC sales was expected to continue to far exceed that of TVs in the foreseeable future (see Appendix 6).

APPENDIX 6

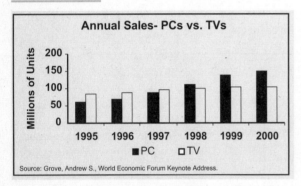

Source: Grove, Andrew S., World Economic Forum Keynote Address.

Due to its interactivity and personalization capability, explosive growth was projected in the use of the web as an advertising medium. Although still small relative to the $300 billion spent on advertising worldwide, ad sales for the web were expected to grow from $1.5 billion in 1998 to at least $8 billion in 2002. While it was commonly believed that 80% of available advertising slots on the Internet went unsold in 1997,[10] ad spending in 1998 was beginning to boom. First half 1998 Internet ad spending had doubled from the year prior to $774 million. This was still a small fraction of TV ad spending, but recent growth in Internet advertising was outpacing the growth in new users. TV advertising spending per viewer in 1998 was stable at approximately $180 per viewer[11] while web ad spending per Internet user had grown from $4 in 1995 to $25 in 1998. This number was expected to grow to $104 by 2003.[12] Additionally, some experts predicted the potential convergence of TV and the Internet to bring even more change and growth to the use of interactive targeted advertising.

Procter and Gamble had experienced such shifts in advertising media before. The print advertising of the 1930s rapidly transitioned into radio advertising in the 1940s. The growth of the television in the 1950s caused 80% of P&G's advertising dollars to be spent on television by 1955.[13] Many believed such a shift was likely to occur again as the benefits of targeted, personalized, and interactive advertising matured with the growth of the PC and the Internet.

Changes for Ad Agencies

A key stakeholder group that was certain to be affected by the development of Internet advertising strategies were the advertising agencies themselves. They depended on media commissions for compensation, and a shift from traditionally expensive television commercials to less expensive Internet ads would force agencies to place additional spots to maintain their current revenues.

The industry as a whole had recently experienced a shift from traditional commission-based compensation. Traditionally, 15% of all media spending would go directly to the agency. This had dropped in recent years as more than 75% of agency commissions were currently below that level in 1998.[14] Companies had begun to explore the concept of linking agency compensation to sales performance. This was in an effort to make the advertising agency a partner in the success or failure of an advertising campaign.

CHARACTERISTICS OF WEB ADVERTISING IN 1998

There were several predominant types of web advertisements in 1998, and new technology and innovations were occurring at a breakneck pace. One of the first types of online ad, and the most common in 1998, was the *banner.* This was essentially the billboard of the Internet world—a rectangular advertisement that would typically appear at the top or bottom of a web page. With increases in bandwidth and new developments in graphical ad technology, banners were becoming more and more animated and interactive. A *button* was a small ad appearing on a web site, generally containing a corporate name or brand. By clicking on banners and buttons, the user would normally be redirected to another site called a *content site* that promoted the advertised product or service. Placement of banners or buttons was becoming increasingly scientific. *Keyword ads* were banners that appeared as a response to content being searched for on an Internet search engine such as Yahoo! or AltaVista. *Sponsorship ads* were banners or buttons that were placed in order to integrate a brand or product with an online article, editorial, or targeted web site.

As the effectiveness of banners and buttons came under increased scrutiny, companies were experimenting with a variety of new advertising technologies specifically designed for leveraging the interactive and multimedia capability of the web. These ads, called *interstitials,* often incorporated a separate window that popped up separately from the web page being viewed. Many included video and sound in an effort to distinguish themselves from other more common ads competing for the eye of the consumer on a web site. Interstitials were controversial due to the high bandwidth required and the intrusive nature of their appearance in the foreground.

INTERNET ADVERTISING TOOLS

Software companies were developing many interactive technologies to take full advantage of the web's advertising and marketing potential.

Enliven by Narrative Communications

Enliven was designed as a web advertising suite that introduced a wide range of "rich-media" innovations. One option, designed in conjunction with Hewlett-Packard, enabled advertisers to incorporate direct local printing capabilities within web ads with the click of a mouse. Amazon.com was one of the first users of this technology, promoting a new book with a banner ad that, when clicked, would print out a five page excerpt. Arch rival barnesandnoble.com was also using Enliven. Their ads had the capability of taking an order for the advertised book, with no need for the user to click through to the main web site.

V-Banner by InterVU

V-Banner allowed video clips to be integrated into traditional ad banners. The recipient did not need any special plug-ins or downloads to view the 3 to 5 second video clips. According to the developers, V-Banner's "branding capabilities and high retention rates make it one of the most effective marketing tools on the web. Video brings the national branding power of television advertising, e-commerce, sponsorship, licensing, promotion and syndication to the web."[15] Advertisers could use V-Banner as a stand-alone tool, a transactional tool, or as an initial tease to a more robust video presentation via video-on-demand.

Comet Cursor by Comet Systems

Comet Cursor changed the user's cursor into a rich-media graphic element. Research indicated that the cursor is the first thing a web user looks at on a web page. The Comet Cursor was position sensitive, meaning it could change according to where it was on the page. For example, a web page could change the cursor to show varying prices or special discounts as the user moved over different products. The cursor also supported animation: it could show a scrolling list of stock quotes as a user went about his or her normal surfing activities.

ONLINE ADVERTISING COSTS AND MEASURES

Pricing Standardization Issues

The cost of placing an ad on the web varied significantly in 1998. Prices were typically quoted in "cost-per-thousand" impressions, or CPM, although an increasing number of sites charged only for actual click-throughs (defined below). According to an International Advertising Bureau study, "56% of deals are hybrid, involving impressions delivered and some performance measurement, such as click-through or cost-per-sale. Forty percent are straight cost-per-thousand or sponsorship deals, while only 4% are strictly performance-based. And 95% of the deals are straight cash."[16] CPM prices had been dropping steadily as the market matured and new entrants increased competition.

The many pricing structures in the online world were indicative of the turmoil revolving around standardized measurement systems. Further, some sites had their own advertising departments and worked individually, while others may also have been part of a network that was served by online advertising specialists. (See Appendix 7 for examples of the types of sites involved in online advertising and online rates.)

Measurement Issues

A key issue in 1998 for advertisers, agencies, and web sites was the lack of consistent and standardized measurement statistics with regard to online advertisements. Indeed, many media buyers were confused enough to avoid advertising in the medium altogether. For example, during one month in 1998 CNN's sites were given statistics on unduplicated visitors that ranged from 2.47 million to 11.79 million.[17] A survey of media buyers by the Association of National Advertisers found that a lack of reliable measurement was the primary reason they did not buy ads on the Internet.

Measurement statistics for web site popularity and advertising effectiveness had evolved throughout the World Wide Web's brief history. The original benchmark was termed a "hit," which occurred any time a file (e.g. a graphics file on a web page and/or the web page itself) was downloaded onto a computer screen. This measurement, while easy to record, was wildly inaccurate: a page with 10 graphics pieces would score 11 hits (10 graphics files plus the parent HTML file) each and every time a person viewed it. A more sophisticated measurement was termed an "impression," which

APPENDIX 7

DoubleClick was a full service online advertising solutions provider. Services ranged from geographic targeting via demographics such as states, zip code, or area codes, to real-time effectiveness reporting, allowing advertisers to change their strategy at any point during a campaign. DoubleClick also created a categorized network of affiliate sites, each belonging to one of seven "affinity groups" such as Automotive, Sports, or Technology. This was an attempt to help advertisers create more targeted campaigns. As of December 1998, the DoubleClick Network had 70 premier affiliates such as Alta Vista (at top-tier search engine), Dilbert (a popular cartoon site) and U.S. News & World Report.

Infoseek, a top-tier search engine, set their rates according to various placement and rotation schemes that were common to many online advertisers. Run-of-Site banner ads, for example, would appear in all areas of the Infoseek site, while keyword banners appeared as a result of a specific keyword search. Infoseek also employed more specific targeting techniques, such as domain or platform origination. For example, Infoseek could determine from which domain type a browser originates (such as .com, .edu, .net, or specific country domains), and/or which platform (such as Windows, Max, Unix, etc.). Ads displayed would be geared toward these specific target groups.

GoTo, a second-tier search engine, employed an auctioning system for determining its ad rates. Advertisers bid on search terms and only paid for click-throughs (rather than impressions) in an effort to optimize their spending and allow the market system to determine their placement rather than large blanket advertising budgets.

ValueClick was a firm whose goal was to impact the market with bargain-basement prices. Like Doubleclick, ValueClick developed a network of popular sites and, like GoTo, charged advertisers a fixed rate per click-through. When ValueClick was launched in July 1997, its rate per click-through was 15 cents. Given an average click-through ratio of 2%, this worked out to be about $3 CPM, compared to a typical CPM at that time of $20.[18] Many experts believed ValueClick was successful in establishing the pricing floor of Internet advertising.

APPENDIX 7 *(continued)*

DoubleClick Network Advertising Rates (sample)			
DoubleClick U.S. Network Rates **(Rates are expressed in cost per thousand impressions)**			
DoubleClick Interest Groups *Base*	*One Filter*	*Two Filters*	*Targeting a Specific Site*
Automotive $50	$51	$52	$55
Business & Finance $40	$41	$42	$45
Entertainment $30	$31	$32	$35
Health $50	$51	$52	$55
News, Information & Culture $40	$41	$42	$45
Search, Directories & ISPs $30	$31	$32	$35
Sports $30	$31	$32	$35
Technology $70	$71	$72	$75
Travel $40	$41	$42	$45
Women & Family $50	$51	$52	$55

Base — runs untargeted throughout the specified interest group.

Targeting Filters — includes frequency, geography, domain, SIC codes, company size, browser type, operating system, service provider.

One Filter — allows the advertiser to select 1 criteria from the targeting menu.

Two Filters — allows the advertiser to select 2 criteria from the targeting menu.

Targeting a Specific Site — allows the advertiser to select a specific site in the specified interest group.

Editorial Keywords — allows the advertiser to "target by keywords" on DoubleClick Network sites - $30 CPM.

Micro Targets — allows the advertiser to choose the following micro targets Specific Company or Specific College - $120 CPM.

AltaVista Keyword Rates	
Key Word Category	*Gross Rate*
Premium & Exclusive	$85
Standard Words	$70
Run of Site	$20

All rates are gross and are expressed in cost per thousand (CPM) ad banner impressions.

APPENDIX 7 *(continued)*

InfoSeek Advertising Rates (sample)

RUN-OF-SITE ROTATIONS

Ad banners rotating throughout all areas of InfoSeek. Minimum monthly investment: $2,500.

Gross Costs Per Thousand

Channel Rotation Types	1 Month	3 Months	6 Months	9 Months	12 Months
1 - 249,000	$29	$28	$27	$26	$25
250,000 - 499,000	$28	$27	$26	$25	$24
500,000 - 999,000	$27	$26	$25	$24	$23
1 million -1,999,999	$24	$23	$22	$21	$20
2 million - 2,999,999	$22	$21	$20	$19	$18
3 million - 4,999,999	$20	$19	$18	$17	$16
5 million plus	$18	$17	$16	$15	$14

CHANNEL ROTATIONS

Ad banners appearing when users request pages from any of InfoSeek's Channels. Advertisers may choose from two options within Channel Rotations. Minimum monthly investment: $2,000.

Gross Costs Per Thousand

Channel Rotation Types	1 Month	3 Months	6 Months	9 Months	12 Months
Channel Topics: Ad banners served on Topic category pages within Infoseek Channels.					
All Impressions	$60	$59	$58	$57	$55

Gross Costs Per Thousand

Impressions	1 Month	3 Months	6 Months	9 Months	12 Months
Channel Context: Ad banners served in targeted Channel environments appropriate to user's queries.					
All Impressions	$35	$34	$33	$32	$30

KEY WORD ROTATIONS

Ad banners that appear as the result of a specific key word search. Minimum monthly investment: $1,000.

Gross Costs Per Thousand

Impressions	1 Month	3 Months	6 Months	9 Months	12 Months
All Impressions	$60	$59	$58	$57	$55

DOMAIN, PLATFORM AND BROWSER TARGETING

Allows advertisers to target audiences by the "domains" from which their browsers originate from (i.e., .com, .net, .edu, or domains for specific countries), by computing platform—from Windows 95 to Mac OS to Unix—or by browser and version (i.e., Microsoft Internet Explorer 4.0, Netscape 3.0).

Impressions	Premium
All Run-of-Site Impressions	25%

recorded a single statistic regardless of the number of files on a web page or how many repeat visits a single user had. A "click-through" was a statistic directly related to an advertisement. It recorded the number of times someone clicked on a standard linked advertisement to get to the advertiser's web site. Often, "click-through ratios" were used to determine the affinity towards the product or service being advertised. Click-through ratios were defined as the ratio of click-throughs to impressions. For example, a site that had 100,000 impressions per month with 1,000 click-throughs would have a ratio of 1%. A less popular site with only 5,000 impressions and 100 click-throughs would have a ratio of 2%. This higher ratio was thought to indicate a higher affinity towards the product or service being advertised and thus more converted sales despite the lower site traffic.

INNOVATORS AND SUCCESS STORIES OF WEB ADVERTISING

There are numerous examples of firms that were attempting to leverage the interactivity of the web to improve their advertising and marketing penetration. Some, like M&M's Candies and Tanqueray, drew the user in with a simple game and the promise of prizes at the end. Others, like P&G's Always brand, used interactive media to educate consumers about products and their variations. Some employed only rich-media advertisements and/or mini-sites, while others had full-fledged web sites behind the ads. All were designed in an attempt to build a relationship with the consumer rather then simply deliver a message. (See Appendix 8 for examples of new interactive methods companies were using to build their brands.)

IMPLICATIONS FOR PROCTER & GAMBLE

The emergence of the Internet as a sales and marketing medium had the potential to radically change the way traditional marketers approached not only retailing, but also brand-building. P&G, the world's biggest advertiser and perhaps the most effective brand company, may have had the most to gain (or lose) from its Internet strategy.

The Internet provided the opportunity to take a brand's value to a new level. P&G had perfected the old brand model of "safety, quality, reliability," but the Internet could add a new level of product information that allowed the consumer to use a product more informatively and efficiently. For example, P&G had developed a "stain detective" on the Tide home page that can help solve any laundry problem.[19] This type of interaction demonstrated that the Internet could be used to establish a stronger bond between products and consumers; an interactive experience personally tailored to each viewer could leave a strong impression when compared to a 30-second television commercial.

There were issues other than marketing and branding that had to be considered. Currently, P&G distributed its products through thousands of retailers around the world. The Internet allowed companies to sell directly to the consumer, eliminating the retailer as a middleman. This had major implications for retail giants such as K-Mart and Wal-Mart. P&G had stated that selling on the Internet was not in their best interests. "We're not going to sell the Tides and Charmins of the world direct to consumers. We really see the value traditional retailers bring to the equation."[20] Indeed, the company had established an elaborate set of guidelines through its Store Link program which addressed the issue of Internet retailing, encouraging its retailer partners to establish an online presence and promote P&G's products. This would indicate that P&G planned to avoid selling through the Internet.

However, the company had recently begun its own online retailing experiments. P&G fragrances, such as Hugo Boss began to be sold directly to consumers. Additionally, Millstone coffee was using the interactive medium to allow customers to personalize coffee blends that would then be shipped directly.[21] These online retailing trials indicated P&G had yet to truly determine whether it would simply be a marketer or also a merchant on the Internet.

FAST Summit

Denis Beausejour envisioned the Internet as the innovation that would eventually unseat television as the dominant advertising medium. In August of 1998, P&G hosted the Future of Advertising Stakeholders Summit (FAST), inviting some the

APPENDIX 8

Marriott

Similar to P&G, Marriott was skeptical of the value of banner ads and felt that providing services online was the best way to reach and make an impact on the customer. Its *marriot.com* site was established to provide online mapping and a hotel locator. It was quickly extended to allow Marriott Rewards members to check account balances, make online reservations, and provide assistance with meeting planning. Eventually, Marriott planned to bring visual aspects to the site. This would provide a reservation service that would show the view from the window of a reserved room. In September 1998, Marriott reported that in the prior month, it had made $5 million from 1 million visitors to the site, or 1% of its total monthly sales.[22]

Tanqueray

In order to generate excitement for its site and to garner online marketing research forms, Tanqueray's strategy was to push the envelope of online interactive games. Its Tanqueray Links Classics game was an entire nine-hole golf game played entirely within an animated and interactive web banner advertisement. It engaged the user by providing nine holes of hitting an olive "golf ball" around various golf scenarios into a martini glass. Since its inception, 12,000 users had played the game, yielding 1,000 registrations.[23] By filling out the registration form at the end of the ten-minute nine-hole round of golf, users would receive various perks. Because direct offers generally only yielded a 2-3% response rate, Tanqueray was very pleased with the high return of its investment in the online banner game.

M&M's Candies

In 1997, M&M's Candies initiated a contest promotion that was built around gray, drab, "Imposter" candies—described as "M&M's wannabes" who lacked the bright, vibrant colors of regular M&M's candies. The campaign was run across all media: Internet, TV, radio, print, and outdoor. It was designed to create an opportunity for online consumers to interact with the characters and work with the Red and Yellow "spokes candies" to find the imposter M&M's candies. One of the primary objectives was to generate repeat visits and "community" to leverage M&M's brand awareness.

Sales of M&M's candies increased by 65% for the duration of the Imposters campaign, versus the same time span for the previous year. From the beginning of the Imposters promotion, traffic to the M&M's Studios increased by 33%, from 288,511 unique visitors to 383,956 unique visitors. Visitors to the Studios site increased their average length of stay by 56%, to 4 minutes 40 seconds, with 82% of that time being spent in the Imposters area. This length of stay has accounted for 28,000 hours of time that users visited the Studios during the Imposter promotion alone. During the campaign, visitors could email friends a copy of the "Imposter: Wanted" poster. More than 11,000 copies of the artwork were emailed, building brand equity by "word of mouth," often considered a more credible source than standard advertising.[24]

world's most powerful marketers to their corporate headquarters in Cincinnati, in an attempt to understand the potential of using the Internet as an effective marketing tool. Technology (especially bandwidth limitations) and difficulties in measuring advertising effectiveness were frequently cited as reasons for limiting online expenditures at P&G, but Beausejour admitted that the major inhibitor was the company itself: "As marketers, we really don't know how to use [the Internet] effectively."[25] Invitees included IBM, Levi's, AT&T, and General Motors, as well as primary P&G competitors such as Unilever and Clorox.[26]

The FAST summit was convened to open a dialogue among marketers, advertising agencies, technologists, and major stakeholders who were grappling with the Internet's implications. Issues were not expected to be resolved, but P&G

decided to push the issue of online advertising, in the hopes that the collaboration of these stakeholders would accelerate the development of effective Internet marketing. As one moderator put it "The point was the event, not the results of the event."[27]

A primary agenda item at P&G's FAST conference was to standardize measurement controls so that the entire process of valuing, purchasing, and gauging the success of online ads could be streamlined. One invitee to the FAST Summit, Thinking Media Corporation, had taken the lead in the measurement process and was awarded a patent for its work in October 1998. Vid Jain, a co-inventor of the process, and Chief Creative Officer at Thinking Media, explains:

> The patent is officially for a "method and apparatus for tracking client interaction with a network resource and creating client profiles and a resource database." That's jargon for what we call "client-side" tracking, which means that we put a kind of "homing pigeon" in each ad that sends information about it to a central database. What's different is that up until now, ad tracking has been done based on information provided by the computers that serve ads to the web browser. Our method lets us track what happens on the user side: who sees which ad, and where, and what's going on inside of them... we can now track not only if someone saw a banner, but how long they spent interacting with it.

Owen Davis, Thinking Media's Managing Director, stated that the process addressed the core of the measurement debate at the FAST Summit. "Client-side tracking is a solution that comes along at exactly the time when issues of accountability for online advertising have become critical. The technique will help provide the kinds of proof of effectiveness advertisers want to see before they begin to allocate bigger budgets to the Internet."

As a result of the event, an ongoing industry coalition, FAST Forward, was established. Representatives on the steering committee included the Internet Advertising Bureau (IAB), the Coalition of Advertising Supported Information Entertainment (CASIE), and the Advertising Research Foundation (ARF).[28] This group would work on developing workable advertising/marketing models while formulating generally accepted and measurable

standards. (See Appendix 9 for FAST Summit overview.)

P&G Store Link Program

P&G recognizes that as technology changes, manufacturers and retailers have to adapt to meet the increased expectations of technology-savvy consumers. The Internet is a key enabler for meeting those needs.

P&G web site

In order to entice their retailers to embrace the Internet, P&G developed the Store Link Program to "allow retailers with web sites to meet their consumers' needs in the online environment."[29] The program had two executions: the Store Finder Tool and a Co-Branded Interactive Ad Program. The Store Finder Tool allowed consumers to link from a brand's Internet ad to a list of local and online retailers that carried the P&G brand. The link could come from brand web sites, ad banners or email messages sent to consumers. Consumers could choose whether they wanted to purchase online or see a list of stores in their area that carried the brand (based on the zip code entered). The Co-Branded Ad Program worked similar to an insert in a local newspaper. P&G provided the artwork and message for the interactive ad banner while the retailer purchased and placed the ad on the Internet. Both programs were open to all P&G retailers that had an Internet site. By performing much of the design work and providing assistance in site development, P&G assisted its retailers in establishing a presence on the web while increasing the company's exposure online.

Interactive Marketing Team

P&G created the Interactive Marketing Team to drive the development and introduction of interactive marketing for their brands. The team consisted of approximately 10 brand managers who received corporate funding to execute interactive projects with select brands. Brand groups jointly funded projects with the Interactive Team to develop Internet advertising and web sites. Based on their work with various brand groups, the Interactive Marketing Team gathered key learnings regarding the Internet and disseminated this information

APPENDIX 9

FAST Summit, August 1998, Procter & Gamble World Headquarters, Cincinnati, Ohio

Principle Goals

- FAST will focus on developing action plans that accelerate the development and use of digital advertising models that are both effective and consumer-acceptable in order to enable interactive digital media to become more available, more useful, and more enjoyable.

- FAST must be driven by committed advertising, media, and technology firms determined to help achieve win/win solutions for the entire industry.

- FAST efforts will focus on both broadening acceptance of the current state of the space (through effective knowledge sharing) as well as accelerating the development of breakthroughs that will more rapidly enable its future potential.

Participants

- Over 40 major advertisers
- Over 30 interactive and traditional agency representatives
- Over 40 content providers and publishers
- Over two dozen measurement companies and technology enablers
- Nearly a dozen representatives of industry associations
- Consumer and privacy advocates, academic representatives and more

Key Focus Areas

- Consumer Acceptance of Online Advertising
- Creating Effective Advertising/Marketing Models
- Broadly Accepted Measurements
- Making Online Media Easier to Buy

throughout the corporation. They also helped brand groups establish relationships with interactive advertising agencies and buy interactive media. Eventually P&G hoped to disband the team and have these interactive capabilities distributed to each of their brand groups.

Changing Relationships with Ad Agencies

Not only had the growth of the Internet drastically changed how P&G approached advertising, it had also changed how P&G dealt with some of its closest business partners, advertising agencies. P&G announced that starting in 1999, it would begin testing performance-based compensation with seven of P&G's brands representing its seven largest agencies.

Traditionally, P&G had paid agencies a commission (13%-15%) on the amount they spent through them on advertising. This made it much more attractive to place a $150,000 TV ad than a $2,000 web banner. The company was seeking "to find a system that is media-neutral". P&G had already started to shift away from television ad spending in the 1990s. (See Appendix 10 for chart on P&G's ad spending.) They hoped this change in pay structure would compel its agencies to look to the Internet more frequently. The goal of the program was to "create effective, breakthrough advertising in record time, while encouraging experimentation and innovation."[26]

The compensation structure change followed a trend in the industry of manufacturers moving away from the traditional commission-based system

APPENDIX 10

Shifting Spending

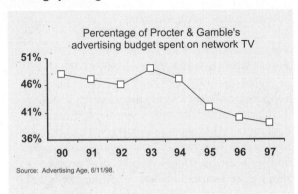

Source: Advertising Age, 6/11/98.

toward payment plans that had a fixed fee plus incentives based on increased sales (straight commission systems represented only 35% of all systems in 1997 versus 61% in 1994). The adoption of a new system could shift more of P&G's advertising dollars to the Internet, which received less than 1% of their total ad spending in 1998.

REDEFINING THE BRAND

P&G Interactive Brand Building

Procter & Gamble was also using the Internet to change the way it approached marketing and brand building. Consumers were starting to demand more from brands than purely functional benefits. The process of learning about and purchasing a product and the relationship developed between a brand and a consumer were becoming increasingly more important (see Appendix 11). Procter & Gamble began to use the Internet to capitalize on this shift and to develop a stronger relationship with consumers through more information and service oriented brands.

In the past, P&G marketed to consumers on television through testimonials (Crest—the toothpaste most often used by dentists), product demonstrations (Bounty—the quicker picker upper), and emotional appeal (the relationship of a mother and baby in a Pampers ad). The Internet had enabled P&G to move beyond passive advertising and provide interactivity, personalization and community to their brands.

APPENDIX 11

Consumers Want More Than Functional Benfits

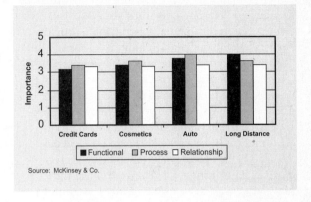

Source: McKinsey & Co.

As P&G further utilizes the web, they will rely on many outside partners and sources of information to expand their learning. P&G is working with their own advertising agencies as well as independent Internet agencies to develop Internet ads and web sites. The company is also partnering with content providers to create sites that interest their consumers and enable them to better target their advertising. For example, P&G is involved with Time Warner in the production of ParentTime.com, a web site dedicated to providing parenting information. Additionally, P&G also formed summer intern and new hire task forces to investigate branding on the Internet and other uses of information technology. Each of these groups provide a unique perspective and enable P&G to learn more about the potential of the Internet.

P&G's Interactive Ads

Consistent with its approach to provide value-added services online to build both its brands and relationships with the consumer, P&G built several stand-alone sites which offered numerous targeted services to its various consumer groups. Some examples include Pampers, Scope, Tide, and Always. Each of these are examples of how P&G was using the Internet to deepen their relationship with consumers and provide value beyond the functional product benefits.

www.pampers.com To attract its targeted audience (new parents) to its site, the Pampers Parenting Institute featured several informational and discussion zones, some even hosted by P&G's own panel of pediatric medical experts. The site's components included "Toilet Training 101," "House Call: Advice and Encouragement for your Baby's Development," as well as other informational articles such as "Well Baby" and "Healthy Baby Skin." Additionally, the Pampers site was experimenting with interactive media: "Ask our Experts" was an email based service for receiving free medical advice online regarding babies and young children. To provide a recurring brand image and service to its customers, visitors could also sign up for a customized electronic newsletter to be delivered via email at regular intervals. The content of the newsletter was customized based on user-input information such as the baby's age.

www.scope.com   P&G's Scope Mouthwash site's main feature was its "Scope Send-a-Kiss" email service. It allowed a visitor to "get fresh with someone online" by offering the option of sending one of five graphical animated kiss messages to a loved one via email. The user could also include a customized message to be sent with the animated kiss. The Scope site offered such informational services as "Breath Protection Tips," frequently asked questions, as well as a feedback zone that allowed emails to be sent directly to someone involved with the Scope brand. Detailed product information was also made available, including ingredients of Scope and a description of the purpose of each of these components.

www.tide.com   The Tide laundry detergent site was another example of P&G's attempt to develop a deeper consumer-brand relationship. This site featured several interactive areas, including a "Neighbor to Neighbor" community section in which users could submit stories relating their experiences with Tide. Users could submit photos of their families with the chance of having them featured on the site. There was also a "Stain Detective" and a "Tips and Timesavers" section, both geared towards educating the consumer on the best ways to make sure their laundry came out as clean as possible. Additionally, Tide.com had a contest area that changed monthly, encouraging repeat visits. Participants would answer questions using their own anecdotes (providing P&G with extremely valuable marketing data), while each entry was given the

chance to win prizes such as new washing machines. Consistent with most P&G web sites, there were areas with extensive product information and email feedback forms.

www.always.com   A final example of P&G's interactive efforts was the Always.com site. This site provided an outlet for young women to learn about the often awkward subject of reproductive development. Advice was given to mothers and daughters from varying perspectives (i.e. how to talk to your daughter or how to approach your mother with questions). The site also provided a forum for web surfers to share experiences and information on various salient subjects. The topics that were posted that went beyond typical Always discussions into areas such as bulimia and clinical depression.

COMPETITORS' ONLINE STRATEGY

P&G's competitors were also very interested in the progression toward interactive online media for advertising. The 15 member steering committee set up during the FAST conference included some of P&G's closest rivals: Unilever, Clorox, and Johnson & Johnson. These and other P&G competitors were also independently making various Internet strategy decisions.

Unilever

Unilever, a $50 billion British-Dutch consumer products superpower, was a primary competitor of P&G in such areas as cleaning products and personal care. Unilever's President and CEO of US operations, Richard Goldstein, had both interest in and questions about harnessing the new online media:

> How can we use interactive media to enhance the emotional appeal of established brands? Can the same strategies that succeeded for online sales of PCs, books, and CDs work for personal care and food products? ... What services will drive the next wave of consumers to new media, and who will create them: Internet service providers? Content sites? Software developers? Online marketers?[31]

Goldstein had reservations about the effectiveness of current Internet advertising technologies like the banner. He called these ads "more of a nuisance and clutter than an attraction." Although involved heavily in the FAST Summit, Unilever was taking several steps independently to develop and test possible solutions to some of his questions and reservations about online advertising.

In July of 1998, Unilever signed independent agreements with the two largest online service providers, America Online and Microsoft Corporation to jointly develop new interactive media and marketing programs for such Unilever Brands as Lipton, Ragu, Dove, and Mentadent. Although advertising spending figures were not released, experts indicated it was considerably more than $20 million over 3 years.[32] Goldstein expected that these deals would result in over one billion impressions of its brands on the Internet in the following three years. AOL reported that as many as 100 Unilever brands including cleaning, personal care, and food and beverages would begin having a "prominent presence" throughout the AOL service.

Unilever was taking other steps toward developing a large presence on the web. The company established an Interactive Brand Center in New York, staffed with dedicated Internet experts and marketing executives. In a separate move, Unilever indicated interest in experimental selling over the Internet by signing a deal with NetGrocer, the first nationwide Internet-based supermarket. NetGrocer would exclusively promote and sell Unilever's brands in several product categories on the its site.

Clorox

Clorox's early experimentation with Internet advertising was targeted towards effectively locating ads on the Internet rather than experimenting with new ad technologies. The company believed that an Internet site bidding war was imminent and establishing an early presence would be a strategic advantage. For example, Clorox partnered with the online site of Kelley Blue Book, Inc. Kelley was considered the bible of used car data and, according to Clorox, a perfect channel for advertisements of its Armor All automotive cleaning and restoration products.[33]

Johnson and Johnson

Independent of its work on the FAST Summit task force, Johnson & Johnson was venturing on its own with respect to Internet marketing. Betting on the potential of rich-media techniques, they joined several other top marketing firms who had partnered with the @Home Corporation (a pioneer in high bandwidth systems and multimedia content) to create and test more elaborate types of online media. J&J began experimenting with rich animation, sound, and full video in its advertising that was made possible with @Home technology.

Other Competitors

Two other large consumer brand firms, Colgate-Palmolive and Kimberly-Clark, were further behind the industry leaders and were taking a less proactive digital strategy.

BEYOND FAST: ISSUES AND CONCERNS

Since the FAST conference, Denis Beausejour was encouraged by the agreements that had been made, but some issues still provided much uncertainty about the future direction of the Internet as a way of building consumer relationships and P&G's brands. As serious as P&G was about interactive advertising and the potential that it showed, Beausejour still had some reservations.

First, despite the hype and promise surrounding the interactivity and multimedia aspects of Internet advertising, there remained some major technical constraints. The current bandwidth limits required file sizes so small that the desired rich content could not be delivered. There was also a limited infrastructure for 2-way message serving and information gathering. How and when would this bandwidth limitation be solved? Could P&G's hope of delivering interactive and animated ads occur with the current infrastructure? With whom, if anyone, should they partner to ensure success?

Beausejour also worried whether P&G could accurately measure the effectiveness of its online efforts. Indeed, there was a lot of work to be done to realize the hyped promise of online ad feedback:

APPENDIX 12

Sales Inroads on the Net

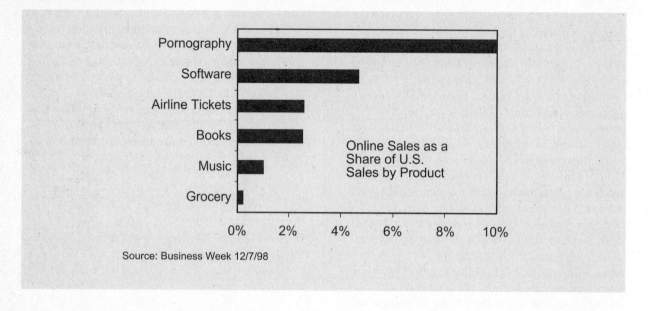

Online Sales as a Share of U.S. Sales by Product

Source: Business Week 12/7/98

One of the promises of interactive media is that we will have a continual feedback loop that instantly measures message effectiveness. So far we have not realized this promise. In fact, we don't even have measures as meaningful as those we've developed to evaluate our television messages and media.[34]

Perhaps the most important issue P&G needed to consider was the feasibility of selling consumer goods over the Internet to end-users. Were P&G customers online and ready to buy? How will the company involve its critical retail partners, especially Wal-Mart and K-Mart? In 1998, only about one-fourth of Internet commerce was direct to consumers. Most of these sales consisted of books, music, software, airline tickets, etc. Less than 0.5% of total grocery sales occurred online (see Appendix 12). The Internet was littered with budding "web-grocers" that were unprofitable. NetGrocer was once seen as the hottest company in online grocers after securing partnerships with AOL and Yahoo! to gain exposure, but a poor infrastructure resulted in extremely high distribution costs, eliminating any profit margins. Peapod, another online grocer, was attempting to perfect the business, but as of the end of 1998 the company had yet to turn a profit.[35]

Distribution issues aside, P&G's product line may be perfectly suited to net retailing. Darlene Mann, a venture capitalist specializing in the web, stated that Internet commerce works best when merchandise is easy to label and doesn't vary meaningfully within each category.[36] P&G has a portfolio of some of the world's best known brands, so consumers who order Tide or Pampers online know exactly what to expect when the product arrives at home.

Endnotes

1. "Digital Media Master: Denis Beausejour," *AdvertisingAge*, June 1998.
2. Procter & Gamble Corporate News Release, October 13, 1998.
3. "Procter & Gamble explains why the web will be The Biggest Medium since TV," *Brandweek*, July 20, 1998.
4. Procter & Gamble Corporate News Release, October 13, 1998.
5. Wingfield, Nick, "A Marketer's Dream," *The Wall Street Journal*, December 7, 1998.
6. *Ibid.*
7. "Branding on the Net; The old rules don't apply. So how do you hustle those wares online?" *BusinessWeek*, November 9, 1998.

8. "Branding on the Net; The old rules don't apply. So how do you hustle those wares online?" *BusinessWeek,* November 9, 1998.

9. Grove, Andrew S., World Economic Forum Keynote Address, February 3, 1997.

10. Anders, George. "Internet Advertising Gaining an Audience," *The Wall Street Journal,* December 6, 1998.

11. "Web vs. TV," http://www.webmagazine.com/features/aug97/webvstv/charts.html, 1998.

12. "Report: Global Online Spending to Hit $15 Billion by 2003." Internet News, www.Internetnews.com/bus-news/1998/08/1901-report.html, August 19, 1998.

13. Beausejour, Denis. "Branding and Bonding Beyond the Banner." Remarks at the Spring '98 Ad-Tech Conference, May 7, 1998.

14. "Use of billings-based compensation plans plummets," *AdvertisingAge,* June 11, 1998.

15. www.interVU.net

16. "IAB: Ad revenue online projected to hit $2 bil in '98," *AdvertisingAge,* November 2, 1998.

17. Stone, Martha, "Don't Believe the Numbers," *Editor and Publisher,* September 19, 1998.

18. "New networks chase per-click ad business," *AdvertisingAge,* July 1997.

19. "Procter & Gamble explains why the web will be The Biggest Medium since TV," *Brandweek,* July 20, 1998.

20. "P&G Launches Cyberspace Cologne Play," *The Wall Street Journal,* November 24, 1998.

21. Horovitz, Bruce. "P&G spins web to snare consumers. Summit will be 'defining moment' of Net advertising," *USA Today,* August 17, 1998.

22. "Have a Pleasant Stay at Marriot.com. Case Studies of Successful Online Campaigns," Ad/Insight, www.channelseven.com/adinsight/case_studies/1998/199810/marriott/index.shtml, October, 1998.

23. "Tanqueray Links Golf Classic Scores a Hole in One," Archive- ChannelSeven.com Case Studies Archive," http://www.turboads.com/richmedia_tech/active/archive/1998/1998_10/case_studies/c19981024.shtml, October, 1998.

24. "Best Cross-Media Integration iAd of 1997," http://www.channelseven.com/adinsight/case_studies/1998/199801/mms/index.html.

25. Horovitz, Bruce, "P&G spins web to snare consumers. Summit will be 'defining moment' of Net advertising," *USA Today,* August 17, 1998.

26. *Ibid.*

27. Hodges, Jane, "P&G tries to push online advertising," *Fortune,* September 28, 1998.

28. Giardina, Carolyn, "P&G summit sparks formation of FAST forward," *Shoot,* September 25, 1998.

29. www.pg.com

30. Beatty, Sally, "P&G To Test Ad Agency Pay Tied To Sales," *The Wall Street Journal,* November 9, 1998.

31. Beatty, Sally, "P&G and Unilever Brainstorm: How Can Internet Ads Be Better?" *The Wall Street Journal,* August 13, 1998.

32. Canedy, Dana. "Unilever Developing Online Programs," *The New York Times,* July 2, 1998

33. Anders, George, "Internet Advertising Gaining an Audience," *The Wall Street Journal,* December 6, 1998.

34. Beausejour, Denis. "Branding and Bonding Beyond the Banner," Remarks at the Spring '98 Ad-Tech Conference. May 7, 1998.

35. Leonhardt, David, "The Meat and Potatoes of Online Shopping?" *BusinessWeek,* December 7, 1998.

36. Anders, George, "Click and Buy; Why, and where, Internet Commerce is succeeding," *The Wall Street Journal,* December 7, 1998.

Indian Motorcycle Company: Taking Hogs Head On

MBA Candidates Hudson, Marisa, McCartney, Ong, and Schreter prepared this case under the supervision of Professor Christopher L. Tucci for the purpose of class discussion rather than to illustrate either effective or ineffective handling of an administrative situation.

As Rey Sotelo, President of Indian Motorcycles, sat on his red and black 1999 Limited Edition Indian Chief, his questions were the same today as they were a few months ago when Indian was reborn in, of all places, a Colorado courtroom. He strapped on his helmet, started the engine, and drove off, reminiscing about that day in October of 1998, when he prepared to show the world what the new Indian Motorcycle Company was made of ...

In October 1998, Sotelo grimaced under the weight of the 850 lb. Indian Chief as he pushed it into the elevator. He was on his way to the Colorado courtroom where the fate of Indian Motorcycle would soon be decided. As Rey glanced around the elevator car at the other members of his prospective Indian Motorcycle management team, a stream of thoughts ran through his head. Would Murray Smith, the CEO of Indian Canada, support a serious effort to reenter the motorcycle market instead of pursuing his preferred brand-based strategy involving Indian label cafes and paraphernalia? Should Indian develop proprietary engine technology or could Indian rely on the strength of the brand to sell "kit" bikes? Even with court approval, given the heavy industry nature of motorcycle manufacture, how could Indian get adequate follow-on financing? The "bing" of the elevator interrupted Rey's thoughts. The door opened, Rey took a deep breath and wheeled the legendary bike to the courtroom.

COMPANY HISTORY

At the turn of the century a bicycle racer named George M. Hend partnered with the famed engineer Carl Oscar Hedstrom. Together the two men founded the Hend Manufacturing Company in Springfield, Massachusetts to fulfill their common dream of manufacturing "motor-driven bicycles for the everyday use of the general public."[1] In 1901, the year the first bike was unveiled, Hedstrom and Hend decided to rename their motorcycles and adopt a name that symbolized a "wholly American product in the pioneering tradition"[2] —and the legendary Indian Motorcycle Company was born.

By 1905, 4 years after the unveiling of the original motorbike, Indian reached production levels of over 1,000 bikes per year. In 1907, spurred by the introduction of the innovative V-twin engine, an American rider won the International Six Days Enduro race in England on an Indian Twin and the name Indian became synonymous with reliability and engineering ingenuity. Indian bikes continued to blow the competition away in domestic and foreign races and prized Indian clients, such as the New York Police Department, were attracted to the machines "patented, leverless, double-grip, twist-of-wrist system." As a result of the overwhelming excitement and positive press surrounding Indian Bikes, by 1913 Indian controlled almost 42% of the US Domestic market and was producing upwards of 31,000 motorcycles a year.[3]

In 1916, Indian joined the war effort by supplying Allied soldiers with more than 41,000 bikes. Although these motorcycles were equipped with yet another proprietary side-valve engine, this move alienated domestic consumers and dealers, strained the production resources of the company, and damaged Indian's reputation. A major competitive blow was the introduction of the Model T Ford, which retailed for the same amount as a V-twin motorcycle ($285), and began Indian's long death spiral towards bankruptcy.[4]

Industrialist Paul DuPont assumed control in 1930 and temporarily resuscitated the dying company, but the Great Depression hit, and demand for motorbikes essentially vanished until America's entry into World War II. Again Indian supported the war effort and subsequently won the Army-Navy Production Award for Achievement in the production of war equipment. While the war effort revived Indian fiscally, the company continued to neglect its distributors, such that, as the government's demand disappeared post V-Day, Indian faced a domestic market with a distribution network in shambles. Indian was unable to capitalize on its patriotic wartime successes, DuPont sold out and the company muddled its way to extinction, finally ceasing production in 1953.

OWNERSHIP: THE MODERN EVOLUTION OF THE INDIAN TRADEMARK

Since the Indian factory was shuttered in 1953, ownership of the Indian brand name and trademark has traveled a most twisted and convoluted road. Although the Indian Motorcycle Manufacturing Company closed its doors, the Indian Sales Corporation, a group owned by Englishman, John Brockhouse, remained active and functioning.[5] After World War II, poorly executed contracts with the US government left Indian in financial trouble. Brockhouse lent money to the struggling Indian, a loan that he called in 1950.[6] Brockhouse then split the company into separate sales and manufacturing companies, maintaining control of the Indian Sales Corporation after the Indian Motorcycle Manufac-

turing Company closed its doors.

Brockhouse continued producing "Indians" through licensing agreements with British manufacturers until 1959, when he realized that one of America's best-known brands was not a good fit on an English bike. Brockhouse then sold the Indian rights to AMC Bikes who exported their motorcycles to the American company Berlinger Corp. When Berlinger dropped the Indian pretense on the imported bikes, the Indian Sales Corporation effectively disappeared, and there was now no clear owner of the Indian name and trademarks.[7]

With no clear owner of Indian, a variety of individuals began producing bikes onto which they slapped the Indian name. The most significant of the bunch was Floyd Clymer, who had tried unsuccessfully to buy Indian from Brockhouse years earlier. In his will, Clymer left the dubious rights to the Indian name to his wife.[8] Clymer's widow filed for registration of the Indian name, in its distinctive scriptive style, with the U.S. Patent and Trademark Office who never officially approved the registration despite no challenges to its ownership.[9] In 1983, after the name was sold a few more times, and a few more aborted attempts to bring imported Indians to America left the USP&TO registered Indian name with Carmen DeLeone, owner of the American Moped Association, who ended up doing almost nothing with the name.

Enter Philip Zanghi, who in 1990, smooth-talked DeLeone into selling half of the Indian rights to him for $1.[10] Zanghi became the first owner to seriously merchandise the Indian logo while vigorously defending the Indian name in court. DeLeone eventually dropped out of the picture as Zanghi raised millions from investors proposing to put the first American made Indian back on the road since 1953. Zanghi was essentially an embezzler and promptly ended up in jail. Around the same time, a man by the name of Wayne Baughman claiming to have the rights to the name was duping another group of investors out of millions of dollars, but somehow was able to avoid jail time.[11]

With all the fraud and confusion over the Indian trademark, a Colorado federal court appointed a receiver to help sort out the twisted mess. Given Indian's rich history as a premier motorcycle manufacturer and the recent history of conmen trying to claim the rights to the Indian name without any real intentions of manufacturing motorcycles, the need for owners that truly intended to produce motorcycles was deemed critical. Therefore, the judge insisted that a working prototype was required in order to win the coveted Indian trademark.

The race for the name was started. Leonard Labriola, a Colorado-based entrepreneur [...] set out to raise $50 million and struck a deal with the receiver to buy the Indian trademark. This deal, which included paying off the creditors that were victims of the Zanghi and Baughman fraud, was set to close on October 1, 1998.

At the same time however, Murray Smith, the owner of the Indian name in Canada, was compiling a group of investors to counterbid for the Indian name. The plan included building a kit-bike Indian prototype, stocked with an S&S V-twin engine, from Rey Sotelo's California Motorcycle Company, a producer of customized motorcycles. They were now asked to produce Indian bikes exclusively and possibly in mass. When Labriola was not able to make good on the October 1 agreement date, Smith and Sotelo made their move, wheeling an 850 pound Indian Chief prototype up twelve floors, into the courtroom, started it up for the judge, struck a deal with the receiver, and once and for all, ending the almost 50 year battle over the Indian name.

Smith secured financial backing from Katama Capital (consisting of Sommerfield Johnson, then Chairman of Coca-Cola Enterprises, and Henry Schimberg, then CEO of Coca-Cola Enterprises), J.L. Albright Venture Partners, and Oxbow Capital Partners, among others. The group settled with the receiver for $23 million to be paid to the cheated Zanhi and Bauman investors. An additional $30 million merger of motorcycle companies, including Smith's Canadian Indian Motorcycle Company, American Indian Motorcycle Company, and Sotelo's California Motorcycle Company and its six related companies, completed the rebirth of the Indian Motorcycle Company.[12]

COMPETITION: THE HEAVYWEIGHT CRUISER MOTORCYCLE MARKET

Typically, heavyweight cruisers are defined as those with engine displacement in excess of 650 cubic centimeters. As a result of favorable demographics, economic environment and the continued popularity and successful marketing of the Harley Davidson brand, the heavyweight segment is growing faster than the overall motorcycle market, and currently comprises approximately half of the total worldwide motorcycle market.[13]

Harley Davidson

Harley Davidson was founded in 1903, two years after Indian Motorcycles. In the early half of the 20th century, Indian and Harley were the fiercest of competitors right up until Indian's demise in 1953. Indian was the incumbent and Harley the attacker, seeking approval from the motorcycle community. Harley Davidson has had some rough points (e.g., One joke about Harley's goes like this, "How do you know when to put more oil in your Harley engine? Answer: When there is no longer oil spilling out on your garage floor"). However, after a few ownership changes during the second half of the 20th century, Harley has become recognized as one of the truly great American success stories, achieving operational and marketing success that many companies dream of but few actually achieve.

Harley Davidson currently dominates the American market, with a forecasted 46.3% market share and projected sales of 177,000 bikes in 2001. It is projected that there will be 1 million Harley owners in the United States who collectively own 1.4 million Harley Davidson motorcycles by the end of 2001. Harley Davidson has also been able to leverage its iconic brand name to gain a steady revenue stream from of a variety of consumer products with the Harley brand name attached, ranging from clothing to roadside restaurants.[14]

Harley recently completed a "dreamers" study to determine how many potential Harley owners are in the marketplace. The study concluded that 17%-18% of the U.S. population would consider buying a motorcycle. Nearly half of these are interested exclusively in Harley-Davidson motorcycles, and more than 80% of that set would at least consider HD in their purchasing process. This study implies that there are roughly 25 million potential Harley buyers in the U.S. RBC discounts this by 80% to get to a serious buyers number implying 5 million potential owners, collectively owning about 7 million motorcycles.[15]

Harley Davidson epitomizes the "Made in America" ideal and its brand name conjures powerful images of quality, performance and mystic to both motorcycle enthusiasts and general consumers.

Japanese Manufacturers: Honda, Suzuki, Kawasaki, and Yamaha

Large Japanese manufacturers are the other large players in this market and enjoy a combined market share of 46.7%. Cost consideration and availability are the predominant reasons consumers typically buy these Japanese "knock-off" cycles.[16] Additionally, these bikes are known for excessive speed capability and have even been coined as "suicide machines."

Other

In North America, a very small portion of the market, equivalent to less than 5%, goes to other premium priced, highly engineered competitors such as BMW and Ducati.[17] BMW has a reputation for performance engineering, but their motorcycles lack the cache that their cars have.

HEAVYWEIGHT MOTORCYCLE DEMOGRAPHICS

Heavyweight motorcycles are viewed as a luxury product and are particularly susceptible to cyclical economic trends. Following a 15-year decline, U.S. motorcycle registrations have rebounded with a total of 4.4 million motorcycles registered forecasted for 2000, up from 3.9 million in 1995. Total sales of new motorcycles are expected to reach $5.5 billion in 2000, representing almost half of total retail sales for this product. Used motorcycles represent 16% of the total motorcycle retail market.[18] Consumers range from biker enthusiasts and thrill-seekers to weekend warriors and those using motorcycles for practical transportation needs. Approximately half of the market is composed of motorcycle enthusiasts who view proprietary engines as a critical prerequisite for a mass produced component manufacturer to be welcomed into the motorcycle community.

Wealthy baby-boomers represent approximately 70% of Harley buyers—the median age of Harley buyers is 45. After peaking in 2005, the population of 45-year-olds will decrease noticeably.[19]

DISSENSION WITHIN THE RANKS: THE MANAGEMENT TEAM

The three-man Indian Motorcycle management team resembled the biking demographic; their interests were extremely diverse. Murray Smith, the CEO of Indian Canada, joined the newly minted American company intent on extending the Canadian marketing strategy into the US endeavor. Ironically, Smith was not interested in developing unique proprietary motorcycle manufacturing. He especially wanted the brand name for his restaurant chain in Canada and for his line of clothing, especially T-shirts. Indian Canada enjoyed moderate success and recognition pursuing a strategy of building kit bikes with the Indian name slapped on. They leveraged the name to promote such business ventures as Indian Motorcycle Café in Toronto. Smith believed the value of Indian was in the name; and the motorcycles were a way to promote the brand. Rey Sotelo and the Henry Shimberg had a different plan: build competitive motorcycles.

Rey Sotelo, the Founder and President of California Motorcycle Company, brought more than 20 years of motorcycle industry experience and is an avid motorcycle enthusiast. His expertise covered sales, research and development, engineering, and customized cycle production. Sotelo knew that in order to be taken seriously in the motorcycle community, Indian would not be able to churn out kit-bikes for long. Indian would need to invest in proprietary technology to assure his ultimate goal be fulfilled; to restore Indian to its former greatness and attack the entire heavyweight cruiser market (including the eight hundred pound gorilla Harley Davidson) head on.

Henry Schimberg, the former Coca-Cola Enterprises CEO, was the key third member of the management team and obviously knew brand equity following his years of marketing and distribution experience with the world's most recognizable brand. Shimberg and Coca Cola cohort Johnson owned the Katama Capital private equity group that invested heavily in Indian. Schimberg left Coca-Cola to become chairman and CEO of Indian Motorcycles, and despite his minimal knowledge of motorcycles, agreed with Sotelo's intuition: Indian had to create its own motorcycles. Shimberg also understood that the strength of Indian was its

EXHIBIT A

Total U.S. Motorcycle Registrations (1945–2000)

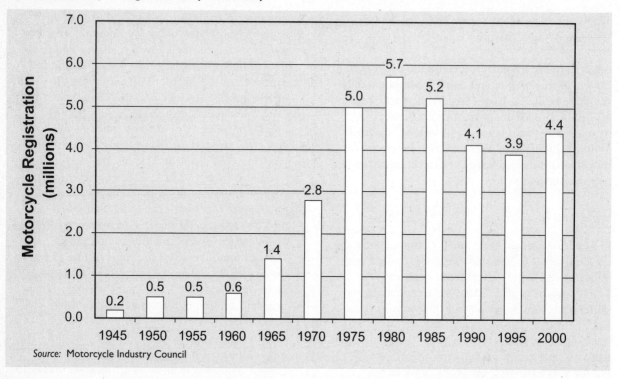

Source: Motorcycle Industry Council

brand name and believed the new company could easily leverage this power with a superior product. His goal was to use his Coca-Cola branding and distribution experience to exploit and build the Indian name.

CHALLENGES FOR INDIAN

As Rey Sotelo twisted the throttle and gave his Chief a little juice, so many thoughts raced through his head. Will we be able to restore Indian Motorcycles as a viable American motorcycle OEM and deliver a premium product worthy of the nostalgic logo? Will we be able to gain momentum and produce high quality machines with cutting edge technology that would satisfy the motorcycle community? Can the current market demographic support two Harley Davidson size producers? Even if a unique product offering is enough to sustain a competitive advantage for Indian as it reenters the motorcycle market, how will the management team reconcile their strategic differences? Are we doing the right thing spending millions developing an

engine or should we really just be focusing on the brand and put out kit bikes? Harley's scale and dominance is such that no matter how good our proprietary engine is, they could easily crush us. Who's to say that the two years engine development time will even yield a functional viable Harley alternative?

EXHIBIT B

U.S. Market Share—2000

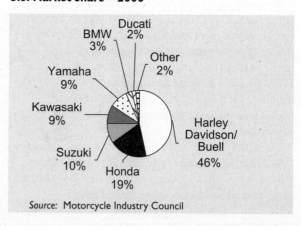

Source: Motorcycle Industry Council

EXHIBIT C

Regional Heavyweight Markets

	North America	Europe	Asia /Pacific	Worldwide
Industry:				
2000 Growth Rate	16.0%	–4.3%	–0.7%	7.8%
5 Yr. CAGR	17.4%	7.2%	9.7%	11.9%
% of W'wide Mkt	50.5%	40.8%	8.7%	1000.0%
Harley/Buell				
2000 Growth Rate	15.7%	9.4%	4.3%	13.8%
5 Yr. CAGR	16.7%	7.2%	10.3%	15.0%
Mkt Share	46.3%	7.4%	20.5%	28.2%

Source: Motorcycle Industry Council, Giral S.A., Australian Bureau of Statistics, Japan Automobile Manufacturer's Association, and Motorcycle & Moped Industry Council.

As the fresh mountain air rushed through his hair, Sotelo looked down at his 1999 Limited Edition Indian Chief, shining just like it did that day in the bright Colorado courtroom, and took a deep breath. This was going to be a long road, but he knew that Indian could be Chief again.

EXHIBIT D

2000 Retail Sales Volume by U.S. Motorcycle Outlets ($11.8 Bn Total Sales)

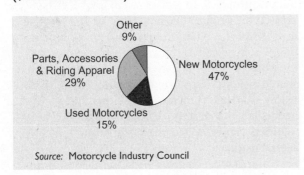

Source: Motorcycle Industry Council

Endnotes

1. Indian Motorcycle Website, http://www.indianmotorcycles.com/, Historical Timeline.
2. *Ibid.*
3. *Ibid.*
4. *Ibid.*
5. Salvadori, Clement, "Riding Around, the Indian Wars," *Rider,* May 1999, p.12.
6. Bricken, Gary, "Indian Motorcycle Lore & Legend."
7. Salvadori, *op. cit.,* p.12.
8. *Ibid.* p.12.
9. *Ibid.* p.13.
10. *Ibid.* p.13.
11. *Ibid.* pp.13-14.
12. Indian Motorcycles Website, http://www.indianmotorcycles.com/, Historical Timeline.
13. RBC Capital Markets research report "Harley-Davidson, Inc. Looking for Adventure," March 15, 2002, p. 4.
14. *Ibid,* p. 5, p. 12.
15. *Ibid,* p. 12.
16. *Ibid,* p. 5.
17. *Ibid,* p. 5.
18. *Ibid,* p. 3.
19. *Ibid,* p. 13.

MBA Jungle

MBA Candidates Devineni, Ruiz, Levin, and Schnaid prepared this case under the supervision of Professor Christopher L. Tucci for the purpose of class discussion rather than to illustrate either effective or ineffective handling of an administrative situation.

"We have succeeded, in part, because our audience is unlike any other. There is no other vehicle that can reach readers in their 20s and young 30s who make six figures or more," said Jungle Interactive's group publisher and 20-year media veteran, Larry Burstein. *"Our audience is truly the new generation of leaders."*[1]

JUNGLE INTERACTIVE MEDIA INC.: LAUNCHING *MBA JUNGLE*

In Spring 2002, Jungle Interactive Media inc., the publishers of *MBA Jungle* and *JD Jungle*, faced several pressing strategic decisions. Despite a severe advertising recession following the bursting of the Internet bubble, Jungle Interactive was about to be profitable by Q3 2002, within two years of receiving venture capital funding from Ridgewood Capital and a strategic investment from Korn Ferry. Annual circulation for *MBA Jungle* and *JD Jungle* exceeded 250,000 magazines, and signs of an advertising rebound were encouraging. Jungle Interactive Media had already published 12 issues of *MBA Jungle* and 5 issues of *JD Jungle*. Nevertheless, the founders and staff contemplated future

opportunities and the possibility of an eventual exit plan. How should the company focus on its growth? Should the company attempt to expand in its core segments (MBA and JD), expand into other graduate magazines, or try to grow through other means? Should the founders consider selling the company to a large media conglomerate?

THE FOUNDERS

John Housman, Sean McDuffy, and John McBride created the original business plan for *MBA Jungle* in 1997 for the Wharton Business Plan Competition. The seeds of the idea were sown earlier in their business school careers. The founders often shared articles from various magazines with their fellow students. They recognized that MBAs needed a voice that spoke directly to them. The founders viewed MBAs as a valuable and underserved market.[2]

Upon graduation from NYU Stern (John Housman) and Wharton (Sean McDuffy and John McBride), the founders pursued their individual careers. John Housman joined McKinsey & Company, and Sean McDuffy and John McBride worked at Goldman Sachs. Despite their individual pursuits, however, the founders remained close, and by the end of 1999 decided to revisit their *MBA Jungle* business plan.

STARTING THE COMPANY

In 2000 the founders raised $6 million of venture capital from Ridgewood Capital and Korn Ferry. Ridgewood Capital was founded in 1998 to take advantage of the high-growth in the technology sector, and at the time had over $300 million of committed capital. Korn/Ferry International, a leading provider of recruitment solutions, invested as a strategic investor in Jungle Interactive Media inc.

The founders approached the investors with the idea of publishing a life-style magazine focused on MBA students and potentially other niche graduate student markets. Revenue sources for the venture would be derived from both print advertising in the magazine and subscriptions. Although some potential venture capital investors were interested in only an Internet website, the founders believed it was important to have both the magazine and the website.

THE BUSINESS PLAN

The Jungle Interactive Media business plan closely followed the traditional print media business model. Revenue was generated from advertisers targeting the niche demographic represented by the magazine and from subscription revenue. Jungle Interactive Media estimated its target audience at over 250,000, however it was hoping to reach a total of 1.2 million people.[3] The larger figure represented the "best-case" scenario if most of the potential readers were subscribing to the magazine. This figure, as it later became apparent, was unrealistic. To reach the target audience, the company provided the magazines for free to most readers in exchange for completing an information form online at the company's websites. Boosting circulation of the magazines and attracting the desired demographics were thought to be key success variables. The company initially tailored its content specifically for the MBA and then for the JD markets. The Jungle Interactive Media business plan departed from the traditional print model in its unique distribution strategy and coupling with the magazine companion websites.

TARGET MARKET

The target audience of *MBA Jungle* comprised potential students taking the GMAT exam for entry into business school, students currently matriculated in an MBA program, and alumni of MBA programs (Exhibit 1). Jon Housman identified the *MBA Jungle* audience as "... a group of people ages 25 to 35, 70% men, who are generally high-income earners." He also commented: "Our publication is really meant for someone in their late 20s to early 30s and not in their 50s. It speaks with a sense of humor, with a sense of fun and style."[4]

Similarly, *JD Jungle* targeted potential students taking the LSAT for entry into law school, students currently matriculated in a law school, and alumni of law schools working as first, second, or third year associates within law firms (Exhibit 2). When *JD Jungle* launched in April 2001, its first issue had an initial base circulation rate of 80,000—making it the largest legal publication in existence.[5]

MBA students represented an appealing demographic for advertisers. Most business students have worked several years and have savings. Business school itself was relatively short, only 18 months, with a 3-month break during which time students earned income through internships. Most business school students could also be expected to

EXHIBIT 1

MBA Statistics

Number of business schools in the U.S.	900
Number of schools accredited by the AACSB	300
Number of people graduating from an MBA every year in the U.S.	> 90,000
Number of International students graduating from an MBA every year in the U.S.	20,000
Number of people taking the GMAT every year	approx. 270,000
People getting a perfect score	approx. 100
People getting 700 or more	approx. 2,000
Percentage of CEOs with MBA	approx. 30%

Source: http://www.foreignmba.com/getin2.shtm

EXHIBIT 2

Law School Statistics, 2000

184 accredited law schools in the U.S.

In 2000, the median annual earnings of all lawyers was $88,280. The middle half of the occupation earned between $60,700 and $130,170. The lowest paid 10 percent earned less than $44,590; at least 10 percent earned more than $145,600. Median annual earnings in the industries employing the largest numbers of lawyers in 2000 are shown below:

Legal services	$96,610
Federal government	87,080
Fire, marine, and casualty insurance	82,170
Local Government	66,280
State Government	64,190

Source: Labor Statistics http://www.bls.gov/oco/ocos053.htm#earnings

69,000 American men and women applied for a JD in the year 2000; law school tuition costs range from about $10,000 a year at a state school to almost $30,000 at a private institution.

Source: http://www.review.com/law/article.cfm?id=law/law_jungle1&tabIndex=2

become future high earners with significant disposable income. For these reasons, business school students represented an enticing target audience for providers of premium goods and services.

Law students also represented an appealing demographic for advertisers. Since law school students are typically younger and have a longer period in school during which time they do not earn income, they were not as appealing of an audience as MBA students. Nevertheless, the JD target audience also represented future high earners that would have significant disposable income. In addition, Jungle acknowledged a need for the young associates at the law firms to have a voice and sense of community when working the long hours after graduation. These young professionals tended to have little free time while earning significant income.

DISTRIBUTION STRATEGY

Jungle Interactive Media used a unique distribution strategy for its magazines. The strategy comprised primarily a controlled distribution system (90%), as well as direct mail subscriptions and limited newsstand sales. Through these outlets, Jungle Interactive Media reached 250,000 people a year, approximately 10,000 of which were reached through subscriptions. The majority of readers were reached through the "controlled channel."

The controlled channel was based upon relationships the company had with the top business and law schools in the world. The company used different methods to reach students at these schools. Most business schools recognized the value of the magazine and the desire of their students to receive the magazine. These schools provided access to their current students, which Jungle utilized to send free subscriptions during their educational career. Some schools also provided links from their respective websites to the *MBA Jungle* website.[6]

Some schools, however, avoided a direct relationship with *MBA Jungle*. Harvard, for example, was "very cautious about giving out student names or affiliating itself with outside organizations."[7] To reach students at such schools, the company used creative methods to reach students, including providing the career services office of such schools with complementary magazines that could be picked up by students. The company found such alternative methods successful in reaching students at schools that would not have a direct relationship with it.

Jungle Interactive Media also sent magazines free of charge to some potential students taking the GMAT and LSAT exams. The company targeted a percentage of these prospective students since it would have been too expensive to reach all of them. The testing companies participated with Jungle Interactive in reaching potential students expressing an interest in the magazines. Jungle also worked closely with alumni associations at the various schools to increase awareness. The company partnered with these associations to send out copies of the magazine so that recent alums would hopefully enjoy the content and pay for a subscription.

Although Jungle Interactive expected significant subscription and newsstand sales of their magazines as well, such sales had so far been less than expected. The company magazines were also available at Barnes & Nobles and Borders bookstores near target schools through a distribution agreement (approximately 800 stores nationwide).[8] Subscriptions were available through the company websites. The company estimated its current subscriptions at 10,000 per year, but expected growth in this distribution channel.[9]

CONTENT

The content of *MBA Jungle* had changed since its launch to reflect the changing interest of its readers. The magazine was initially positioned as an irreverent magazine to reflect the boom times of the Internet bubble and the high-flying economy. Although still focused as a lifestyle magazine targeted toward MBA students, the content had shifted toward more serious articles on finding jobs and getting ahead in a career. Nevertheless, the magazine retained its edge as reflected by the inclusion of Bill Shapiro, a former Maxim magazine Executive Editor, as *MBA Jungle*'s Editor-in-Chief.

The content of *JD Jungle* was very similar to that of the *MBA Jungle*. One main exception for *JD Jungle*, however, was that the company was also heavily focused on recent law-school graduates. Therefore the issues that the magazine addressed were not limited to life in graduate school but post degree-life as well.

ADVERTISERS

Jungle Interactive Media matched its advertisers to target its demographics. Advertisers primarily included companies building brand equity with potential employees as well as lifestyle premium brands. Advertisers could be generally divided into two categories: companies that wanted to attract MBAs as potential employees and companies that wanted to attract MBAs as potential customers. During the early days of *MBA Jungle*, many of the advertisers included Internet consulting companies recruiting new employees. With the bursting of the Internet bubble, however, such firms had been replaced with more traditional employers such as banks (e.g., Goldman Sachs, Merrill Lynch) and blue chip companies (e.g., Sun, IBM, Booz-Allen). Lifestyle advertisers included such companies as Hugo Boss, Brooks Brothers, Sony, and Jaguar.[10]

Attracting and retaining advertisers was an involved process for the company. The typical investment was 12 to 24 months before a potential advertiser would sign up. Advertisers were concerned about the longevity of a new magazine, as well as its ability to deliver the promised demographics. The advertisers also wanted to ensure that the content of the magazine would in no way harm their own brand equity. In fact, the advertisers expected the content to help build the brand with the demographic. According to James Winter, Manager of Business Development at Jungle, the niche audiences that read *MBA Jungle* and *JD Jungle* were very attractive to the advertisers. While the company did not have a circulation reaching that of most mainstream magazines, the value was provided by Jungle's reach of the key demographic.[11] For this reason, premium advertisers from BMW to Goldman Sachs were consistent advertisers in the publication. "Jungle Interactive was founded on the premise that we can do a better job targeting the young and affluent audiences that advertisers want and need to reach," said Housman. "*MBA Jungle* has been extremely successful in this regard, and *JD Jungle*, our second launch in the past year, will round out our ability to deliver quality demographics to top brands and companies."[12]

COMPETITION

According to Winter, Jungle Interactive viewed itself as the only current player in its segmented space. The company viewed magazines such as "Yahoo! Internet Life" as potential competitors, but the influence and popularity of such magazines had decreased. The company viewed the potential entry of a large media company into the space as its greatest competitive threat. A large media company would be able to operate a magazine targeted at professions within a portfolio of other magazines, thus realizing economies of scope and scale. However, Jungle Media believed that through its relationships, their own magazines had significant first-to-market advantages.[13]

GROWTH OPPORTUNITIES

Jungle Interactive identified several areas for growth. Foremost, the company believed it could expand its circulation of existing magazines. Nonetheless, the company recognized that the readership for these magazines was very limited. The absolute number of students in MBA and JD schools were limited and the life of a reader was short since the magazines lost relevance for most readers as they became further removed from school (although *JD Jungle* still pertained to graduates recently out of school but lost pertinence soon thereafter). The company, on a minor scale, also published books targeted at its core audience on topics of interest to their readers, thus providing another potential source of growth.

As part of its strategy, the company was trying to transition readers of its print magazines to relationships with the companion websites. Website initiatives included resume collection and services such as Feedback Exchange. Jungle Media purchased Feedback Exchange in 2000 to realize possible market synergies. Feedback Exchange provided various surveying capabilities with its most popular being feedback to students from recruiters visiting their campus. The recruiters also received feedback from the interviewed students about their perception of the company and the personnel representing them. These surveys not only helped the company's bottom line but also provided valuable information on their key demographic.[14] Through obtaining results related to those that they surveyed, Jungle could help counsel their advertisers on the reach and strength of their brand equity. Yet, this strategy would move the company away from its traditional role of print media and into an unproven area.

The company also entertained the option of creating lifestyle magazines for other professions such as engineering and medicine. John Housman joked, "We're thinking about Lion Tamer Jungle [next]."[15] While expanding to other professions seemed to be a very appealing growth opportunity because the company could utilize its capabilities across various graduate programs, the demographics for these markets were not quite as appealing to advertisers due to the longer time in school and time before students reached their prime earning years.

The company was also optimistic about a rebound in the advertising market. As the economy continued to recover from a recession, potential advertiser expenditures were expected to increase commensurately.[16]

THE FUTURE

When asked about future growth opportunities, Housman responded, "one [opportunity] is growing vertically, within the *MBA Jungle* brand there are different layers of business that we can add on to the magazine. There is also the horizontal, in that there are a number of different verticals that we can add."[17] The growth of *MBA Jungle* and *JD Jungle* had been remarkable, having achieved a circulation of over 250,000 and profitability within 2 years of launch. However, the company was at an important crossroads. Had it already exhausted its growth potential serving its targeted niche? Should the company consider expanding into other graduate programs (i.e. *Engineering Jungle, MD Jungle*)? Would the company be more valuable as part of a large media company? Would a large media company be interested in Jungle Interactive? These questions confronted the founders as they continued to grow their business.

Endnotes

1. www.kornferry.com/pr/pr_01_0430_jungle_interactive_secures.asp
2. Interview with James Winter (Dir. Business Development, Jungle Interactive) March 29, 2002, by Syam Devineni, Salvador Garcia-Ruiz, and Larry Schnaid.
3. *Ibid.*
4. http://www.npost.com/interhousman.html
5. www.kornferry.com/pr/pr_01_0117_jungle_interactive.asp
6. Interview with James Winter.
7. McClain, Dylan Loeb, "A Magazine Seeks Management Potential," *The New York Times,* August 6, 2000, p. 13.
8. www.npost.com/interhousman.http
9. Interview with James Winter.
10. *Ibid.*
11. *Ibid.*
12. www.kornferry.com/pr/pr_01_0117_jungle_interactive.asp
13. Interview with James Winter.
14. *Ibid.*
15. Smith, P. Kelly, "Business School Showed Them a Perfect Market," *Entrepeneur Magazine,* July 2001, p. 35.
16. Interview with James Winter.
17. www.npost.com/interhousman.http

BroadVision

This case was prepared by Jean-Claude Charlet (MBA '98), under the supervision of Erik Brynjolfsson, Visiting Associate Professor of Operations, Information, and Technology, Stanford University Graduate School of Business. Special thanks to Ken Kronenberg for his insightful comments and editing work.

This case was made possible by the generous support of The R. Denzil Alexander Fund.

Using the new media of the one-to-one future, you will be able to communicate directly with consumers, individually, rather than shouting at them, in groups. Until recently, it has not been economically realistic for businesses to collect, analyze, and understand the data necessary to communicate with customers in a 1:1 fashion. But no longer.
The One-To-One Future, *Don Peppers and Martha Rogers*

Pehong Chen, President, Chairman of the Board, and CEO of BroadVision, Inc., leans back in his chair with a sigh of satisfaction. It is 3.00 p.m. on this sunny Wednesday July 23, 1997, in Los Altos, California, and the conference call with the press just ended. As he looks back on the four years that have just passed, he feels proud of his achievement. BroadVision seems well on its way to become "the leading supplier of enterprise-class solutions for personalized, one-to-one business on the Internet," as the press communiqué puts it. In

The case was prepared as the basis for class discussion rather than to illustrate either effective or ineffective handling of an administrative situation.

today's conference call, Pehong has just announced to the press record second quarter 1997 results, with revenues worth $6.0 million for the period, up by 161% over 1996. Although the net loss for the period is still $2.1 million, these results are more than encouraging. Some major contracts have been signed recently, strengthening the company's leading position in the emerging market of personalization software for Internet-based services. Leaders on their respective markets such as Sabre Interactive, IBM Europe, JP Morgan or Spain's Telefonica have just chosen BroadVision's One-To-One™ solution, and relying on the choice of these high-profile customers, Pehong Chen's deepest wish is that many other Fortune 500 companies will follow.

THE ONE-TO-ONE INTERNET REVOLUTION

BroadVision is a publicly owned company headquartered in Los Altos, California, that develops and markets one-to-one software applications that enable companies to profile visitors to their Web sites. With this information gained through the use of Broad Vision's One-To-One™ software, the companies can then customize their marketing messages to the individual needs of these potential customers.

Founded in May of 1993 by Pehong Chen, a remarkable entrepreneur with three high tech start-ups to his credit, BroadVision seems well positioned to become "the leading supplier of enterprise-class solutions for personalized, one-to-one business on the Internet." Chen speaks candidly about his business strategy and what it takes to build a company such as his.

The Precursors: Direct Marketing and Database Marketing

The idea of approaching customers on a more personalized basis is not new. Direct marketing, mail order, and database marketing are based on the same concept. However, BroadVision goes further. It deals with the concept of "mass customization," i.e., the way a company can talk to each customer differently given a very large customer base. This technological breakthrough was made possible by the Internet, the first true global reach medium, and the automation of tasks allowed by new cutting-edge technologies. The biggest difference between past marketing techniques and BroadVision One-To-One™ software is the level of granularity. "What the database marketers are saying is that there is a big pond of fish there, so let's go in and try to catch the *biggest* one," says Chen, "while we aim at talking to *each* customer differently. The idea of treating users and customers differently does not exist in that world. So far, a medium of communication has never been a dialogue, a two way communication."

Direct marketing, for example, does not compete with mass customization because mail is a very broken process. Typical mail return rate is very low, less than 1%, which represents a huge waste of money. People who actually return may not even be the most profitable customers of a company. So relevancy is at stake. Lacking is the

FIGURE 1

Intelligent Interactivity Goes Beyond Today's One-Way Web Experience

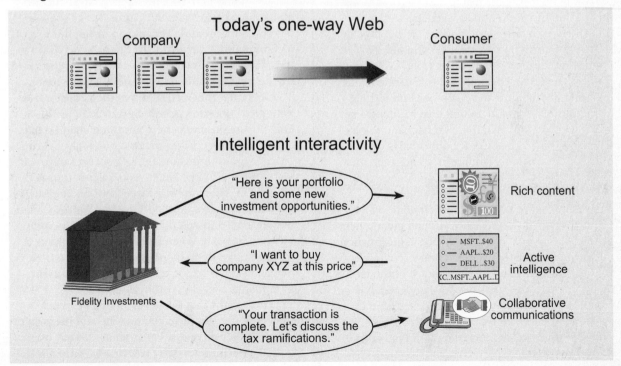

Source: Forrester Research, Inc.

interactivity that a marketer can get through a poll, for example, but not through direct marketing.

The 1:1 Concept

To increase customer satisfaction, develop customer loyalty, and contain the high costs associated with new customer acquisition and customer support, businesses are turning their attention from mass marketing of generic products to "one-to-one" marketing and mass customization of products and services. The Web allows for easy implementation of these one-to-one techniques on a mass basis. To capitalize on this opportunity, businesses require software application solutions that exceed the capabilities of currently available Web software products, many of which were designed for publishing static content, or "brochureware." To address this need, BroadVision introduced the BroadVision One-To-One™ application system, which allows businesses to develop and manage personalized Web sites. One-to-one Web sites interactively profile each visitor and dynamically match information to them based on their profile and the business rules specified by providers of the site and its services. In contrast to traditional push or pull technologies, this avoids end-users the difficult and painful task of finding their way through overloads of information to find the relevant data nuggets.

The idea of one-to-one business is a compelling strategy set forth by Don Peppers and Martha Rogers in their best-selling book *The One-To-One Future.* The driving principle of one-to-one marketing is getting to know the customer. Establishing a dialogue and a sense of community with customers creates a bond between the merchant and the individual customer. The ultimate objective is to own a piece of the customer's mindshare and to provide customized services to each customer according to his or her personal preferences—whether expressed or inferred. All this must be done while protecting the customers' privacy and giving them a sense of power and control over the information they provide. One-to-one marketing also allows a vendor to identify and take advantage of the moment when a customer's purchasing decision is most likely to occur and to be prepared for that moment, one step ahead of the competition. BroadVision One-To-One™ aims at embodying all these principles.

FIGURE 2

BroadVision's Interactive Business Lifecycle

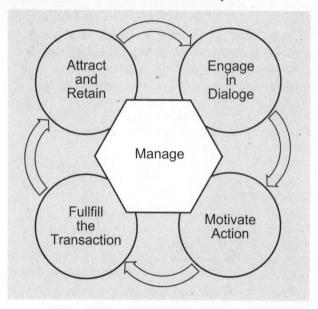

If the concepts of one-to-one business and mass customization on the Internet are going to revolutionize e-commerce in the near future, BroadVision's top-management insists that it should not be an end in itself. The higher goal is measurable return on investment. This is one of the key factors differentiating BroadVision from the rest of its competitors, according to Chen. BroadVision's top management takes a view that the Internet will be the next telephone or the next fax machine. The technology is well-suited to the needs of marketers; the question is how best to achieve this end. "In any business, there are three main aspects to dealing with customers. First, you want to attract and engage your customers. As a second step, you want to retain them. Finally, you wish to transact with them. Those are the three key building blocks for doing business. And because the Web is a multi-dimensional and voluntary environment (people hit your Web site when they want to, as opposed to you calling them by phone), the three-step mechanism has become much easier than in the past, thanks to mass customization."

That means that whatever number of customers you might have, be they the end users (Internet), other businesses (Extranet), or your own employees (Intranet), you will be able to reach them personally by sending personalized messages to them, automatically and at a low cost. Those users have very distinct nature of features, and little time to spend on the Web. However, by using One-To-One, marketers can now develop a relationship with each of them and try to know who they are, what they want, and provide that to them in real time.

Trust and Privacy

In order to develop such relationships successfully with their customers, Internet-based companies need to create an atmosphere of trust and respect of the customers' privacy. This is why BroadVision joined the Electronic Frontier Foundation's TRUSTe initiative and supports Firefly's Open Profiling Standard (OPS). These two emerging industry standards will compel companies to disclose publicly what they intend to do with the information provided by the end user, while empowering customers at the same time and letting them decide what information they wish to disclose. This is a very sensitive issue for all Internet software companies, and even more so for BroadVision. Its rules-based system enables marketers to define "If...then..." business rules that will send selected messages to the PC screen in accordance with customer profiles. If a customer is a single 30-year-old male who earns $100,000 a year and is visiting a car dealer Web site with BroadVision One-To-One™ software, the marketer of the site will be able to send him an advertising message for a car corresponding to his profile, for example, a brand new Mercedes convertible. If another customer is a 40-year-old man, married, with two children, the ad might be for the latest Plymouth Voyager instead. The efficiency of the whole process relies on the amount of information each customer agrees to disclose to a particular Web site, or on the information that the Web site can grab by observing the customer's behavior (pages visited, time of connection, bookmarking...). Without trust, no information will be disclosed, and the system will not work.

Customers will disclose accurate personal information if they believe they will benefit. That will happen if and only if (1) they feel they have total control of the information they provide, and (2) they have something to gain in return for releasing

the information. As Harvard Professor Anne Wells Branscomb states in her book *Who Owns Information,* typical consumers will be perfectly willing to give out information about themselves if a quid pro quo is offered by the party interested in getting that information from them. Consumers also trust reliable brand names, so establishing brand recognition early on is crucial.

BroadVision tries to convince customers that they engage in a win-win situation when they disclose personal information. Merchants benefit as well by gaining a better understanding of individual customers, thereby enabling them to offer individually targeted motivations and create more effective advertising, yielding a higher profit margin. The merchant's customers get personalized service that reflects their individual preferences without making them feel that their privacy is in jeopardy. This gives them a sense of power and confidence. As they experience the benefits of increased personalized service, they become more willing to provide further information, resulting in a feedback loop that continues to increase the benefits to both merchant and customer. Finally, the customers get better value because the merchant will be able to offer better prices and service because of higher profit margins.

Rules-Based vs. Collaborative Filtering

Collaborative filtering systems such as are used in Firefly software might be more in phase with this idea of trust. However, a collaborative filter makes recommendations to a customer based on the preferences this customer has declared to the Web site and thanks to the opinions of other customers with similar tastes. The system may be viewed as being more objective than BroadVision's rules-based system, since in the Firefly case the customer relies on other anonymous customers, while in the BroadVision case, marketers determine messages delivered. Pehong Chen does not see it that way, though. In his opinion, the meaning and importance of trust must be viewed in terms of objectivity and relevance of the information. He answers: "we provide an environment for people to offer expert opinion about certain things. One can assume that collaborative filtering recommendations are safer and more objective than the ones experts can make through our rule-based system. The only thing is how relevant are they? It is a very different philosophy. Our firmly held view is that businesses like to control their own destiny." In the end, it is a question of balance between the revenues a business wants to enhance and the service or advice it wants to give to customers.

The philosophies indeed appear very different. For Firefly, rules-based personalization softwares such as BroadVision's One-To-One™ are focused on an old paradigm of marketing. "'Customization' is a banned word around here," says Saul Klein, Senior VP of Brand and Strategy at Firefly. "'Customization' to us equals rules-based systems, in which the company decides how to control the environment. You 'customize' for people who fit a criterion. In contrast, we're building Web sites dynamically based on each person's profile. There is a basic philosophical difference here: the rules-based system is centered on the seller, while collaborative filtering focuses on the buyer."

If an Internet-based business really wants to develop its service and provide value, it probably can benefit from both approaches, collaborative filtering and a rules-based system. It is interesting to compare BroadVision's rules-based system with collaborative filtering softwares such as those developed by Firefly Networks or NetPerceptions. They reflect two different approaches to personalization. BroadVision does not compete directly with Firefly, but the way it challenges the solution offered by the Boston-based company gives evidence of a mix of defiance and interest. According to the CEO of BroadVision, collaborative filtering can be applied only to a limited number of domains, likely in an unreliable way, and that is not business efficient.

Applicability   Asked to compare the two solutions, Chen replies straightforwardly: "the polite answer is that both systems are complementary. The not so polite answer is that I really don't see there being a lot of value in collaborative filtering in the real business world. It's probably valuable in a very limited range of domains like buying books at Amazon, buying CDs from CD-Now or stuff that can be influenced by word of mouth and trend. But if you're a Fortune 500 company, you serve a particular clientele. I just cannot come up with any scenario in which your interest as a customer would be influenced by somebody else's buying the same thing. Why would that be of any value to you? If I

buy stock, it's because I have a particular investment profile. I don't really care whether my neighbor buys the same stock or not. Companies that do collaborative filtering are going to tell you this is the nicest thing since sliced bread. I'm very skeptical of that, and so are our customers."

Reliability   Even in domains related to taste, collaborative filtering applications can be challenged, in BroadVision's perspective. "Who do you trust more, an expert or people in general?" asks Chen. What bothers him most about collaborative filtering is its unproved reliability. "Contrary to what they say, collaborative filtering requires a tremendous amount of knowledge in setting up the right framework. We've looked at this. We've got lots of Artificial Intelligence PhDs in our company. This topic is hard and extremely specific. To do this right is so domain-specific that the model you build for movies doesn't really work for music. Even for music, one class of music probably doesn't work for another class of music. So unless you don't care about the validity of the recommendations, or the recommendation does not impact a big financial decision, you should be careful with these engines. You buy a CD for $15 and books for $9.95, you don't really care. But if it's a major decision you're making, you probably trust an expert more than what everybody else is saying. That is where our solution comes in."

Business Efficiency   Finally, Chen argues that with collaborative filtering, the company has no control. It is a black box in which one receives inputs from the customers and which mysteriously formulates recommendations, whatever the result is. "Again we're in total complementarity with their approach. But ours is more pro-business. We say to companies: You can set whatever rules you want to interact with your customer. By the way, you can add any of those options that enable you to match tastes, such as a collaborative engine, if you want."

The question for end-users remains whether BroadVision's rules-based system is not the most extreme marketing tool that companies have ever had. If marketers know their customers' profiles and can set up business rules targeted specifically at each of them, should not customers be frightened of how this technology will be used? "Let's face it," answers Chen. "You're being marketed every day. From the business standpoint, if I've got a blue shirt that doesn't sell, why could not I entice you and say 'Hey, buy this blue shirt now, it will only sell for $50 over the next two hours'? Amazon shouldn't care, they just sell books and they are a distributor. If somebody says books 1 and 28 are really great and they can sell a lot more of them, that is fine for them. Collaborative filtering is a perfect match for companies like that. But there are not a whole lot of companies like Amazon that could basically act as a really impartial distributor. Most companies have a product to sell or some number of products to sell. Most companies are not distributors or aggregators of content."

Pricing Issues

Whatever kind of personalization software a company chooses, the final aim is to enhance the customer's experience while at the same time assuring the company a fast return on investment. Therefore, in the new personalized Internet environment enabled by BroadVision software, another issue of concern, both for companies and users, is pricing. What impact will personalization softwares have on selling prices on the Web? On the one hand, intelligent agents, such those used for BargainFinder (http://bf.cstar.ac.com/bf/), help customers find the cheapest price on the Web for the product they are looking for (a specific CD for example). That technology should drive prices down because it allows customers to compare different prices automatically. The price war between Barnes & Noble and Amazon.com on the Web is a good example of such a mechanism (Amazon dropped its prices by 30% when Barnes & Noble went online). On the other hand, with BroadVision's technology, which enables the delivery of targeted messages to each customer, companies will be able to price each user differently, according to his or her profile. It is also true that customers would be able to take advantage of the system by registering under two different names and using two different profiles. Just by selecting different yearly incomes, for example, the customer might get very different quotes for airfares.

Does Personalization Equate with Higher Profits for Companies?

If the pricing issue is still wide open, because the return on investment is a major concern for

companies investing in personalization softwares for their Web-based business, the next major concern should be cost. What kind of new costs will enterprises face? Will these new costs be compensated by the savings gathered through lower distribution and packaging costs?

New kinds of employees   Companies will have to develop new internal qualifications, such as "customer managers." These key specialists will look at the customer (as opposed to the product) as the unit of interest. Their role will be to understand each customer on a more personal basis, in order to satisfy the customer's need. To achieve fine-granularity personalized interaction, a mix of people and applications must then make qualitative judgments about digital content and match that content with specific user behavior, preferences, categories, demographics, etc.

Other costs   If companies want to reach their customers on a more personal basis, they need to create specific content to address all their different needs. They must switch from high distribution and packaging costs to Web content development costs. There is a tradeoff between a higher level of personalization and higher costs. Nevertheless, automated mass customization on the Internet cannot be compared to direct marketing in terms of cost, neither on the efficiency side, nor on the expense side. The average cost per mail drop is somewhere between 50 cents to three or four dollars, depending on what is sent out. When millions and millions of copies of a leaflet are sent out, there is a lot of money involved. Each campaign, each market survey, can easily go up to a million dollars. Chen considers cost as a long-term investment: "Direct marketing is about each drop," he comments, "while our software can be there forever."

Cost of software and implementation budget   One thing is certain, namely that venturing beyond Web brochureware isn't cheap either. An average business customer will spend about $200,000 to license BroadVision software, and about as much in consulting fees for implementation. The process of getting to know the customer and implementing the application correctly can take a few months, up to a year or year-and-a-half, depending upon the business concerned.

One-To-One as a Competitive Advantage

Companies that invest now in personalization software understand the value of trust and loyalty. Their best competitive advantage in the future will be that they can keep their customers for much longer than in the past. They are going to be able to predict their customers' next big purchase and act to satisfy their needs. Most of the time in today's business environment, there is a disconnect in the feedback loop between the customer and the provider. To help its customers reverse this trend, BroadVision's strategy is to start working with companies as upstream in the implementation process as possible. The good point is that firms do not have to wait for huge aggregate data, like for warehousing techniques, before being able to know enough about their customers profiles. Pehong Chen insists that "a lot of things are actually happening in real time on the Internet. For instance, recently there have been currency crises in Southeast Asia. If you, as a customer, show a keen interest in that, we, as an online bank equipped with BroadVision software, will be able to detect that in fairly real time. Your interest actually gives us a great indication that you may be interested in investing in Asian mutual funds, because over the past few weeks you have read all those articles about the currency crisis and have come back five times on this specific fund Web-page. The bank can therefore send you an e-mail with some target information and say, 'Shall we talk?' So the 70% robot will help us detect your interests automatically, giving that remaining 30% an opportunity to engage you in and sell you something."

BROADVISION INC., THE COMPANY

Positioning, Strategy, Business Model

International presence   One-To-One™ finds its prospects among the world's thousand largest companies. BroadVision strives to become the equivalent of SAP in the Internet market. To build its brand equity, the company is implementing an "Intel inside" strategy. Customers will be invited to highlight the fact that "this service is being powered by BroadVision One-To-One™," which should give a great deal of name recognition. The company also aims at making its Web site, www.broadvision.com, which will soon schedule an online service, one of the hottest on the Internet. An important part of BroadVision's strategy is to grow quickly in the international market, and 50% of the company's business is currently outside of the United States. Major contracts have been signed in Europe and Asia. From a competitive point of view, that is one of the company's current strengths. Chen explains this deliberate choice: "I think we've made the right decision. In certain markets, we got in early, and we can actually dominate them. We're seeing the exact result we predicted. In Asia and Europe, we're doing very, very well. In the States, the market is huge and also very competitive, which means opportunity for us. We can now grow in the US market, all the more so because our resources, unlike other companies, are spread thin across the world, while our competitors tend to just focus on the US and then go from there. But in the Internet software market, we believe it will be too late for them. This is why we've maintained a presence in all three places, the US, Europe, and Asia. Going forward now, we are going to put a lot more investment and resources into the U.S."

One player dominates   BroadVision believes that in its market, a few big players are going to dominate, and they want to lead the way. "Take the search engines, for example," explains Chen. "You will find Yahoo! and probably four or five other names. It's finished. If you are just entering this market today, it's hopeless. You're not going to get there. Any new medium is dominated by four or five players. That's already happened with TV and radio. Yahoo! currently represents 38,000,000 Web pages viewed per day. The next closest competitor accounts for only half that number. It's gone. There's no hope."

A small repeat customer base   BroadVision does not aim at becoming a mass-market software manufacturer, but rather follows the example of Cisco, which does repeat business with its solid customer base. "Engage, retain, and transact," says Pehong Chen. "Those are the three key elements of Internet business. We do a great deal of business with our customers, all 300 of them. I'm going to try to make them happy, to solve their problems. I'm going to sell more stuff to them. That's our opportunity. The strategy is simple," he continues. "We need to stay on top of this food chain. Partner with the right people. Deliver the results. Because once this ball starts rolling, it will snowball. We want to avoid competing with Oracle, Microsoft, or Netscape at this level. We don't have the volume, and we don't have the resources to do that anyhow. So that is a very clear strategy: Stay on top of the hill, where the air is fresher. The business model is simple too. We need to provide solutions and applications. And we bundle services around our products. We created a nine-step process to help our customers visualize, conceptualize, and internalize the value of mass customization. It's like teaching them how to use a telephone to call their customers. We need to tell them how to do that."

Revenues   Revenues so far come mostly from selling the software (about 70%), followed by consulting and training (approximately 30%). The revenue model is based on licensing the One-To-One product line: development license, Dynamic Command Center (DCC) license, deployment license, and professional services. All licenses come with a mandatory 18% maintenance and support contract. Each customer will need to purchase at least one development license. Each merchant will need at least one DCC. And customers who are aggregators may have many merchants under their "aggregation," each of which would require a DCC. The deployment license is the engine that powers the customer's online service. Its pricing is based on the number of subscribers, and the number of services linked into the subscriber database. As the customer's business grows by increasing subscribers and services, BroadVision receives additional revenues automatically. Finally, BroadVision interactive services generate revenues on a time and material basis, education services charge fees for training courses, and support services sell technical support contracts. BroadVision's business is much more than just the product itself. The whole business model is wrapped around the idea of service.

Products

BroadVision One-To-One™ supports large user and content databases, high transaction volumes, intelligent agent matching, and easy integration with existing business systems. It also incorporates a suite of management tools that empower non-technical business managers, content editors, and Web masters to dynamically control application behavior from their desktops. (For more details about the product, see Figure 3.)

Customers

BroadVision's customers are global 1,000 companies. These companies use BroadVision One-To-One™ to build, operate and manage Web sites or broadband interactive services. BroadVision's main target sectors include telecommunication companies, financial services firms, and Web retailers. A point worth noticing is the portability of BroadVision's solution. As an open solution, BroadVision was meant to be platform-, network-, and bandwidth-independent. As a result, while most of the customers target the Internet, some contracts have been signed with companies developing interactive TV solutions, such as OpenTV (formerly Thomson-Sun Interactive), or Hong-Kong Telecom. A list of the biggest customers so far include: Kodak, HP, The World Bank, France Telecom, NTT, Sabre, Virgin.net, Prodigy, Olivetti, Sema, US West, and Grolier interactive. Olivetti, for example, used BroadVision's One-To-One™ solution to launch the first virtual shopping center in Italy, through "Cybermercato," a site that can dynamically match merchant information to each user shopper's profile each time that he/she visits the mall. Thanks to BroadVision, NetRadio Network, the first 24-hour Internet-only radio network, will provide personalized radio services over the Web, so that listeners can customize their favorite music [or] sports program. EarthWeb, the leading online service for Internet and Intranet software and site developers, teamed up with BroadVision to customize its marketing and sales effort to meet the needs of each individual customer. FirstAuction, a live, real-time auction offering computer, consumer electronics and general merchandise to the Internet shopping community, uses BroadVision to allow users to create their own profiles corresponding to their bidding history.

Two of the most ambitious users of the BroadVision platform are Kodak and Banco Santander. BroadVision announced on 25 August 1997 that it will provide key-technology used in the "Kodak Picture Network," an online initiative that marks the debut of Kodak into the Internet. It will

FIGURE 3

BroadVision One-to-One™ Interactive Architecture

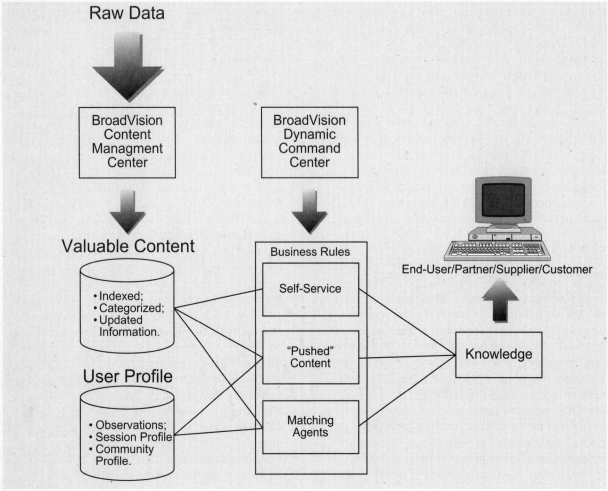

Source: Aberdeen Group, Inc.

make it much easier and more convenient for customers to access and reprint their photos as well as choose various ways of displaying and sharing their pictures. BroadVision One-To-One™ enabled Kodak to quickly build a scaleable Internet application that will support millions of transactions and dynamically personalize each user's experience with the service. Consumers will be able to have their pictures placed on-line simply by checking a box on their photofinishing envelope at more than 30,000 photo counters. They may then log into the Kodak Picture Network through their own Internet connections to view their photos, order reprints, and share pictures via e-mail and the Web with family and friends. BroadVision's back-end integration features allow Kodak to retrieve and transfer

consumers' pictures from an image storage system that is indexed and managed by a Sybase database running on servers from Sun Microsystems. Using BroadVision's extensibility features, Kodak will handle payment and taxes by customizing BroadVision objects that handle these functions. Eventually, Kodak will incorporate BroadVision's more advanced personalization and targeting capabilities that will enable consumers to receive one-to-one services, such as specialized photo albums. This is a great example of using the Internet as a new channel to reach new markets.

Building on its excellent reputation in the banking industry and leveraging the success of its previous sign-ups in that sector, BroadVision was able to sign a contract with Spain's most profitable bank,

Banco Santander, to build an Internet banking service. With Banca SuperNet, an online service launched in May 1997, Banco Santander was the first bank in the world to offer its customers personalized online banking services. Customers are now able to access their accounts to conduct standard banking practices from their desktops and conduct transactions outside of Banco Santander as well. For instance, a Banca SuperNet user can transfer funds to any financial institution. In addition to a fully operational online service, Banca SuperNet is customized to each individual user. Visitors to the site can choose one of four different site "styles" for the presentation of information, each defined by a different set of fonts, colors and styles. Within each of those four "styles," another four options are available. These four options let the user choose what is most important to view first. For some, it might be a credit card balance; for others, it might be to follow certain companies in the stock market. Banco Santander is committed to exploring avenues of personalization, with additional functions set to be unveiled every two weeks. One of these upcoming projects is an alert capability, letting the user know if something happens in their account. For example, a user can be notified if his account goes below $500. This alert can either be by phone or via e-mail. "We had one objective with the Internet banking service: to increase customer loyalty," said Jorge Mata, head of multimedia banking at Banco Santander. For Banca SuperNet, Banco Santander is leveraging its telephone banking operation. The bank has pledged that customer service will answer e-mail from the Internet in less than 24 hours. Customer requests will be responded to either by e-mail or phone, depending on the preferences of the customer.

Competitors

BroadVision is an Internet applications company. Dynamic Web application platforms are an emerging class of software that combine Internet technologies, database, middleware, messaging, and transaction processing to create sophisticated resource-leveraging corporate Web sites. BroadVision, therefore, does not compete directly with Netscape, Oracle, Microsoft, or IBM (which are platform companies). Its focus is on codifying the business rules into a system to make a customer's online business more compelling and profitable. Even Netscape application servers fall short as far as profiling and personalization are concerned. Neither does BroadVision compete directly with successful applications companies such as SAP and PeopleSoft, which are confined to the Intranet world. From a certain standpoint, BroadVision aims at becoming the new SAP for Internet commerce personalization software solutions.

Among the other Internet software companies, we can distinguish two different kinds of competitors for BroadVision. First, in the personalization field, the artificial intelligence and collaborative filtering companies such as Firefly, NetPerceptions, and Open Sesame, even if there is more complementarity than competition between BroadVision and each of them. Then comes another set of companies such as Connect Inc., Open Market, and Interworld. But they are more e-commerce-oriented types of softwares, and most of them fall short in terms of personalization, do not offer dynamic pricing capability, or do not support an open API for payment, taxing, and shipping. Another of BroadVision's strengths is its scaleability. Customers like Sabre Interactive have switched to BroadVision One-To-One™ because the previous software they were using could not handle the large number of simultaneous sessions and transactions their business was generating. "Connect Inc.'s OneServer product, for example," says Chen, "seems to be more of a result of a long legacy than something optimized for the Internet. In recent experience, our main competitors have failed due diligence analysis conducted by our customers." But even thirty-year industry veteran Gordon Bridge, who left AT&T in November 1995 to become the new CEO of Connect Inc., a ten year-old Apple spin-off based in Mountain View, California, which employs 125 people, denies competing directly with BroadVision: "We run into companies such as Open Market, but believe it or not, our competitors continue to be internal MIS departments that, in fact, are trying to build it themselves."

If BroadVision seems not to be too concerned with Bridge's perspective and competition, another side of the competition could threaten their consulting services, namely the new trend toward "interactive architects," hybrid consulting companies such as Organic Online or Interactive Solutions that specialize in full-service Web development. "Your business is in jeopardy . . . Deliver interactivity or you'll never see your customers again!," a message on young Boston startup Interactive Solutions' home page warns provocatively.

What would keep these new players from challenging BroadVision's leadership in the consulting part of their business? Some of them are already very successful: Organic has helped big names such as Microsoft, Netscape, Yahoo!, and Levi-Strauss develop their Web sites. Moreover, one step beyond personalization softwares, BroadVision will be challenged by fierce competition from big players in the broader market for Internet commerce solutions, as research done by Forrester predicts. Finally, some direct competitors could emerge in the near future, and BroadVision seems to particularly fear the application servers they believe Netscape is developing. Even if these products are not in commercial release yet, the most direct threat could come from their Mountain View neighbors. But as Connect Inc.'s CEO Bridge predicts, in this emerging market, the competition might well not be born yet. "In the next months, you will see an increase in the number of small companies because this is a huge market, and you will see a whole cadre of acquisitions too," he predicts.

Finance

BroadVision has been in business for three years and is backed by powerful VCs and strong international corporate investors. The company has been successful in attracting a list of bluechip companies around the world as customers and partners. In September 1997, BroadVision announced that Carl Pascarella, president and chief executive officer of Visa USA had been elected to the company's board of directors. "Carl Pascarella is a savvy business strategist who brings decades of experience in building one of the fastest growing and most successful companies in the world," said Pehong Chen. "As the top executive in one of the world's leading financial services companies, we expect Carl to contribute significantly to BroadVision's strategy and growth, particularly in financial services, which has become a major focus for BroadVision over the past year."

The market and recent history seem to support Chen's self-confidence. The company has experienced fast-paced growth and has become accustomed to announcing record revenues each quarter since it went public in 1996. Revenues for the second quarter of 1997 were $6.0 million, a 161 % increase over revenues of $2.3 million in the

second quarter of 1996. The net loss for the period was $2.1 million, or $0.10 per share, compared to $2.2 million, or $0.13 per share, in the year-earlier quarter. For the six months that ended on 30 June 1997, revenues were $11.3 million, a 205% increase over the $3.7 million reported for the first six months of 1996, resulting in a net loss of $4.6 million, or $0.23 per share, compared to the corresponding figures in 1996 of a loss of $3.9 million, or $0.22 per share (see Exhibit 1 for a detailed balance sheet and income statement). The stock price is fairly stable. On 11 September 1997, BroadVision's stock (BVSN) was traded at $7.125 per share on the NASDAQ, while its introduction price for its IPO in June 1996 was $7.00. However, the mood of the market for Internet software companies can change quickly. Connect Inc., one of BroadVision's main competitors (NASDAQ: CNKT), saw its stock price fall to $1, from a high at $10 after underachieving badly in the first quarter of 1997 as customers delayed purchase decisions or built their own applications. Connect Inc. announced some improvement in its financial statements for the second quarter of 1997, with revenues up to $3.2 million, up by 26% compared to the second quarter of 1996, and with a loss that narrowed to $3.2 million, from the $4 million deficit of the second quarter of 1996. Its stock price was traded at $2 on 11 September 1997. Connect Inc.'s CEO Gordon Bridge explains that, "before, analysts were projecting that we would do something around $25 million in revenue, compared with the $10 last year. And now, they are projecting that we will do somewhere between $13 million and $15 million of revenue. Again, if you looked at the previous plan, this company would have had to generate $30 or $40 million of revenue before it broke even. Well, if we execute our current plan, we could break even at numbers that are substantially below those figures."

Pehong Chen remains confident as he looks toward the future. He firmly believes, as the experts at Aberdeen consulting firm report, that relationship management is not an electronic commerce niche. The continued expansion of computing from PCs to lap tops and ultimately to smart cards will dramatically increase end-user information. Serious Internet businesses in financial services and computer-related sales already recognize that consumer data represents the competitive advantage in electronic commerce. And BroadVision's CEO has firmly decided not to let someone else reap what he has sown.

RELATED WEB SITES

Amazon	http://www.amazon.com
Banco Santander	http://www.bancosantander.es
BargainFinder	http://bf.cstar.ac.com/bf
Barnes&Noble	http://www.barnesandnoble.com
BroadVision	http://www.broadvision.com
CDNow	http://www.cdnow.com
Connect Inc	http://www.connectinc.com/
Earth Web	http://www.earthweb.com/
Firefly	http://www.firefly.net
First Auction	http://www.firstauction.com
Grolier	http://www.club-intemet.fr
Interworld	http://www.interworld.com
Kodak Picture Network	http://www.kodakpicturenetwork.com
NetPerceptions	http://www.netperceptions.com
Net Radio Network	http://www.netradio.net/
Open Market	http://www.openmarket.com/
Open Sesame	http://www.opensesame.com
OpenTV	http://www.opentv.com
Organic	http://www.organic.com/
TRUSTe	http://www.etrust.org
Virgin Net	http://www.virgin.net/

EXHIBIT I

BroadVision, Inc. and Subsidiaries Condensed Consolidated Balance Sheet and Consolidated Statements of Operations

BroadVision, Inc. and Subsidiaries Condensed Consolidated Balance Sheet (In thousands)		
	June 30, 1997	December 31, 1996
ASSETS		
Current assets: (unaudited)		
Cash and short-term investments	$12,389	$19,720
Accounts receivable, net	7,129	5,548
Other current assets	645	317
Total current assets	20,163	25,585
Property and equipment, net	3,563	3,024
Other assets	388	321
Total assets	$24,114	$28,930
LIABILITIES AND STOCKHOLDERS' EQUITY		
Current liabilities		
Accounts payable and accrued expenses	$3,075	$3,484
Unearned revenue	1,610	2,625
Deferred maintenance	1,439	924
Current portion of long-term liabilities	365	294
Total current liabilities	6,489	7,327
Long-term liabilities	490	587
Stockholders' equity		
Equity	39,806	39,318
Deferred compensation	(1,806)	(2,033)
Accumulated deficit	(20,865)	(16,269)
Total stockholders' equity	17,135	21,016
Total liabilities and stockholders' equity	$24,114	$28,930

EXHIBIT I *(continued)*

BroadVision, Inc. and Subsidiaries Consolidated Statements of Operations (In thousands, except per share amounts)				
	Three Months Ended June 30,		Six Months Ended June 30,	
	1997	1996	1997	1996
	(unaudited)		(unaudited)	
Revenues				
Software licenses	$4,098	$1,564	$7,246	$2,663
Services	1,929	738	4,072	1,037
Total revenues	6,027	2,302	11,318	3,700
Cost of revenues				
Cost of license revenues	425	93	639	189
Cost of service revenues	1,001	331	2,144	497
Total cost of revenues	1,426	424	2,783	686
Gross profit	4,601	1,878	8,535	3,014
Operating expenses				
Research and development	1,802	1,277	3,482	2,193
Sales and marketing	4,257	2,486	8,461	4,093
General and administrative	700	320	1,446	638
Total operating expenses	6,759	4,083	13,389	6,924
Operating (loss)	(2,158)	(2,205)	(4,854)	(3,910)
Interest and other income	187	51	408	94
Interest and other expense	(138)	(26)	(150)	(62)
Net loss	$(2,109)	$(2,180)	$(4,596)	$(3,878)
Net per share	$(0.10)	$(0.13)	$(0.23)	$(0.22)
Shares used in computing net loss per share	20,219	16,822	20,111	17,699